"This latest work on the incarnation and nativity is an excellent example of serious scholarship served up in a [illegible] most readable manner. No birth in history had such prophetic preparation, which is a powerful, central theme in these pages that celebrate the start of the greatest life ever lived. This is a welcome antidote to the cheap sensationalism in recent books on Jesus that try to demolish every reason for regarding Christmas as 'the most wonderful time of the year.'"

Paul L. Maier, Professor of Ancient History, Western Michigan University; author, *In the Fullness of Time*

"*The First Days of Jesus* is a revealing look at the earliest days of Jesus in Matthew, Luke, and John set against some of the skeptical takes on these passages. Add to this a taste of Jewish messianic expectation and you have a nice overview of the start of Jesus's career and where it fits in God's plan. Solid yet devotional, it is a great introduction to the first days of our Lord."

Darrell L. Bock, Executive Director of Cultural Engagement, Howard G. Hendricks Center, and Senior Research Professor of New Testament Studies, Dallas Theological Seminary

"*The First Days of Jesus* combines Scripture passages, historical background, scholarly insight, and practical application to cast Christ's incarnation in fresh light. Few tasks are more urgent than for today's Christians worldwide to rediscover and deepen their connections with their origins. This book is a valuable resource for achieving that aim. Like the star of Bethlehem itself, this volume leads those who seek God to find him afresh in the events of Jesus's historical appearance, the prophecies that preceded, the apostolic testimony that accompanied, and the social world that God split wide open when he sent his Son."

Robert W. Yarbrough, Professor of New Testament, Covenant Theological Seminary

"Köstenberger and Stewart admirably unpack the birth narratives of Matthew and Luke along with that beautiful first movement of John's Gospel against both the grand sweep of biblical history and the nitty-gritty details of first-century events and culture. The result may dismantle a few of your nativity-scene notions about the Christmas story even while building up your faith in and commitment to the Word become flesh."

George H. Guthrie, Benjamin W. Perry Professor of Bible, Union University

"Köstenberger and Stewart provide for us a faithful and useful guide to the early days of Jesus. This book should serve well those desiring to learn about the early chapters in the Gospels and those who desire to preach and teach these narratives."

Thomas R. Schreiner, James Buchanan Harrison Professor of New Testament Interpretation, The Southern Baptist Theological Seminary

"Written with exceptional clarity, *The First Days of Jesus* pays close attention to the key biblical texts on Christ's nativity in an illuminating way. It deals briefly yet helpfully with critical scholarship and presents the events surrounding Jesus's conception and birth in both a canonical and a chronological fashion. It addresses unashamedly the difficulties with these birth stories, tackling the problem of variant accounts, the use of sources, the nature of prophecy and typology, and much more. It challenges us readers to respond to the Word of God with the obedience of faith, like Mary did, and with praise, worship, and witness, as the shepherds did. I know of no other book that so masterfully weaves together these infancy narratives on so many fronts. I thoroughly enjoyed it and highly recommend it!"

Gregg R. Allison, Professor of Christian Theology, The Southern Baptist Theological Seminary

"There is more to Christmas than you may think. Cut through the layers of tradition and the fog of nostalgia, and discover the scandal of how it all started. The Bible has more to say about Jesus's earliest days than you might expect, and this book is a reliable guide. *The First Days of Jesus* blends world-class scholarship with real-world concern for everyday Christians. Here attention to detail, in the text and in history, complements warm devotion and pastoral care."

David Mathis, Executive Editor, desiringGod.org; Pastor, Cities Church, Minneapolis

"In this accessible and reliable guide to how the Gospels present the early years of Jesus Christ's life, Köstenberger and Stewart provide an exceptionally helpful study, informed by the best of modern scholarship. Drawing on what we know of the historical context, they expound with clarity both the meaning of the biblical text and its relevance for modern readers. In doing so, they enable us to grasp afresh how a detailed appreciation of Jesus's first days contributes significantly to a deeper understanding of his whole life."

T. Desmond Alexander, Senior Lecturer in Biblical Studies, Union Theological College, Belfast, Northern Ireland, UK

THE FIRST DAYS OF JESUS

THE FIRST DAYS OF JESUS

THE STORY OF THE INCARNATION

ANDREAS J. KÖSTENBERGER
& ALEXANDER E. STEWART

FOREWORD BY JUSTIN TAYLOR

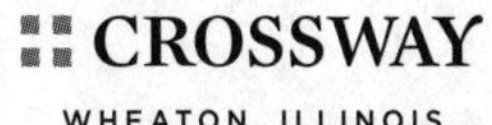
WHEATON, ILLINOIS

The First Days of Jesus: The Story of the Incarnation

Published by Crossway
1300 Crescent Street
Wheaton, Illinois 60187

Cover design: Adam Green

Cover image: Robby Sawyer

First printing 2015

Printed in the United States of America

All emphases in Scripture quotations have been added by the author.

Trade paperback ISBN: 978-1-4335-4278-7
ePub ISBN: 978-1-4335-4281-7
PDF ISBN: 978-1-4335-4279-4
Mobipocket ISBN: 978-1-4335-4280-0

Library of Congress Cataloging-in-Publication Data

Köstenberger, Andreas J., 1957–
The first days of Jesus : The story of the incarnation / Andreas Köstenberger and Alexander Stewart ; foreword by Justin Taylor.
pages cm
Includes bibliographical references and index.
ISBN 978-1-4335-4278-7 (tp)
1. Jesus Christ—Nativity. 2. Messiah—Prophecies. 3. Jesus Christ—Messiahship. I. Bible. English. Selections. English Standard. 2015. II. Title.
BT315.3.K67 2015
232.92—dc23 2015000584

Crossway is a publishing ministry of Good News Publishers.

VP 25 24 23 22 21 20 19 18 17 16 15
15 14 13 12 11 10 9 8 7 6 5 4 3 2 1

CONTENTS

LIST OF CHARTS, DIAGRAMS, AND MAPS

FOREWORD

One New Testament scholar described the Gospel of Mark as a "passion narrative with an extended introduction."[1] This is why Andreas Köstenberger and I coauthored *The Final Days of Jesus*: if you want to understand who Jesus is, you have to understand the most important week of his earthly ministry.[2] The Gospel writers, like Jesus himself, set their faces to Jerusalem and refused to look back (Luke 9:51, 53).

But something built into the human spirit *wants* to go back, to see how it all started. God himself, of course, begins the biblical storyline, "In the beginning" (Gen. 1:1). And the story of Jesus, as the preincarnate Word, likewise starts, "In the beginning" (John 1:1).

Although we would never complain about how the Spirit of God chose to guide his inspired writers, we sometimes wish the narrative of Jesus's first days would slow things down and add some more detail. Obviously we cannot add more chapters to the Bible. God has given us everything we need to worship him in a way that pleases and glorifies his great name and equips us for every good work (2 Tim. 3:16–17). But we can slow down. And we can go deeper. This is where Köstenberger and Stewart, gifted biblical theologians and New Testament scholars, can help us.

People say that familiarity breeds contempt, but when it comes to Bible reading, I've found that familiarity is more likely

---

[1] Martin Kähler, *The So-Called Historical Jesus and the Historic, Biblical Christ* (1892; repr., Philadelphia: Fortress, 1964), 80.

[2] Andreas J. Köstenberger and Justin Taylor, with Alexander Stewart, *The Final Days of Jesus: The Most Important Week of the Most Important Person Who Ever Lived* (Wheaton, IL: Crossway, 2014).

to produce *laziness*. I tend to skim when I already know the story. How many times in my life have I read or heard preached the following familiar words?

> In those days a decree went out from Caesar Augustus that all the world should be registered. This was the first registration when Quirinius was governor of Syria. And all went to be registered, each to his own town. And Joseph also went up from Galilee, from the town of Nazareth, to Judea, to the city of David, which is called Bethlehem, because he was of the house and lineage of David, to be registered with Mary, his betrothed, who was with child. And while they were there, the time came for her to give birth. And she gave birth to her firstborn son and wrapped him in swaddling cloths and laid him in a manger, because there was no place for them in the inn. (Luke 2:1–7)

We've heard it so many times that we assume we know what it all means.

But then we start to ask questions. Who was Caesar Augustus? When did he rule? Over what exact area did he rule? Why did he want all the world to be registered? Who was Quirinius? Is the Syria in this passage the same as the modern country of Syria? Don't some Bible scholars say that Luke's history about the timing of the census is inaccurate here? Why did Joseph have to go to Bethlehem instead of registering in Nazareth? How big was Bethlehem? Why did Mary need to go with him? And why doesn't it say she rode on a donkey—is that in another account, or is that just what we've seen on TV? How exactly is betrothal different from engagement? Where is the innkeeper? And what kind of an "inn" was this—a cave, a room in a house, or an ancient hotel?

These are fourteen questions off the top of my head, and we've only covered seven verses. As we keep reading, the questions keep coming. Even though we've read or heard it dozens of times, it is humbling to recognize just how much we still don't know.

The book you hold in your hands has no gimmicks or clever sales pitches. It won't reveal a "gospel" you never knew. (If it did, you should throw it away [Gal. 1:8].) It doesn't purport to finally disclose the secrets of Jesus's childhood or what he did in Egypt. Instead, it takes us back to Scripture, the only infallible source with an account of how God became man and dwelt among us.

I think you will find several benefits in reading *The First Days of Jesus*:

First, this book can help you *slow down*. The biblical narrative contains details that you probably haven't noticed before. These details reflect historical realities you probably didn't know before. And these biblical and historical realities have implications for your life that you probably haven't thought of before. Köstenberger and Stewart guard us from racing through familiar words and guide us in seeing what we have not yet fully seen.

Second, this book can help you *go deeper*. The incarnation—God become man—is a deep mystery. Pastor-theologian Sam Storms poetically captures some of the paradoxes at play:

> The Word became flesh!
> God became human!
> the invisible became visible!
> the untouchable became touchable!
> eternal life experienced temporal death!
> the transcendent one descended and drew near!
> the unlimited became limited!
> the infinite became finite!
> the immutable became mutable!
> the unbreakable became fragile!
> spirit became matter!
> eternity entered time!
> the independent became dependent!
> the almighty became weak!
> the loved became the hated!
> the exalted was humbled!
> glory was subjected to shame!
> fame turned into obscurity!
> from inexpressible joy to tears of unimaginable grief!
> from a throne to a cross!

from ruler to being ruled!
from power to weakness![3]

The wonder of the incarnation deserves a lifetime of thought, and this book is a faithful resource to prompt deeper reflection on the foundation of our salvation.

Third, this book can help you *make connections*. Even though the Bible devotes only four and a half chapters (out of 1,189) to Jesus's first days, Köstenberger and Stewart show us that the incarnation is the hinge of redemptive history—with the Old Testament leading up to it and the rest of the New Testament flowing from it. Reading this book will help you see how the whole story line fits together.

C. S. Lewis once confessed that in his own reading, "devotional books" did not produce in his mind and heart the results they promised. He suspected he was not alone: "I believe that many who find that 'nothing happens' when they sit down, or kneel down, to a book of devotion, would find that the heart sings unbidden while they are working their way through a tough bit of theology with a pipe in their teeth and a pencil in their hand."[4] You may want to contextualize away the pipe depending on your own preferences and convictions, but I think the advice is sound, and I found this to be the case when reading *The First Days of Jesus*.

This is not the dry-as-dust formula of dumping data and dates onto the pages of a book. This is not a book of theology void of history or a volume of history minus theology. It is a work of confessional theology rooted in historical investigation and devoted to a careful reading of Scripture, all designed to help us worship our God and Savior, Jesus Christ. I hope you find this book as meaningful and fruitful as I did.

Justin Taylor
Maundy Thursday, 2015

[3] Sam Storms, "The Most Amazing Verse in the Bible," February 20, 2010, http://www.samstorms.com/all-articles/post/the-most-amazing-verse-in-the-bible.
[4] C. S. Lewis, "On the Reading of Old Books," in *God in the Dock: Essays on Theology and Ethics*, ed. Walter Hooper (Grand Rapids, MI: Eerdmans, 1970), 205.

INTRODUCTION

SEPARATING FACT FROM FICTION

Christmas is the most wonderful time of the year—at least according to Andy Williams's famous rendition of Edward Pola and George Wyle's Christmas song that can be heard in malls and on radio stations across America throughout the month of December. Pola and Wyle provide several reasons for this assertion:

It's the most wonderful time of the year
With the kids jingle belling
And everyone telling you, "Be of good cheer."
It's the most wonderful time of the year.

It's the hap-happiest season of all,
With those holiday greetings and gay happy meetings
When friends come to call.
It's the hap-happiest season of all.

There'll be parties for hosting,
Marshmallows for toasting,
And caroling out in the snow.
There'll be scary ghost stories
And tales of the glories of
Christmases long, long ago.

It's the most wonderful time of the year.
There'll be much mistletoeing
And hearts will be glowing

When loved ones are near.
It's the most wonderful time of the year.[1]

For all of the shallow reasons that Williams sings about, he rightly taps into many people's perceptions of Christmas as a sentimental time to reconnect with family and friends. This superficial sentimentality sums up Christmas for many people in our modern Western culture.[2]

CULTURAL CHRISTMAS

When you think of Christmas, what first comes to mind? Perhaps you think of the manger scene with shepherds and wise men, presents, a Christmas tree, decorations, shopping, relatives, Santa Claus, Christmas cards, snow, caroling, or the January credit card bill. Despite what some Christians may want to believe, Christmas, as celebrated by many Americans, is a cultural, not a religious holiday. If Jesus were to be completely removed from the equation, Americans could continue to celebrate Christmas with hardly an interruption. People would still decorate their houses and workplaces, give and receive presents, take the day off work, go to parties, stand in line with their children or grandchildren to see Santa Claus at the local mall, listen to wonderful songs on the radio about Rudolph the Red-Nosed Reindeer, Jack Frost, and world peace, and watch an endless stream of movies featuring Santa Claus as the main character. These are some of the ways in which we celebrate Christmas in America (and other countries have their own Christmas traditions). Christians, of course, may also attend a special Christmas pageant at their church, maybe even with some live animals. Even live animals, however, can't compete with the main feature of Christmas for every child: presents!

Cultural Christmas doesn't need Jesus. There is too much money at stake for retailers to depend upon a first-century Jew-

[1] Edward Pola and George Wyle, "It's the Most Wonderful Time of the Year," performed by Andy Williams, Columbia Records, 1963, record.

[2] See the helpful booklet containing a series of messages by Josh Moody, pastor of College Church, *How Christmas Can Change Your Life* (Wheaton, IL: College Church, 2013). Audio versions of these messages are available at http://www.college-church.org/av_search.php?seriesid=101.

ish messianic baby to bring in the revenue. The financial side of Christmas has thoroughly shaped and molded its cultural expression. Our economy needs Christmas. What would happen if Americans stopped overspending and going into debt each December? As every economist would tell you, the economy would be dealt a serious blow. Even families that try to scale back find it very difficult because of all the expectations from relatives and friends. Although other countries and cultures have Christmas traditions of their own, at least in America (and much of the Western world), Christmas is synonymous with commercialism.[3]

THE BATTLE FOR CHRISTMAS

Christians, of course, have not allowed the almighty dollar or superficial sentimentality to take over Christmas without a fight. Throughout the month of December, churches proclaim the *real* reason for the season through special services and events. We know it's all about *Jesus* (or at least it once *was* all about Jesus), and we want it to be all about Jesus *again*.

We engage in this battle for Christmas, however, with one hand tied behind our back—solidly rooted in the very culture that is obscuring or ignoring the original reason for the season. We find ourselves making up *spiritual* reasons for our cultural practices. For example, we give gifts to each other to remind ourselves of God's great gift of *Jesus* to the world or of the gifts of the *wise men* to *Jesus*. That may sound nice, but is it true? Or do we give gifts because our parents did and everyone else we know does? What kind of parent would you be if you didn't give your child a Christmas present? Or—God forbid—if you didn't celebrate Christmas at all? Very little is intrinsically spiritual with these kinds of expectations; they are almost entirely cultural. Of course, there's nothing inherently wrong with observing such rituals. The difficulty comes in trying to understand and communicate accurately the *real* significance

[3]Both Linus and Lucy lamented this fact long ago in *A Charlie Brown Christmas* (1965). Linus: "Christmas is . . . getting too commercial." Lucy: "We all know that Christmas is a big commercial racket. It's run by a big eastern syndicate, you know." Charles M. Schulz, *A Charlie Brown Christmas*, directed by Bill Melendez, aired December 9, 1965, on CBS.

of Jesus's birth as a human child when its *true* meaning is buried beneath so many layers of culture-related traditions.

Examples abound. What does the decoration of an evergreen tree have to do with Jesus's coming to earth to rescue God's creation? We may tell ourselves that it symbolizes everlasting life because it is *ever-green*, but is that really the reason we set up a Christmas tree each year? Similarly, we may point to candles as a symbol of Jesus as the Light of the World, holly as a symbol of the crown of thorns that was placed upon Jesus's head, the color red as a symbol of Jesus's blood shed on the cross, the Yule log as a symbol of the cross, mistletoe as a symbol of reconciliation, and bells as a symbol for ringing out the good news. Even if some of these associations and symbols date back centuries, they fail to explain why we incorporate these traditional elements in our Christmas celebrations today. If we're honest, we have to admit that we celebrate Christmas the way we do primarily because of our cultural traditions, even though they have little (if any) real connection to Jesus's actual coming to this earth as a baby.

Now please don't misunderstand what we're trying to say here. We are not advocating that all true Christians reject these traditions as mere trappings of culture. Far from it. Traditions can be deeply meaningful and enhance our spiritual experience, and as long as they don't clash with biblical information, they can certainly be used to celebrate key events such as the birth of Jesus by the Virgin Mary. So if you are looking for an argument against the use of Christmas trees or the giving of presents, you are reading the wrong book (though the Puritans made a pretty good run at it; these pious forebears rejected Christmas observances on account of their religious beliefs).[4] We're simply trying to draw attention to the difference that exists between the *traditional* ways in which we celebrate Christmas based upon our culture and the *reality* and *significance* of Jesus's coming to this earth to enact God's grand rescue plan to restore and reclaim humanity. In this regard, it's helpful to

[4] See Andreas J. Köstenberger, "A Puritan Christmas," *Biblical Foundations* (blog), December 16, 2006, http://www.biblicalfoundations.org/a-puritan-christmas.

recognize the many ways in which our cultural traditions, often unintentionally, distort our understanding of the actual import of Jesus's coming as the long-awaited culmination of God's plan.

GOING BACK IN TIME

In order to appreciate the significance of Messiah's coming—and so to understand the *true* meaning of Christmas—we need to travel back in time, back to the first Christmas, before this event even carried that name. We can't offer you a time machine (sorry!), but we can point you to the earliest written witnesses to the first Christmas: the canonical Gospels of Matthew and Luke. (Mark's Gospel picks up the story of Jesus when he's a grown man and does not discuss Jesus's birth. John's Gospel does not mention Jesus's birth directly but surprisingly contributes quite a bit to our understanding of the significance of Jesus's coming—more on that later.) These Gospel authors wrote their accounts on the basis of others' eyewitness testimony; neither Matthew nor Luke (nor even John) was there on that fateful night in Bethlehem. Luke even explicitly alerts his readers to his use of eyewitness testimony in his preface:

> Inasmuch as many have undertaken to compile a narrative of the things that have been accomplished among us, just as those who from the beginning were eyewitnesses and ministers of the word have delivered them to us, it seemed good to me also, having followed all things closely for some time past, to write an orderly account for you, most excellent Theophilus, that you may have certainty concerning the things you have been taught.[5]

Luke provides an account of a careful ancient historian motivated by a desire to present an accurate narrative of the events surrounding Jesus's birth, life, death, and resurrection in order to strengthen his readers' faith. Similarly, while Matthew says nothing of his sources, his Gospel would have likely begun circulating by the late AD 50s to early 60s, early enough that surviving

[5] Luke 1:1–4.

eyewitnesses could still have provided oral source material and confirmed the published contents of his Gospel.

The fact that Matthew and Luke were personally absent from the events they record does not lessen the value of their testimony. Their Gospels reveal a concern for careful and accurate reporting; one detects a complete lack of the fanciful and over-the-top types of stories that various gnostic authors invented about Jesus in the second century.[6] The Gospels are akin to the ancient genre of *bios*, or biography, not fiction.[7] Although we cannot know for certain which eyewitnesses passed on the accounts, likely candidates include Jesus's mother, Mary, as well as his half-brothers James and Jude, both of whom (especially James) served as leaders in the early church and would certainly have known the stories surrounding Jesus's birth. We can safely assume that Joseph had died by the time Jesus began his public ministry because none of the Gospel accounts mention him, but Joseph must have passed on his account of the angel's messages to others, whether Mary, his sons, Jesus, or some other close friends or relatives.

The New Testament Gospel accounts of Jesus's birth—the so-called infancy narratives—provide a different perspective than most modern popular presentations. They are far richer and deeper than can be communicated in a children's Christmas pageant, a still manger scene on a fireplace mantle, or a Christmas card. The baby would not have had a halo and—despite the famous line from "Away in a Manger," "but little Lord Jesus, no crying he makes"—almost certainly would have cried.

Perhaps the hardest aspect of Jesus's coming for modern read-

---

[6] Gnosticism was the first Christian heresy, both denying the goodness of material substance and thus Jesus's human flesh and denying Jesus's full and ultimate divinity.

[7] See the classic work by Richard A. Burridge, *What Are the Gospels? A Comparison with Graeco-Roman Biography*, 2nd ed. (Grand Rapids, MI: Eerdmans, 2004). Andrew T. Lincoln argues that the genre of ancient biography allowed for legendary embellishment in infancy narratives. *Born of a Virgin?* (Grand Rapids, MI: Eerdmans, 2013), 57–67. However, Matthew and Luke doubtfully invented Jesus's virgin birth independently; they more likely passed on the traditions they had received about Jesus's infancy, traditions that family members preserved and that were widespread in earliest Christianity. Richard Bauckham cogently argues that we can trace Luke's genealogy in particular back to Jesus's immediate family members. *Jude and the Relatives of Jesus in the Early Church* (London: T&T Clark, 1990), 315–73. For an extensive discussion of ancient historiographical practices, see Craig S. Keener, *Acts: An Exegetical Commentary: Introduction and 1:1–2:47* (Grand Rapids, MI: Baker, 2012), 51–220.

ers to appreciate is its Jewish context, particularly its connection to the Old Testament. Even as the Gospel infancy narratives are more meaningful than contemporary cultural versions, they lack many of the details that have been added over the centuries. For example, they don't tell us about the nature of the stable (cave, open-air, wood, etc.); whether there even *was* a stable; whether or not animals grazed nearby; or how many wise men traveled to Bethlehem. The wise men almost certainly did *not* arrive on the night of the birth, as most mass-produced manger scenes depict, and a star most likely would not have been suspended right above the roofline. A careful reading of the New Testament infancy narratives in their historical context will help you separate fact from fiction and clear away the brush so you can truly encounter and be changed by the Christ of Christmas.

A GUIDEBOOK

One might best describe this book as a guidebook for reading and encountering the Gospel infancy narratives. No book, no matter how well written, could ever function as a substitute for the narratives themselves, so each chapter will begin with the relevant text of Scripture to be discussed. Each chapter will examine a section of the biblical text with an eye toward proper understanding and application. Sometimes this will require attention to historical and cultural details. At other times it will require looking at connections with the Old Testament or later events in Jesus's life. We aim throughout to present the most important information in a clear and understandable way in order to enable you to grasp and be changed by a biblical understanding of Christmas.

In our companion book, *The Final Days of Jesus*, we set forth two complementary ways of reading the Gospels, vertically and horizontally.[8] Reading the Gospels *vertically* means reading each one (or at least a portion of it, such as its infancy narrative) from beginning to end as a self-contained story in its own right. Reading

---

[8] Andreas J. Köstenberger and Justin Taylor, with Alexander Stewart, *The Final Days of Jesus: The Most Important Week of the Most Important Person Who Ever Lived* (Wheaton, IL: Crossway, 2014), 18–19.

the Gospels *horizontally* means exploring how each presentation relates to the others in a complementary fashion, jointly witnessing to the same historical reality, statements, and events. Both types of reading are valuable; both should be done sequentially. In the present case, since both Matthew's and Luke's infancy narratives (not to mention John's prologue) are so unique and coherent, it makes sense to start with a vertical reading of their respective accounts and to draw horizontal connections once we have completed the vertical readings. This will involve comparisons of various aspects of the Matthean and Lucan infancy narratives, such as their respective genealogies or other elements in their stories; it will also involve comparisons of Matthew's and Luke's accounts on the one hand and John's on the other.[9]

In that vein, our approach to the biblical text will essentially be *biblical*, *exegetical*, *historical*, and *devotional*. *Biblical* means that we will look at how the infancy narratives connect with Old Testament prophecies and in some cases point forward to later fulfillment. We will also try to consistently relate the infancy narratives to the larger story of Scripture.

Exegetical means that we will give careful attention to the words of the actual text.[10] While a biblical approach looks at the entire forest, an exegetical approach carefully examines the individual trees.

Historical means that we will situate and discuss the infancy narratives within their first-century context in ancient Palestine. Critics of Christianity often use a supposedly historical approach to mock certain aspects of the infancy narratives. Some of this criticism is patently superficial and skeptical and stems from a prior rejection of any possibility of God's supernatural intervention in history. If God exists, however, we have no reason to rule out the possibility of supernatural events such as the virgin birth or angelic appearances simply out of a misguided desire to be historical

---

[9] See chaps. 1 and 10 (especially the section, "Matthew and Luke in Harmony") and chap. 14, respectively.

[10] The word *exegetical* comes from the Greek and means literally, "leading or drawing out." Using an exegetical approach is roughly synonymous to what we mean by engaging in inductive Bible study. On this issue, see R. Alan Fuhr and Andreas J. Köstenberger, *Inductive Bible Study: A Method for Biblical Interpretation* (Nashville, TN: B&H Academic, forthcoming).

or scientific. Beyond these biased critiques, some scholars raise legitimate historical questions that we will address, such as the dating of Quirinius's census that precipitated Joseph's and Mary's journey to Bethlehem and the differences between Matthew's and Luke's accounts of Jesus's birth.[11]

Finally, *devotional* means that we will aim to discuss the scriptural texts in such a way that you, the reader, will be drawn closer to God. We don't write simply to convey information; we want you to be delivered and transformed by the same God who has delivered and is transforming us. This devotional aspect does not imply that we will ignore difficult issues or reject logic and rational argument. Christianity, rightly understood, does not entail a rejection of reason![12] Our attention to the devotional aspect of this material rather emphasizes the fact that, especially in a case like Jesus's birth, information alone is insufficient. The technological revolution we are witnessing in our lifetime notwithstanding, an increase in knowledge by itself will never be able to fix humanity's greatest problems—sin, alienation, and death. Only God can do that. We hope that this book will draw you closer to the One who did not abandon a rebellious creation but set out to rescue it at great expense to himself. God's plan of redemption was conceived even before creation, was set in motion the moment humanity rebelled against its Creator, and was accomplished by the birth, life, death, and resurrection of Jesus of Nazareth. It will achieve its consummation when Jesus returns to reclaim and restore God's creation once and for all. What a glorious day that will be!

But we're getting ahead of ourselves. Let's rewind so that, with the help of sound historical research and a careful reading of the relevant texts, we will be able to put ourselves in the place of the people who lived at the time when the original Christmas—the birth of the Christ-child—took place.

---

[11] Quirinius's census is mentioned in Luke 2:2.

[12] This is the underlying premise of Andreas J. Köstenberger, Darrell L. Bock, and Josh Chatraw, *Truth Matters: Confident Faith in a Confusing World* (Nashville, TN: B&H, 2014); and the book by the same authors, *Truth in a Culture of Doubt: Engaging Skeptical Challenges to the Bible* (Nashville, TN: B&H, 2014).

THE FIRST DAYS OF JESUS ACCORDING TO MATTHEW, LUKE, AND JOHN

SCRIPTURE PASSAGE	EVENTS RECORDED
Matthew 1:1-17	Jesus's ancestry
Matthew 1:18-25	The virgin birth
Matthew 2:1-12	The visit of the *magoi*
Matthew 2:13-15	Escape to Egypt
Matthew 2:16-18	Herod's order to kill boys under two years of age
Matthew 2:19-23	Return of Jesus's family to Nazareth
Luke 1:5-25	The foretelling of John the Baptist's birth
Luke 1:26-38	The foretelling of Jesus's birth
Luke 1:39-45	Mary's visit to Elizabeth
Luke 1:46-56	Mary's song (*Magnificat*)
Luke 1:57-66	The birth of John the Baptist
Luke 1:67-80	Zechariah's prophecy (*Benedictus*)
Luke 2:1-7	The birth of Jesus Christ

SCRIPTURE PASSAGE	EVENTS RECORDED
Luke 2:8-21	The angelic announcement to the shepherds
Luke 2:22–38	Jesus's presentation at the temple; the prophecies of Simeon (*Nunc Dimittis*) and Anna
Luke 2:39–40	Return of Jesus's family to Nazareth
John 1:1-5, 18	The Word's preexistence and agency in creation
John 1:6–8, 15	The witness of John the Baptist
John 1:9–14	The Word's assumption of flesh
John 1:16–17	Culmination of the law, grace, and truth

PART 1

VIRGIN-BORN MESSIAH

1

THE LONG-AWAITED MESSIAH

SON OF ABRAHAM, SON OF DAVID

MATTHEW 1:1-17

The book of the genealogy of Jesus Christ, the son of David, the son of Abraham.

Abraham was the father of Isaac, and Isaac the father of Jacob, and Jacob the father of Judah and his brothers, and Judah the father of Perez and Zerah by Tamar, and Perez the father of Hezron, and Hezron the father of Ram, and Ram the father of Amminadab, and Amminadab the father of Nahshon, and Nahshon the father of Salmon, and Salmon the father of Boaz by Rahab, and Boaz the father of Obed by Ruth, and Obed the father of Jesse, and Jesse the father of David the king.

And David was the father of Solomon by the wife of Uriah, and Solomon the father of Rehoboam, and Rehoboam the father of Abijah, and Abijah the father of Asaph, and Asaph the father of Jehoshaphat, and Jehoshaphat the father of Joram, and Joram the father of Uzziah, and Uzziah the father of Jotham, and Jotham the father of Ahaz, and Ahaz the father of Hezekiah, and Hezekiah the father of Manasseh, and Manasseh the father of Amos, and Amos the father of Josiah, and Josiah the father of Jechoniah and his brothers, at the time of the deportation to Babylon.

And after the deportation to Babylon: Jechoniah was the father of Shealtiel, and Shealtiel the father of Zerubbabel, and Zerubbabel the father of Abiud, and Abiud the father of Eliakim, and Eliakim the father of Azor, and Azor the father of Zadok, and Zadok the father of Achim, and Achim the father of Eliud, and Eliud the father of Eleazar, and Eleazar the father of Matthan, and Matthan the father of Jacob, and Jacob the father of Joseph the husband of Mary, of whom Jesus was born, who is called Christ.

So all the generations from Abraham to David were fourteen generations, and from David to the deportation to Babylon fourteen generations, and from the deportation to Babylon to the Christ fourteen generations.

OUR STORIES AND GOD'S STORY

All the world's a stage,
And all the men and women merely players,
They have their exits and their entrances,
And one man in his time plays many parts.[1]

Our lives are original stories. Each one is different from every other. We are copyrighted, with no possibility of plagiarism. Every story has a unique and different beginning. The conflicts, heroes, and villains all vary. Some stories end sooner than others. The lives of the rich, powerful, famous, or influential are memorialized for future generations in biographies or autobiographies, while the poor often die in anonymity. However, a dark shadow hangs over each of our plots. The inescapable reality of sickness, death, and loss makes every one of our stories a tragedy to some degree or another. Yet as Scripture makes clear, death will not have the final word. For those in Christ, resurrection will triumph.

The Bible is also a story, *God's* story. It recounts the Creator's involvement with his creation, how he made a beautiful and good world, and how he fashioned humankind in his image and as his representatives to share in his rule. Created in God's image, we are able to think, feel, love, choose, perceive beauty, and enjoy God's

[1] William Shakespeare, *As You Like It*, ed. Agnes Latham (London: Methuen, 1967), 2.7.139–142.

good creation. The Bible also recounts how things went terribly wrong, how the human race rejected God's rule and embraced the rule of sin and death. As a result, our lives are now marked by suffering, sickness, sin, hurt, and, finally and inescapably, death. Tragically, our ancestors threw off God's good rule and became slaves to the evil rule of sin and death, and we all, whether we like it or even acknowledge it, share in the same fate.

The Bible continues to tell the story of how God did not simply walk away from his creation in the midst of turmoil and rebellion but purposed to rescue it at great cost to himself through the sacrificial death and subsequent resurrection of his Son, Jesus. What's more, God's story continues beyond Jesus's resurrection. A future day is coming when the Messiah will return physically to his creation to remake the heavens and the earth, to wipe away every tear, and to remove sin and death—the realities that have kept his creation under their spell—forever.

The two halves of God's story pivot around one central point: the coming of Jesus to rescue God's wrecked and ruined creation—BC and AD. Jesus's coming was the great game-changer of history. This chapter will look at the unfolding of God's story leading up to the day when God himself visited his creation through the incarnation, with a view toward the way in which God's story impacts the unfolding stories of our lives. Our involvement in *God's* story has the ability to rewrite *our* stories—to change their endings. Put another way, become a part of God's story, and he will write yours. This chapter will present God's story, and the epilogue will return to the question of how we let God write our stories.

GOD'S STORY: A GENEALOGY?

It would be interesting to know how many of you reading this book skipped the genealogy in Matthew 1:1–17 reproduced at the beginning of this chapter. Perhaps some of you skimmed it. Maybe a very few read every word, whether out of a desire to be spiritual, a respect for God's Word, an obsessive-compulsive personality, or some other reason. Genealogies typically hold very little interest for most people in the twenty-first-century Western world (those with a passion for genealogical research excepted). Lists of ancestors bore most of us. In our present culture, we are lucky to keep memories alive for three generations, maybe four if we are the nostalgic type or had a famous ancestor.

Our general lack of interest in genealogies creates an interesting situation when it comes to Jesus's family tree in the first chapter of Matthew's Gospel. Consider the following four facts.

First, based upon evidence from the earliest Christian writings following the New Testament, a collection known as the apostolic Fathers, Matthew was the *most widely used* Christian Gospel in the first two centuries. Many of the early Christian writers possessed some form of Matthew's Gospel.

Second, when the earliest Christians began to assemble the books that would become the New Testament, they placed Matthew's Gospel *first*. This tradition has remained to this day, and all modern Bibles start the New Testament with the Gospel of Matthew, indicating its foundational position.

Third, Matthew began his Gospel with a *genealogy*. Even ancient authors knew that it was important to put attention-getting or particularly important material at the beginning of a speech or book in order to arouse people's interest. The fact that Matthew began his Gospel with Jesus's genealogy indicates its importance. The entire New Testament begins with these verses!

Fourth, the Old Testament book of Ezra bears witness to the fact that genealogies played a crucial role in Jewish society following the return from Babylonian *exile*. Some men who claimed to belong to the priesthood were excluded because their names were not found in the genealogies and they could not prove their credentials or pedigree.[2] Such evidence was needed at this point in Israelite history in order for those returning from exile to claim family property and offices. At the time of Jesus's birth, many viewed Herod the Great negatively because he was a half-Edomite by ancestry and not a pure Jew. Ancestry was culturally,

[2]See Ezra 2:59–63.

religiously, and politically important in the era we call Second Temple Judaism—that is, the period between the reconstruction of the temple in 516 BC and the Roman destruction of Jerusalem and the temple in AD 70.

These considerations confront us with a question: What are we missing when we skip or skim over the genealogy found in Matthew 1:1–17? To answer this question, we need to embark on a brief journey through the Old Testament to trace the unfolding of God's story leading up to the opening verses of Matthew's story about the coming of the Messiah.

THE BEGINNING OF TIME

A Distant Promise

In the early days of humankind, when the first people rejected God's rule and things went radically wrong, the Bible records a somewhat enigmatic promise. In judgment of Satan, the deceiving Serpent, God declares the following: "I will put enmity between you and the woman, and between your offspring and her offspring; he shall bruise your head, and you shall bruise his heel."[3] While a bit strange and enigmatic, this prophecy in essence declares that one day a *descendant of the woman* (that is, a human being) will crush the head of the Serpent, Satan (a created, angelic being who had previously rebelled against his Creator).

Imagine someone reading through the Bible for the first time without knowing its ending. This hypothetical reader just read how God created an amazing, beautiful world and how Adam and Eve believed the Serpent's lie and chose to throw off God's rule to grasp hold of all the "good things" God was holding back from them. What a breathtaking disaster! Within the course of one chapter, the world has gone from beautiful, orderly, and joyful to marred, cursed, and sorrowful. Genesis 3 ends with the world dark and broken and with God barring his image bearers and representatives from access to the tree of life. At this point,

---

[3]Gen. 3:15.

the reader desperately needs a piece of good news, and God does not disappoint. While the Serpent and humanity will continue their conflict, one day a human being, an offspring of the woman, will, at great cost to himself—the "bruising of his heel"—crush the Serpent's head.

Our hypothetical reader immediately begins to wonder, who is this descendent of the woman? When will he come and conquer the Serpent, setting everything right in God's creation? At this point, the text offers few clues as to his identity; all that is known is that he will be human and a descendant of Eve.

C. 2100 BC

God Chooses a Family

The reader doesn't have to wait long for additional clues because God soon narrows the messianic line down to a particular family: the family of *Abraham*.

> Now the Lord said to Abram, "Go from your country and your kindred and your father's house to the land that I will show you. And I will make of you a great nation, and I will bless you and make your name great, so that you will be a blessing. I will bless those who bless you, and him who dishonors you I will curse, and in you all the families of the earth shall be blessed."[4]

God chooses a particular man from the great mass of humanity in order to reveal himself and his plan further. As the stories about Abraham in Genesis soon make clear, he is far from perfect.[5] He makes many mistakes—lies repeatedly, acts out of unbelief—but, more than anything else, he lives a life marked by faith in God's promises. God has told Abraham that he will make his descendants a great nation and that through Abraham's offspring all the nations of the earth will be blessed. Our reader is filled with expectation. Is Abraham the one? Is this the "seed of the woman"

[4] Gen. 12:1–3.
[5] Genesis 12–25.

who will overcome the Serpent and set things right again in God's creation?

As the narrative of Abraham's life progresses, it becomes clear to the reader that he is not the Promised One, but rather, one of his descendants will be the source of God's blessing to the whole world. Our reader does not yet know the precise identity of the promised offspring of the woman, but the search has been narrowed down considerably; that person will be a descendent of Abraham.

Further Clues

Abraham, of course, had a multitude of descendants, starting with Ishmael (Abraham's son but not through his wife, Sarah, and thus ineligible to receive God's promise), and followed by Isaac, Jacob, and Jacob's sons. Do the subsequent Old Testament narratives narrow things down still further? As Jacob, Abraham's grandson, lies on his deathbed in Egypt, he summons his twelve sons and prophesies concerning each one of them.[6] Things take an interesting turn when he utters the following prophecy concerning his son Judah: "The scepter shall not depart from Judah, nor the ruler's staff from between his feet, until tribute comes to him; and to him shall be the obedience of the peoples."[7] This both narrows down God's promise to Abraham and expands its scope. Abraham's seed through the line of Judah will bring blessing to the nations through a *kingly ruler* (symbolized by the scepter) who will receive tribute and obedience from the peoples of the earth.

C. 1000 BC

It will take hundreds of years, but in due course the reader discovers that this prophecy finds initial fulfillment in a descendent of Judah named *David*. When God first chooses David to be king

---

[6] Genesis 49.

[7] Gen. 49:10. The ESV contains a footnote noting some translational difficulties in this verse: "By a slight revocalization; a slight emendation yields (compare Septuagint, Syriac, Targums) *until he comes to whom it belongs*; Hebrew *until Shiloh comes*, or *until he comes to Shiloh*." *The ESV Study Bible*, ed. Wayne Grudem (Wheaton, IL: Crossway, 2008), 134. Fortunately, the different options do not affect the primary sense of the prophecy.

and Samuel the prophet anoints him,[8] our hypothetical reader can connect the dots and breathe a sigh of relief. Jacob's ancient prophecy concerning the line of Judah is finally beginning to see fulfillment! Going back even farther, the reader can connect these dots to God's promise to Abraham and to his initial announcement of judgment to the Serpent. Is David the one? Is David the seed of the woman who will overcome the Serpent and set things right in God's world? Has the promised deliverer, the "seed of the woman," finally arrived?

The Davidic narratives in the Old Testament soon make clear that David will not fulfill the original messianic promise. Like Abraham, Jacob, and Judah before him, David's life is marked by sin and failure even as he is known for his faith and called "a man after God's heart."[9] As in the cases of Abraham and Judah, however, God narrows the focus to a descendent of King David. At one point during David's kingly reign over Israel, God sends the prophet Nathan to give David the following promise: "And your house and your kingdom shall be made sure forever before me. Your throne shall be established forever."[10] A *descendent of David* will rule on his throne and over his kingdom forever.

Did God's Promises Fail?

Prospects look fairly bright with Nathan's promise to David that God will establish his kingdom and throne forever, but matters do not seem to go as planned. David's kingly descendants regularly stray from God's laws and ways and often lead the nation into idolatry (the worship of other gods) and rejection of God's rule. The Old Testament prophets[11] declare God's words, warnings, and promises during this period of national decline. Each in his own way, the prophets warn the people of judgment for rejecting the Lord and envision a future time when God will set things right in

[8] 1 Sam. 16:1–13.
[9] Acts 13:22; cf. 1 Sam. 13:14.
[10] 2 Sam. 7:16.
[11] That is, those featured in the portion of the Hebrew Scriptures called "The Prophets": Isaiah, Jeremiah, Ezekiel, and the twelve so-called Minor Prophets.

all the earth through a descendent of David. The wolf will lie down with the lamb; swords will be beaten into plowshares.[12] A Davidic ruler will usher in world peace and blessings for the nations.

722 BC / 605-586 BC

Our reader soon learns that because God's people fail to repent, he eventually sends them into exile through the conquest of the foreign nations of Assyria (722 BC) and Babylon (605–586 BC). Although they return from exile and resettle the land, they experience nothing that could remotely be described as the fulfillment of God's messianic promises. Some of the Old Testament writers struggle with this lack of fulfillment. The psalmist expresses this pain poignantly in Psalm 89:

> You have said, "I have made a covenant with my chosen one;
> I have sworn to David my servant:
> 'I will establish your offspring forever
> and build your throne for all generations.'" . . .
>
> "My steadfast love I will keep for him forever,
> and my covenant will stand firm for him.
> I will establish his offspring forever
> and his throne as the days of the heavens.
> If his children forsake my law
> and do not walk according to my rules,
> if they violate my statues
> and do not keep my commandments,
> then I will punish their transgression with the rod
> and their iniquity with stripes,
> but I will not remove from him my steadfast love
> or be false to my faithfulness.
> I will not violate my covenant
> or alter the word that went forth from my lips.
> Once for all I have sworn by my holiness;
> I will not lie to David.
> His offspring shall endure forever,

[12] Isa. 11:6, 2:4.

his throne as long as the sun before me.
Like the moon it shall be established forever,
a faithful witness in the skies."

But now you have cast off and rejected;
you are full of wrath against your anointed.
You have renounced the covenant with your servant;
you have defiled his crown in the dust.
You have breached all his walls;
you have laid his strongholds in ruins.
All who pass by plunder him;
he has become the scorn of his neighbors.
You have exalted the right hand of his foes;
you have made all his enemies rejoice.
You have also turned back the edge of his sword,
and you have not made him stand in battle.
You have made his splendor to cease
and cast his throne to the ground.
You have cut short the days of his youth;
you have covered him with shame.

How long, O Lord? Will you hide yourself forever?
How long will your wrath burn like fire? . . .

Lord, where is your steadfast love of old,
which by your faithfulness you swore to David?[13]

This passage powerfully affirms the surety of God's promises to David while simultaneously crying out in pain: Why has God abandoned his promises? Why has he broken his covenant? We put our hope in him and have been devastated: "Where is your steadfast love of old, which by your faithfulness you swore to David?"

400s BC

The Old Testament ends with the messianic promise unfulfilled, looking ahead to God's future action of bringing salvation. From

[13] Ps. 89:3–4, 28–46, 49.

what our hypothetical reader sees, the promised offspring of the woman has not (yet) come. The world has not yet been set right. Blessing has not come to the world through Abraham's descendants. The scepter has departed from the line of Judah. David's kingdom has been defeated and lost, and no Davidic ruler reigns to mediate God's blessings to the nations. The Old Testament ends looking to the future for closure and fulfillment. While the Second Temple period is anything but silent, the prophetic voice has ceased.[14] The waiting has begun.

TURN OF THE ERA

With this background in place, we read the opening words of Matthew's Gospel with new eyes: "The book of the genealogy of Jesus Christ, the son of David, the son of Abraham."[15] The entire New Testament begins with a verse that declares *Jesus* to be the Son of David, the Son of Abraham, the long-awaited Messiah! Jesus's descent from David would turn out to be foundational for later New Testament theology.[16]

The Book of the Genealogy

The genealogy proceeds to establish Jesus's identity—traced back to David, the descendent of Judah, the descendent of Abraham, whom we know from the Old Testament narratives to be the descendent of Eve.[17] Finally, our reader finds resolution to the tension introduced in Genesis. *Jesus* is the promised seed who will set everything right! The entire Old Testament progressively narrows down the identity of God's Messiah until the day he finally arrives—the day God comes to his creation to undo the work of the fall, destroy the works of the Devil, and begin to set things right.

Four features of Matthew's listing of Jesus's family tree deserve comment. To begin with, the first two Greek words of the New

---

[14] For a discussion of Second Temple Jewish expectation during the Intertestamental period, see the appendix.

[15] Matt. 1:1.

[16] Acts 2:29–36; 13:22–23; Rom. 1:3; 15:12; 2 Tim. 2:8; Rev. 5:5; 22:16.

[17] Jesus's genealogy in Luke 3:23–38 makes this point explicit and traces Jesus's ancestry all the way back to Adam.

Testament, *biblos geneseōs* ("The Book of the Genealogy"), mirror the language used to introduce creation itself and the genealogy connected to Adam.[18] The use of this language points the attentive reader back to the creation of the world and links Jesus's genealogy to God's original plan for his creation.[19]

Second, the inclusion of four *women* in the genealogy is unusual, particularly in light of the fact that each of the women was an outsider to Israel with a questionable background. Most ancient genealogies excluded women, particularly women who may have tarnished the family line. Matthew does the opposite. Tamar was a Canaanite who disguised herself as a prostitute in order to seduce Judah.[20] Rahab was a Canaanite prostitute who lied to protect the Israelite spies and helped overthrow Jericho.[21] Ruth was a Moabite woman who moved to Israel upon the death of her husband.[22] Finally, Bathsheba was the wife of Uriah the Hittite; King David married Bathsheba after fathering a child by her and killing her husband.[23] The inclusion of these non-Israelite women foreshadows the spread of the gospel to the Gentiles and bears witness to the grace of God that actively seeks to forgive and restore sinners and to reach out to those who are marginalized and viewed as outsiders.

Third, Mary falls in line with these other women by conceiving a child in an *unusual*, *questionable*, or *surprising* manner. The family tree itself anticipates the virgin birth of Jesus by breaking its normal pattern of presenting information. The chain of generations consistently reads, "[father's name] *was the father of* [son's name]." Matthew repeats this pattern for every single father-son pair until Joseph: "Joseph the husband of *Mary, of whom Jesus was*

[18] See Gen. 2:4: "These are the generations [*biblos geneseōs* in the Septuagint, the ancient Greek translation of the Hebrew Bible] of the heavens and the earth when they were created, in the day that the Lord God made the earth and the heavens"; and Gen. 5:1: "This is the book of the generations [*biblos geneseōs*] of Adam. When God created man, he made him in the likeness of God."

[19] In this regard, Matthew shares an affinity with John's Gospel, which likewise opens with establishing a connection between Jesus's coming into this world and God's original creation (John 1:1; see also vv. 3–5). We will explore this in greater detail in chap. 13 below.

[20] Genesis 38.

[21] Joshua 2; 6:25.

[22] See the book of Ruth. The Moabites were particularly despised in Israel's history. Deuteronomy 23:3 states, "No Ammonite or Moabite may enter the assembly of the Lord. Even to the tenth generation, none of them may enter the assembly of the Lord forever."

[23] 2 Samuel 11–12.

born, who is called Christ [Messiah]."[24] The Greek language itself specifies clearly that Jesus is the biological son of Mary but not of Joseph.[25] Thus, although Joseph was Jesus's *legal* adoptive parent, he was not his *biological* father. The alert reader takes note of this curious way of putting things but must wait until the end of the chapter to receive additional details regarding this startling change in the pattern of listing Jesus's ancestry.

Fourth, by dividing salvation history into three periods of fourteen generations each (Abraham to David, David to the exile, the exile to Jesus), Matthew communicates the theological truth that *God* was in *control* throughout even the most difficult periods of Israel's history—the Babylonian exile—to move history toward this climactic point in the coming of Jesus the Messiah. Interestingly, Jewish apocalyptic (end-time) literature commonly divided history into set time periods to indicate God's control and guidance of history. Such divisions also aided memorization in a primarily oral culture, and the use of the number fourteen may have even emphasized the link to David via gematria (numerology).[26]

The Genealogies in Matthew and Luke

Many have pointed out the differences between the genealogies in Matthew and Luke,[27] as well as how they differ from Old Testament genealogies of Jewish history. We cannot explore the subject in depth here, but scholars have suggested several ways to explain the variations. Some have posited that Matthew traces Joseph's genealogy while Luke follows Mary's, perhaps reflected in Matthew's decision to link Jesus to David through Solomon while Luke runs his lineage through Nathan.[28] This position, while popular, is less convincing because both genealogies seem to run through Joseph

---

[24] Matt. 1:16.

[25] The relative pronoun "of whom" is feminine.

[26] Many scholars believe that the number fourteen was important for Matthew because the numerical value of David's name is fourteen. One arrives at this number by using the ancient practice of gematria (numerology) in which each consonant carries a numerical value. The consonant *d* (*dalet*) equals four and the consonant *w* (*vav*; our English *v*) equals six. "DaWiD" thus equals fourteen (*d*[4] + *w*[6] + *d*[4] = 14). If Matthew indeed had this kind of numerical symbolism in mind, it would further strengthen Jesus's connection to his ancestor David.

[27] See Luke 3:23–38.

[28] Luke 3:31.

and because it would have been very unusual in antiquity to begin a genealogy with the mother.

Scholars have also commonly explained the differences by pointing to levirate marriage. Particularly in the period lacking biblical evidence between the exile and Joseph, we have difficulty identifying when a genealogy focuses on legal or biological fatherhood, since under Jewish law at that time a man could father a son under his deceased brother's name, a practice called "levirate marriage." Adoptions could further complicate the picture.

More commonly today, Matthew's genealogy is described as a dynastic document focused on the royal line while Luke's is linked more closely with a biological family tree.[29] Craig Keener notes, "modern scholars more frequently argue that Matthew provides the legal line of royal inheritance; but those who wish can connect this lineage with Luke's physical line by means of two adoptions."[30]

Other factors contribute to the smaller differences. Matthew and Luke were likely depending on the Septuagint, the ancient Greek translation of the Hebrew Bible, which differed in some respects from the Hebrew texts available to us, particularly in the spelling of names. Matthew also evidently skipped some generations by linking a son to a grandfather or great-grandfather. In addition, some extrabiblical Jewish sources for these genealogies that have been lost may have contained variations or corruptions. Synthesizing various available genealogies would have also been a complicated process.

All of these factors likely play a role in explaining the differences between Matthew's list of Jesus's ancestry and other available genealogies, but we should also remember that ancient genealogies were often written for specific purposes and were less concerned with scientific exactness than are modern genealogies. Matthew intended his genealogy to show Jesus's concrete historical and legal connection to *David* and beyond that to God's covenant with

[29] See R. T. France, *The Gospel of Matthew*, The New International Commentary on the New Testament (Grand Rapids, MI: Eerdmans, 2007), 32–33; Richard Bauckham, *Jude and the Relatives of Jesus in the Early Church* (London: T&T Clark, 1990), 315–73.

[30] Craig Keener, *A Commentary on the Gospel of Matthew* (Grand Rapids, MI: Eerdmans, 1999), 75.

Abraham. Matthew accomplished this purpose legitimately even if his genealogy skipped, for example, Ahaziah, Joash, and Amaziah between Joram and Uzziah in order to keep the number to fourteen—a strategy that facilitated memorization and highlighted Jesus's connection to David by way of gematria.[31]

The Mystery Revealed

With Matthew's genealogy, God has at last revealed the identity of the hero of his story. We know who the long-awaited deliverer is. In this way, Matthew strikes a note of fulfillment, climax, and consummation. The messianic hope has found its fulfillment in Jesus. The Messiah has come! This chapter has covered a lot of ground by tracing the development of God's story through the Old Testament narratives. In the epilogue we will return to the relationship between God's story and the individual stories of our lives. Jesus's birth, life, death, and resurrection marked the turning point of God's story, but the story is not yet over. Jesus has not yet returned, and his followers are even now called to join him in his mission. Jesus's birth is not just a past event with no significance; Jesus changed the course of history and even now, two thousand years later, can change the course of your life. But we are getting ahead of ourselves. The following chapters will slow down and focus much more closely on the events surrounding Jesus's birth. Matthew's narrative begins by answering the question, "How did the Messiah's birth come about?"

---

[31] See the discussion above. Compare Matt. 1:8–9 with 1 Chron. 3:10–12; Uzziah is likely an alternative name for Azariah.

2

GOD WITH US, BORN OF A VIRGIN

MATTHEW 1:18-25

Now the birth of Jesus Christ took place in this way. When his mother Mary had been betrothed to Joseph, before they came together she was found to be with child from the Holy Spirit. And her husband Joseph, being a just man and unwilling to put her to shame, resolved to divorce her quietly. But as he considered these things, behold, an angel of the Lord appeared to him in a dream, saying, "Joseph, son of David, do not fear to take Mary as your wife, for that which is conceived in her is from the Holy Spirit. She will bear a son, and you shall call his name Jesus, for he will save his people from their sins." All this took place to fulfill what the Lord had spoken by the prophet:

> "Behold, the virgin shall conceive and bear a son,
> and they shall call his name Immanuel"

(which means, God with us). When Joseph woke from sleep, he did as the angel of the Lord commanded him: he took his wife, but knew her not until she had given birth to a son. And he called his name Jesus.

6 OR 5 BC

The Long-Awaited Child Is Born

Matthew's narrative loses no time in moving from the introductory genealogy, which established Jesus's ancestry in conjunction with Abraham and King David, to an account of Jesus's birth. As we saw in the previous chapter, the legal and biological connection to Abraham and David was necessary for Jesus to be the fulfillment of the Old Testament promises God had made to Abraham and David concerning their seed, but by itself, descent from Abraham and David was not enough. Abraham had many descendants, as did David. What made Jesus *the* descendent, who would bless and rule the nations forever? Why not some other descendent of Abraham or David? What made Jesus special and unique as *the* seed of Abraham and *the* Son of David?

These questions can be and have been answered in many ways. First, the Gospel narratives in Matthew, Mark, Luke, and John present *Jesus's own teaching and healing ministry* as evidence of his identity.[1] *John the Baptist*, a highly respected prophet and holy man in the eyes of the common people of the day, bore witness to who Jesus was. Paul drew attention to the *resurrection* as the final and definitive proof of Jesus's identity and vindication by God.[2] The *miraculous events* and *supernatural announcements surrounding Jesus's birth* reported in the infancy narratives come alongside these other lines of evidence to provide their own special contribution to establishing the truthfulness of Jesus's claims. Jesus was not just *a* son of David; he was *the* long-awaited descendant of David who would fulfill God's promises to his people and ultimately set things right in the world. He was, as we shall soon see, God with us.

A "Father's" Perspective

Matthew's infancy narrative is told from the perspective of *Joseph*, Jesus's legal adoptive father. Told from this "paternal" vantage point,

[1] This purpose is particularly evident in John's presentation of Jesus's miracles as signs: see especially John 2:11; 4:54; 6:13–14; 9:1–3; 12:37–40; and 20:30–31. Jesus's miracles demonstrated that he was God's supernaturally sent Messiah. See Andreas J. Köstenberger, "The Seventh Johannine Sign: A Study in John's Christology," *Bulletin of Biblical Research* 5 (1995): 87–103.

[2] Rom. 1:4.

they provide an account of Joseph's character and actions. Luke's narrative, as we will see in future chapters, provides *Mary's* perspective on the events that unfolded. The different points of view may possibly reflect different sources. Perhaps Matthew interviewed or gained access to oral or written accounts through some of Joseph's sons or close friends and relatives while Luke drew information from Mary or her relatives. We don't know the answers to some of the questions; we can only speculate based on the way in which Matthew and Luke wrote their respective accounts.

Different sources are a distinct possibility, but since two of Jesus's half-brothers, James and Jude, were active in the leadership of the early church (especially James), it is probable that *both* Matthew *and* Luke would have had access to similar sources and accounts that could be traced back directly to Jesus's family members and relatives. If so, Matthew and Luke each may have exercised their authorial prerogative to select particular elements in the story of Jesus's birth that were in keeping with their larger overriding purpose for writing their respective Gospels. On the one hand, Matthew may have told the infancy narrative in his Gospel from Joseph's perspective because the paternal viewpoint would have most interested a Jewish audience. Luke, on the other hand, may have chosen to depict the story of Jesus's birth from his mother, Mary's, point of view because it echoed a key theme in his Gospel, namely Jesus's consistent concern for women and others with comparatively low status in the culture of his day.

It may also be that Luke chose to tell Mary's story because she was Jesus's *real* mother while Joseph was only Jesus's *adoptive* father. Matthew, while also acknowledging this fact in narrating the virgin birth, may have chosen to tell the story from Joseph's perspective *despite* the fact that he was not Jesus's real father because of his overriding concern to present Jesus as born in the line of David, following the paternal ancestral family tree.[3]

[3] Andrew T. Lincoln, in *Born of a Virgin?* (Grand Rapids, MI: Eerdmans, 2013), pits Matthew's presentation of Jesus as the Son of David against his narration of the virgin birth, claiming that these two elements contradict each other. However, it is much more likely that Matthew affirmed both Joseph's paternal link to Jesus in a legal and adoptive sense and Mary's maternal link to Jesus through the overshadowing work of the Holy Spirit. See our further interaction with Lincoln below.

NINE MONTHS PRIOR TO JESUS'S BIRTH (7 OR 6 BC)

The first sentence in verse 18 introduces the remainder of chapter 1: "Now the birth of Jesus Christ [or Jesus the Messiah] took place in this way." Matthew is very selective in the information he includes in his account. For example, he does not mention the lives of Mary and Joseph in Nazareth, the appearance of the angel to Mary, Mary's visit to Elizabeth, the census, the trip to Bethlehem, the lack of room in the inn, or the manger. Nothing Matthew writes contradicts Luke's account; he simply omits this information, either because he was unaware of it or, perhaps more likely, because he chose to highlight other aspects of the story of the Messiah's birth in keeping with his own purposes for writing his Gospel.

This unavoidable selectivity brings the material Matthew chooses to include into sharper focus. He begins by noting the important fact that *after* Mary and Joseph had been betrothed but *before* they had come together in a sexually consummated marriage, she became pregnant by the Holy Spirit. Because ancient Jewish betrothal involved a legally binding contract, it differed quite substantially from our modern idea of engagement. Betrothal could be broken only by an official divorce, and sexual activity during this period was viewed as adultery and could carry the death penalty.

If it were not for the final phrase, "from the Holy Spirit," Matthew would be doing nothing more than reporting a small-town scandal about a young woman's pregnancy. Such a scandal would have brought incredible shame on the girl's family and could have resulted in her death.

The final phrase, however, changes everything. Matthew is reporting not a shameful scandal but an instance of miraculous, divine intervention into human history. The phrase itself could legitimately communicate the *source* (*from* the Holy Spirit), the *cause* (*because* of the Holy Spirit), or the *means* (by *means* of the Holy Spirit) of Jesus's birth. Whichever way we translate the phrase, the essential fact remains unchanged: this was no ordinary human conception; God was at work! The Holy Spirit was associated with

God's creative activity in the Old Testament,[4] and Matthew's description of the Holy Spirit's role in Mary's virginal conception sets the account apart from any alleged Greco-Roman parallels, since parallels from the broader pagan world all depend upon a god having sexual intercourse with a human. Matthew excludes any hint of such activity from his description of the conception.

Matthew, of course, is commenting on the situation after the fact. How were Joseph, Mary's parents, or the other villagers to know that this pregnancy was a result of divine intervention and not of sexual promiscuity, immorality, or rape? They were no more likely to believe Mary's claims to purity and innocence than we would be likely to believe such a claim by someone today. Mary was in a very difficult, shameful, and potentially dangerous position. Who would believe her?

SOMETIME AFTER JESUS'S CONCEPTION IN MARY'S WOMB (C. 6 BC)

After this brief presentation of the fundamental facts surrounding the conception of Jesus in Mary's womb, Matthew introduces Joseph as a man who was just and righteous. This description sets Joseph apart as a man who characteristically lived in accordance with God's standards. This righteousness moved Joseph, in the present case, to seek a merciful solution to Mary's apparent infidelity. At this point, Joseph likely doubted that Mary was innocent, but his character compelled him to act in a way that would reduce her shame and shield her from the potentially deadly consequences of adultery. A quiet, private divorce seemed his only alternative. It was clear to Joseph that he must divorce Mary since she was carrying a child that he did not father, but he desired to divorce her as mercifully as possible. If he proceeded with the marriage and pretended that the child was his, he could have exposed himself to public shame, since it was generally viewed as immoral to engage in sexual activity during the betrothal period.

---

[4] See Gen. 1:2.

The First Dream

While Joseph was weighing his options and trying to come to a just yet merciful decision on the basis of his human wisdom, God intervened to set him on a course that he would have never chosen for himself. An angel of the Lord appeared to Joseph in a dream one night and gave him additional information and a command that fundamentally altered his mental list of pros and cons surrounding his decision. First, the angel commanded him not to be afraid to marry Mary since the child was a result of the activity of the Holy Spirit. This confirmation of the child's divine source shattered Joseph's human understanding of the situation: the child was not the shameful result of immorality. Second, the angel informed Joseph that the child would be a male child, a son. Finally, the angel commanded Joseph to name the son Jesus, because "he will save his people from their sins."[5]

What is the significance of the name Jesus? The Greek name Jesus is equivalent to the Hebrew name Joshua, which, reflecting the angel's comment, means "Yahweh saves." The name Jesus therefore points to Yahweh's willingness and ability to save his people and recalls Joshua's role in leading God's people into the possession of the land that God had promised. Jesus was a common name in first-century Palestine, and parents often named their sons Jesus as an expression of their hope that God would one day act to save and deliver his people as he had done in the past.[6]

The angel commanded Joseph to name the boy Jesus because he would realize these hopes. The Hebrew prophets had repeatedly promised that God would one day save his people from their sins. A statement in the book of Isaiah epitomizes this hope: "All we like sheep have gone astray; we have turned—every one—to his own way; and the LORD has laid on him the iniquity of us all."[7] Many Jews around the time of Jesus's birth understood that their sin and

[5] Matt. 1:21b.

[6] Richard Bauckham, building upon the research of Tal Ilan, provides evidence to argue that Jesus was the sixth-most popular name in Palestine during the first century. *Jesus and the Eyewitnesses: The Gospels as Eyewitness Testimony* (Grand Rapids, MI: Eerdmans, 2006), 85.

[7] Isa. 53:6. See also Isa. 40:2; Jer. 31:31–34; Ezek. 36:25–27; Dan. 9:24; Zech. 13:1.

idolatry as a people had led to Babylon's conquest of their land and the resultant exile, and they realized that things had never been the same. They knew that sin was a problem that must be dealt with in order for God to show favor to his people again and to deliver and restore them. John the Baptist's message, "Repent, for the kingdom of heaven is at hand,"[8] was well received by the common people of Palestine because they knew that repentance from sin and a turn toward righteousness were necessary in order to take part in God's coming kingdom.

The angel's statement about salvation from sins finds a counterpart near the end of Matthew's Gospel at the Lord's Supper: "And he took a cup, and when he had given thanks he gave it to them, saying, 'Drink of it, all of you, for this is my blood of the covenant, which is poured out for many for the forgiveness of sins.'"[9] Jesus's death on the cross accomplished and enabled the forgiveness of sins. Matthew anticipates this reality earlier in his Gospel when he recounts Jesus's healing of a paralytic:

> And behold, some people brought to him a paralytic, lying on a bed. And when Jesus saw their faith, he said to the paralytic, Take heart, my son; your sins are forgiven. And behold, some of the scribes said to themselves, "This man is blaspheming." But Jesus, knowing their thoughts, said, "Why do you think evil in your hearts? For which is easier, to say, 'Your sins are forgiven,' or to say, 'Rise and walk'? But that you may know that the Son of Man has authority on earth to forgive sins"—he said to the paralytic—"Rise, pick up your bed and go home."[10]

Jesus fulfills the promise of his name, "Yahweh saves," by saving God's people from their sins through his death on the cross.

Prophetic Fulfillment: Virgin Birth

Matthew interrupts the flow of the narrative in Matthew 1:22–23 in order to comment on how Jesus's unusual supernatural con-

---

[8] Matt. 3:2.
[9] Matt. 26:27–28.
[10] Matt. 9:2–6.

ception, issuing in the virgin birth, served as a fulfillment of Scripture.[11] This is the first of Matthew's numerous fulfillment quotations, which he often introduces with some form or variation of the phrase, "this happened to fulfill the word of the Lord to the prophet. . . ." Each individual narrative concerning Jesus's infancy in Matthew's Gospel explicitly centers on the fulfillment of Scripture. Whereas the genealogy broadly presents Jesus as the fulfillment of the entire history of God's people contained in the Old Testament, these individual quotations focus on specific elements of Jesus's birth that fulfilled Old Testament prophecies. As we will see, Matthew's understanding of prophetic fulfillment is much broader than our common twenty-first-century conception of prophecy-fulfillment.

Matthew's first fulfillment quotation comes from the book of Isaiah.[12] On the surface, it seems like a straightforward fulfillment of prophecy, but readers have raised three main issues that we need to address. First, philosophically, what is the likelihood that Jesus is the result of a virginal conception? Second, theologically, does a virgin birth contradict the Christian belief that Jesus was fully human? Third, historically, is Jesus's birth a legitimate fulfillment of this passage in Isaiah? The first question has to do with the possibility of the miracle itself and is easier to address; the second question deals with the theological reason for a virgin birth, while the third question concerns the originally intended meaning of Isaiah's reference to a young woman conceiving a son.

The only reason to doubt the possibility of the miracle itself would be a prior commitment to philosophical naturalism, that is, the belief that the material world is all that exists and that there is no such thing as God or supernatural intervention. From this perspective, miracles just don't happen. This worldview assumes that science can explain everything, but such an approach demands more from science than it can produce. If one, however, acknowledges the existence of a God powerful enough to create

[11] Although a virgin birth technically differs from a virgin conception, we use the two phrases synonymously to refer to the virgin conception of Jesus.
[12] Isa. 7:14.

all that exists, there remains no reason to doubt that such a God could intervene in history in this supernatural kind of way. This is indeed the God who is presupposed on every page of the Bible and who has been worshiped and served by human beings from the creation of the world. Could a God who spoke the universe with its countless galaxies into existence be unable to cause a virgin to conceive? Although atheists commonly embrace philosophical naturalism, the majority of the world's population finds atheism unsatisfactory. Some things science cannot and will never be able to explain.

Moving from the philosophical to the theological arena, the questions arise: Why the virgin birth? And why is it important? In a recent book, Andrew Lincoln has advanced several arguments against the historicity of the virgin conception.[13] Essentially, Lincoln argues that only two sources mention the virgin birth, Matthew and Luke. Other New Testament authors are relatively silent on Jesus's birth and refer to him as "born of a woman," "born of the seed of David according to the flesh," and "the son of Joseph."[14] In this way, Lincoln contends, those other biblical writers present Jesus as a fully human descendant of David through the line of Joseph. Matthew makes the same point by emphasizing that Jesus shared Joseph's legal ancestry through adoption. Conversely, Lincoln argues that, theologically, the virgin conception undermines Jesus's full humanity.

However, Lincoln's discussion unduly dichotomizes the virgin conception and Jesus's human descent in the line of David. Even if Matthew and Luke were the only sources attesting to the virgin conception, surely such evidence suffices—unless, of course, they were wrong or made up the material. However, while some suggest that these Evangelists employed a literary genre that allowed them to fabricate the account of the virgin conception, such an

---

[13] Lincoln, *Born of a Virgin?* For a review of *Born of a Virgin?*, see Andreas J. Köstenberger, "Born of a Virgin?" The Gospel Coalition, February 17, 2014, http://www.thegospelcoalition.org/article/born_of_a_virgin. See also the fuller review at Biblical Foundations (blog), http://www.biblicalfoundations.org/wp-content/uploads/2014/02/Born-of-a-Virgin.pdf (accessed February 24, 2014).

[14] See Gal. 4:4; Rom. 1:3; and John 1:45, respectively.

appeal fails to do justice to the character and genre of the Gospels. Furthermore, arguing that a virgin conception diminishes the full humanity of Jesus underestimates God's creative ability. The virgin birth is a miraculous event, and we have no reason to think God could not or did not supernaturally provide what was necessary for Jesus to be fully human even without the contribution of a human father.

So why is the virgin birth theologically important? John Frame helpfully summarizes the main reasons:

> The virgin birth is doctrinally important because of: (1) The doctrine of Scripture. If Scripture errs here, then why should we trust its claims about other supernatural events, such as the resurrection? (2) The deity of Christ. While we cannot say dogmatically that God could enter the world only through a virgin birth, surely the incarnation is a supernatural event if it is anything. To eliminate the supernatural from this event is inevitably to compromise the divine dimension of it. (3) The humanity of Christ. This was the important thing to Ignatius and the second century fathers. Jesus was really born; he really became one of us. (4) The sinlessness of Christ. If he were born of two human parents, it is very difficult to conceive how he could have been exempted from the guilt of Adam's sin and become a new head to the human race. And it would seem only an arbitrary act of God that Jesus could be born without a sinful nature. Yet Jesus' sinlessness as the new head of the human race and as the atoning lamb of God is absolutely vital to our salvation (Rom. 5:18–19; 2 Cor. 5:21; Heb. 4:15; 7:26; 1 Pet. 2:22–24). (5) The nature of grace. The birth of Christ, in which the initiative and power are all of God, is an apt picture of God's saving grace in general of which it is a part. It teaches us that salvation is by God's act, not our human effort.[15]

Viewing the virgin birth as part of God's initiative in salvation reminds us to cast it in a long line of supernatural births. Reflecting upon our discussion of the "seed of the woman" from Genesis

[15]John M. Frame, "Virgin Birth of Christ," in *Evangelical Dictionary of Theology*, ed. Walter A. Elwell, 2nd ed. (Grand Rapids, MI: Baker Academic, 2001), 1249–50.

3:15 in the last chapter, we see that barrenness and other obstacles constantly threatened the progression of the seed and that God often intervened supernaturally to ensure the seed's survival. (Sarah's conception of Isaac and Rebecca's conception of Jacob and Esau come immediately to mind.) Jesus's virgin birth thus represents the final and most supernatural birth in the succession of births in fulfillment of God's promise immediately following the fall in the book of Genesis.[16]

Moving from a theological to a historical question requires a closer look at the original context of Isaiah's reference to the virgin conceiving a son in Isaiah 7:14. Between 740 and 732 BC, Syria and Israel tried to force king Ahaz of Judah to join their military coalition against Assyria. When he refused to join their alliance, they invaded with the intention of deposing him and setting up a king in Judah who would join their side. Rather than trusting God, Ahaz appealed to Assyria for help. Assyria did help but at a very high cost: in essence, Judah became a vassal state of Assyria and was forced to pay heavy tribute. This series of events is known as the Syro-Ephraimite War.[17]

In the midst of this crisis, the prophet Isaiah came to King Ahaz with a word of encouragement and an invitation to trust God: "Be careful, be quiet, do not fear, and do not let your heart be faint. . . . It shall not stand, and it shall not come to pass. . . . If you are not firm in faith, you will not be firm at all."[18] Ahaz, however, doubted God and did not think God would deliver. In Ahaz's mind, his only hope was Assyria. Ahaz refused to trust God or receive a sign of God's commitment to rescue, and Isaiah responded:

> Therefore the Lord himself will give you a sign. Behold the virgin ['*almah*] shall conceive and bear a son, and shall call his name Immanuel. He shall eat curds and honey when he knows how

[16] Gen. 3:15.
[17] More details can be found at 2 Kings 15:29–37 and 2 Chron. 28:1–19. See the helpful discussion of Isaiah 7–9 in Robert B. Chisholm, *Handbook on the Prophets* (Grand Rapids, MI: Baker Academic, 2002).
[18] Isa. 7:4a, 7b, 9b.

> to refuse the evil and choose the good. For before the boy knows how to refuse the evil and choose the good, the land whose two kings you dread will be deserted.[19]

The narrative continues:

> And I went to the prophetess, and she conceived and bore a son. Then the LORD said to me, "Call his name Maher-shalal-hash-baz;[20] for before the boy knows how to cry 'My father' or 'My mother,' the wealth of Damascus and the spoil of Samaria will be carried away before the king of Assyria." . . . Behold, I and the children whom the LORD has given me are signs and portents in Israel from the LORD of hosts, who dwells on Mount Zion.[21]

The sign or promise in both passages assured the Israelites that, by the time the child was old enough to speak and choose between right and wrong, the impending threat from Syria and Israel would be over. The meaning of the child's symbolic name in Isaiah 7:14, Immanuel, indicated God's presence with his people to save and deliver, while the child's symbolic name in Isaiah 8:3, Maher-shalal-hash-baz, pointed to the speed by which God would do away with these nations threatening Judah.

God's sign to Ahaz in Isaiah 7:14 likely had an immediate fulfillment that directly related to the original historical situation in the Syro-Ephraimite War. The Hebrew word translated "virgin," *'almah*, denotes a young woman who in most contexts in the Old Testament was also an unmarried virgin.[22] The young woman could have been a member of the royal family but was more likely the "prophetess" of Isaiah 8:3. Given the flow of the narrative, Isaiah's own son probably fulfilled the prophecy. The parents might

---

[19] Isa. 7:14–16.

[20] As the ESV footnote explains, "*Maher-shalal-hash-baz* means *The spoil speeds, the prey hastens*." *The ESV Study Bible*, ed. Wayne Grudem (Wheaton, IL: Crossway, 2008), 1255.

[21] Isa. 8:3–4, 18.

[22] *The ESV Study Bible* expresses this matter well: "Although some claim that the word translated **virgin** (Hb. *'almah*) refers generally to a 'young woman,' it actually refers specifically to a 'maiden'—that is, to a young woman who is unmarried and sexually chaste, and thus has virginity as one of her characteristics (see Gen. 24:16, 43; Ex. 2:8, 'girl')." *ESV Study Bible*, 1254.

easily have given the child two names, particularly when they chose the names symbolically as signs or portents.[23]

How does a historical fulfillment of the prophecy in Isaiah's day relate to Matthew's use of Isaiah 7:14 in Matthew 1:23 to refer to Jesus? To answer this question, it is important to look at the birth of one more child in the context following Isaiah 7:

> But there will be no more gloom for her who was in anguish. In the former time he brought into contempt the land of Zebulun and the land of Naphtali, but *in the latter time* he has made glorious the way of the sea, the land beyond the Jordan, *Galilee of the nations*.
>
> The people who walked in darkness
>   have seen a great light;
> those who dwelt in a land of deep darkness,
>   on them has light shone.
> You have multiplied the nation;
>   you have increased its joy;
> they rejoice before you
>   as with joy at the harvest,
>   as they are glad when they divide spoil.
> For the yoke of his burden
>   and the staff of his shoulder,
>   the rod of his oppressor,
>   you have broken as on the day of Midian.
> For every boot of the tramping warrior in battle tumult
>   and every garment rolled in blood
>   will be burned as fuel for the fire.
> *For to us a child is born,*
>   *to us a son is given*;
> and the government shall be upon his shoulder,
>   and his name shall be called
> Wonderful Counselor, Mighty God,
>   Everlasting Father, Prince of Peace.
> Of the increase of his government and of peace
>   there will be no end,

[23] Note how the name switches back from Maher-shalal-hash-baz to Immanuel in Isa. 8:8.

> on the throne of David and over his kingdom,
> to establish it and to uphold it
> with justice and with righteousness
> from this time forth and forevermore.
> The zeal of the LORD of hosts will do this.[24]

This passage is linked to the prior prophecies by reference to the birth of a son, but unlike the previous passages, the description of the child here easily and quickly leads to a picture of one who is more than human and will accomplish a deliverance that extends far beyond the original historical context of the Syro-Ephraimite War. Significantly, the translators of the Hebrew Old Testament into Greek in the Intertestamental period translated the Hebrew word *'almah* with the Greek word *parthenos*, a much more specific term for "virgin." This may indicate that even before Jesus was born, Jewish readers viewed the prophecy in Isaiah 7:14 in light of Isaiah 9:1–7 and thought that the birth of the promised child would be supernaturally accomplished "in the latter time."[25] Matthew clearly knew the further prophecy in Isaiah 9:1–7, because he later invoked part of this passage to describe Jesus's ministry in Galilee.[26]

All of this leads us to interpret Isaiah's reference to the virgin conceiving a child in terms of double fulfillment. The prophecy makes complete sense in its original historical context, but other factors within the context—the name Immanuel and the description of the child in Isaiah 9:6–7—also point forward in time to the birth of another child. Jesus was the true and final embodiment of Immanuel, "God with us," the one who would sit "on the throne of David and over his kingdom, to establish it and uphold it with justice and with righteousness from this time forth and forevermore."[27]

---

[24] Isa. 9:1–7.
[25] Isa. 9:1.
[26] Matt. 4:15–16; cf. Isa. 9:1–2.
[27] Isa. 9:7b.

6 OR 5 BC

Jesus's Birth

The actual birth of Jesus takes place quickly at this point in the narrative. Matthew notes that Joseph woke up and did what the angel of the Lord had commanded. He proceeded with the marriage to Mary but refrained from sexual intercourse with her until after Jesus was born. Joseph's obedience to the angel was essential for Joseph to count as Jesus's legal father and to establish Davidic descent through Joseph, even though he had no biological connection to Jesus. Culturally, Joseph's naming of the child confirmed his acceptance of Jesus as his own.[28]

Matthew omits some of the details that Luke includes in his account, but in contrast, not contradiction, to Luke, he uses Joseph's perspective to highlight selectively two points about the identity and purpose of Jesus. Jesus was Immanuel, God with us, and he came to save his people from their sins. What is more, because Jesus came not only to save believing Jews, this means that he came also to save those of us from our sins who are non-Jews! But we'll discover more about this in the next chapter. For now it is worth reflecting on the freedom and peace that come from the reality of having one's sins forgiven. Paul, quoting Psalm 32:1–2, celebrates with these words: "Blessed are those whose lawless deeds are forgiven, and whose sins are covered; blessed is the man against whom the Lord will not count his sin."[29] The celebration of Jesus's birth is a celebration of the completion of the purpose of his life. He came to save his people from their sins! Have you experienced the joy of knowing that your sins have been forgiven by God?

---

[28] Matt. 1:25.

[29] Rom. 4:7–8.

3

CONFLICT BETWEEN TWO KINGS AND TWO KINGDOMS

MATTHEW 2:1-12

Now after Jesus was born in Bethlehem of Judea in the days of Herod the king, behold, wise men from the east came to Jerusalem, saying, "Where is he who has been born king of the Jews? For we saw his star when it rose and have come to worship him." When Herod the king heard this, he was troubled, and all Jerusalem with him; and assembling all the chief priests and scribes of the people, he inquired of them where the Christ was to be born. They told him, "In Bethlehem of Judea, for so it is written by the prophet:

"'And you, O Bethlehem, in the land of Judah,
are by no means least among the rulers of Judah;
for from you shall come a ruler
who will shepherd my people Israel.'"

Then Herod summoned the wise men secretly and ascertained from them what time the star had appeared. And he sent them to Bethlehem, saying, "Go and search diligently for the child, and when you have found him, bring me word, that I too may come and worship him." After listening to the king, they went on their way. And behold, the star that they had seen when it rose went before them until it came to rest over the place where the child was. When they saw the star, they rejoiced exceedingly with great joy. And going into the house they saw the child with Mary his mother, and they fell down and worshiped him. Then, opening their treasures, they offered him gifts, gold and frankincense and myrrh. And being warned in a dream not to return to Herod, they departed to their own country by another way.

WITHIN A YEAR OR TWO AFTER JESUS'S BIRTH (C. 5 OR 4 BC)

The Visit of the Wise Men

The visit of the wise men is a well-known feature of the Christmas narratives, even among non-Christians who know very little about the Bible. This popularity, of course, is accompanied by many misconceptions. For example, the Bible nowhere states the number of the wise men. Perhaps there were three, since Matthew mentions three distinct gifts, but that is, at best, a guess and inference based upon no historical evidence. Also, despite many depictions of the nativity scene, the wise men would not have visited Jesus on the same night as the shepherds; they arrived later.

Apart from the addition of trivial ideas, popular presentations of the wise men often miss the main points that the narrative's author originally intended to convey. First, the account of the wise men points powerfully forward to the universal scope of Jesus's kingdom: just as non-Jewish people pledged their allegiance to Jesus as King through worship and gifts, so this King would not limit his kingdom to Palestine.

Second, the account narrates two different responses to Jesus and invites us as readers to identify with the wise men. It implicitly asks us whether we will respond to Jesus with worship and allegiance or with hostility and opposition, fearing the loss of our own "kingdoms."

Finally, the narrative powerfully communicates the conflict between two kingdoms: the kingdom of *God*, which was invading and reclaiming lost humanity, and the kingdom of this *world*, which would fight tooth and nail to stop it. Matthew introduces these two kingdoms in the first verse of chapter 2 by referencing two kings: "Jesus was born in Bethlehem of Judea in the days of Herod the king."[1]

37–4 BC

In the Days of Herod

Herod was a famous, dangerous, brilliant, paranoid, successful, cruel, lucky, and long-living king. He was the client king of Judea under Roman authority from 37–4 BC. We possess a good deal of information about Herod's life and reign through various ancient sources, particularly the Jewish historian Josephus, who concludes his account of Herod's life with the following words.

> He was a man who was cruel to all alike and one who easily gave in to anger and was contemptuous of justice. And yet he was as greatly favoured by fortune as any man has ever been in that from being a commoner he was made king, and though encompassed by innumerable perils, he managed to escape them all and lived on to a very old age. As for the affairs of his household and his relation to his sons, he had, in his own opinion at least, enjoyed very good fortune since he had not failed to get the better of those whom he considered his enemies, but in my opinion he was very unfortunate indeed.[2]

Herod's character, at least near the end of his life, is illustrated by one of the last stories Josephus recounts of his reign. When Herod knew that he was near death, he summoned notable Jews from the entire nation to the hippodrome and instructed his sister, Salome, and her husband, Alexas, to have soldiers slaughter everyone in the hippodrome upon his death. He did this because he knew that the majority of Jews would rejoice at his death (because of his heavy taxation and tyranny), and he wanted to ensure that genuine mourning gripped the entire nation at his funeral.

---

[1] Matt. 2:1.

[2] Josephus, *Ant.* 17.191–192. All Josephus quotations come from *Josephus*, trans. H. St. J. Thackeray et al., Loeb Classical Library (Cambridge, MA: Harvard University Press, 1926–1965).

Fortunately for the Jews at the time, Salome and Alexas did not carry out Herod's instructions. Josephus comments:

> Even if one approves of Herod's earlier treatment of his relatives as having been due to his love of life, one may nevertheless see from his latest instructions that the man's character had nothing human to recommend it, and this conclusion is unavoidable if, when he was about to leave this world, he took care to leave the entire nation in a state of mourning over the loss of their dearest ones, and gave orders to do away with one member of each household, although they had done nothing wrong or offended him in any way and had not been accused of any other crime.[3]

How would you like to be remembered by history as a person whose "character had nothing human to recommend it"? Much more could be written about Herod's achievements and cruelty, but it is better to focus at this point on information directly relevant to Herod's role in Matthew's infancy narrative.

Herod had ten wives and many children, and palace intrigue was thick throughout Herod's reign.[4] This included plots, assassination attempts, deception, and treachery by almost everyone around him. Over the years this led Herod to execute his wife Mariamne and his sons Alexander, Aristobulus, and Antipater, among many other relatives and conspirators. Herod lived among people he could not trust, and he regularly feared for his life and throne. This uncertainty and upheaval led Herod to make six different wills; he changed the wills based upon whom he thought he could trust (and alternately, which son had recently plotted to kill him).

MARCH OR APRIL 4 BC

Herod's Death

Herod's death can be dated with a high degree of historical certainty to the spring of 4 BC between a lunar eclipse on March

---

[3]Josephus, *Ant.* 17.174–181.

[4]For more information about Herod's life see Harold W. Hoehner, "Herodian Dynasty," in *Dictionary of New Testament Background*, ed. Craig A. Evans and Stanley E. Porter (Downers Grove, IL: InterVarsity, 2000), 485–94.

HEROD'S TEMPLE IN THE TIME OF JESUS

Herod began construction of this magnificent temple in 20/19 BC, during the eighteenth year of his reign. The main construction phase was completed within about a decade. Detailed descriptions of the temple exist in Josephus (*Jewish Antiquities* 15.380–425; *Jewish War* 5.184–247) and in early rabbinic writings (esp. Mishnah, *Middot*). The Roman army under Titus destroyed the temple during the capture of Jerusalem in AD 70. The temple was 172 feet (52 m) long, wide, and high (about 16 to 20 stories tall).

Temple Architectural Plan

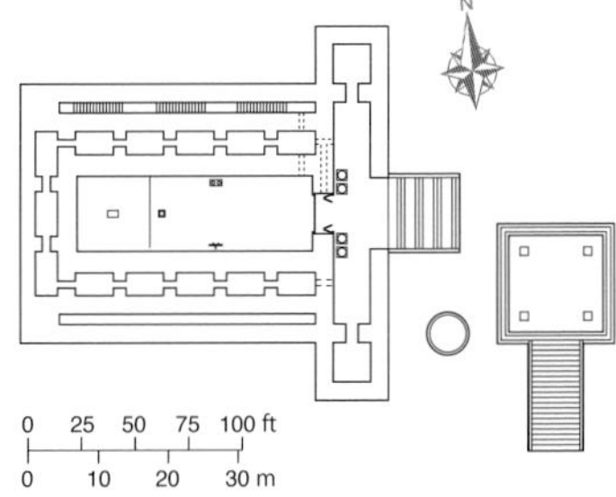

A massive curtain separated the Holy Place from the Most Holy Place. When Jesus died, this curtain was torn in two from top to bottom (Matt. 27:51; Mark 15:38; Luke 23:45).

The inner sanctuary was surrounded on three sides by three stories of chambers, containing 38 cells that housed supplies and vessels for the ritual ceremonies.

There was an upper chamber above the sanctuary, which allowed access (through holes in the floor) for cleaning of the gold-covered walls below. A ladder (shown partly cut away in this section) gave access to the upper roof level.

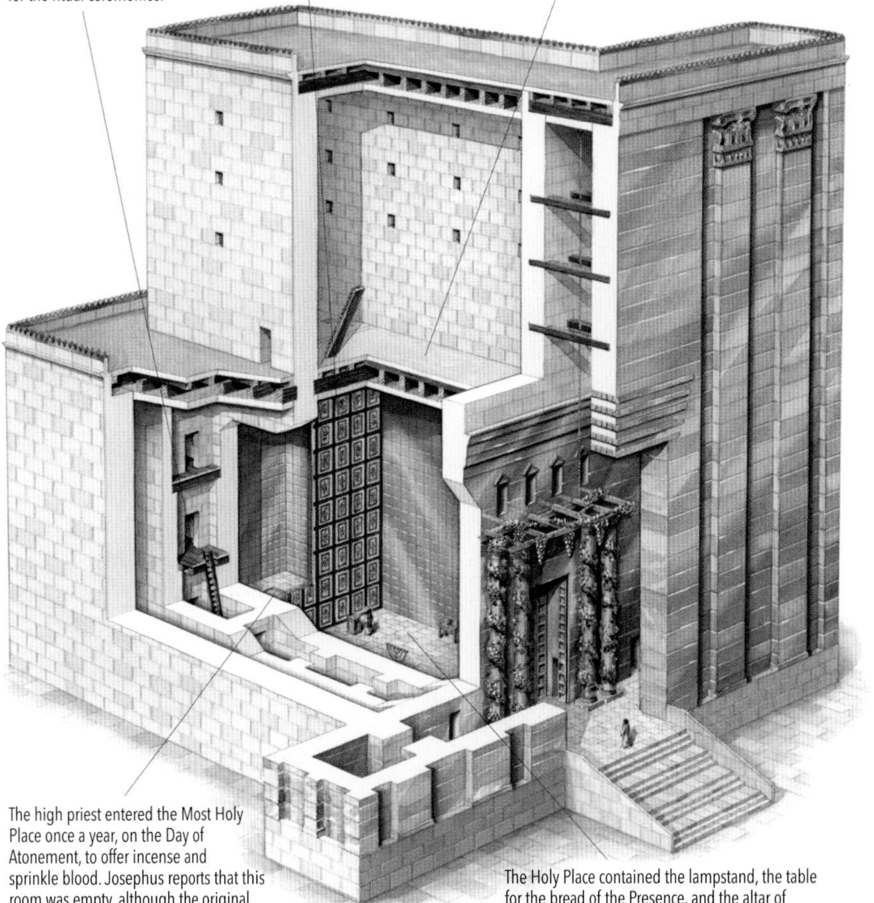

The high priest entered the Most Holy Place once a year, on the Day of Atonement, to offer incense and sprinkle blood. Josephus reports that this room was empty, although the original emplacement of the ark of the covenant in the "Foundation Stone" was still visible.

The Holy Place contained the lampstand, the table for the bread of the Presence, and the altar of incense. An angel of the Lord appeared to Zechariah on the right side of the incense altar (Luke 1:11).

HEROD'S TEMPLE COMPLEX IN THE TIME OF JESUS

When the Gospels and the book of Acts refer to entering the temple or teaching in the temple, it is often not a reference to Herod's temple itself, but rather to this temple complex, including a number of courts and chambers that surrounded the temple. These latter structures were the great and wonderful buildings referred to by the disciples in Matt. 24:1; Mark 13:1–2.

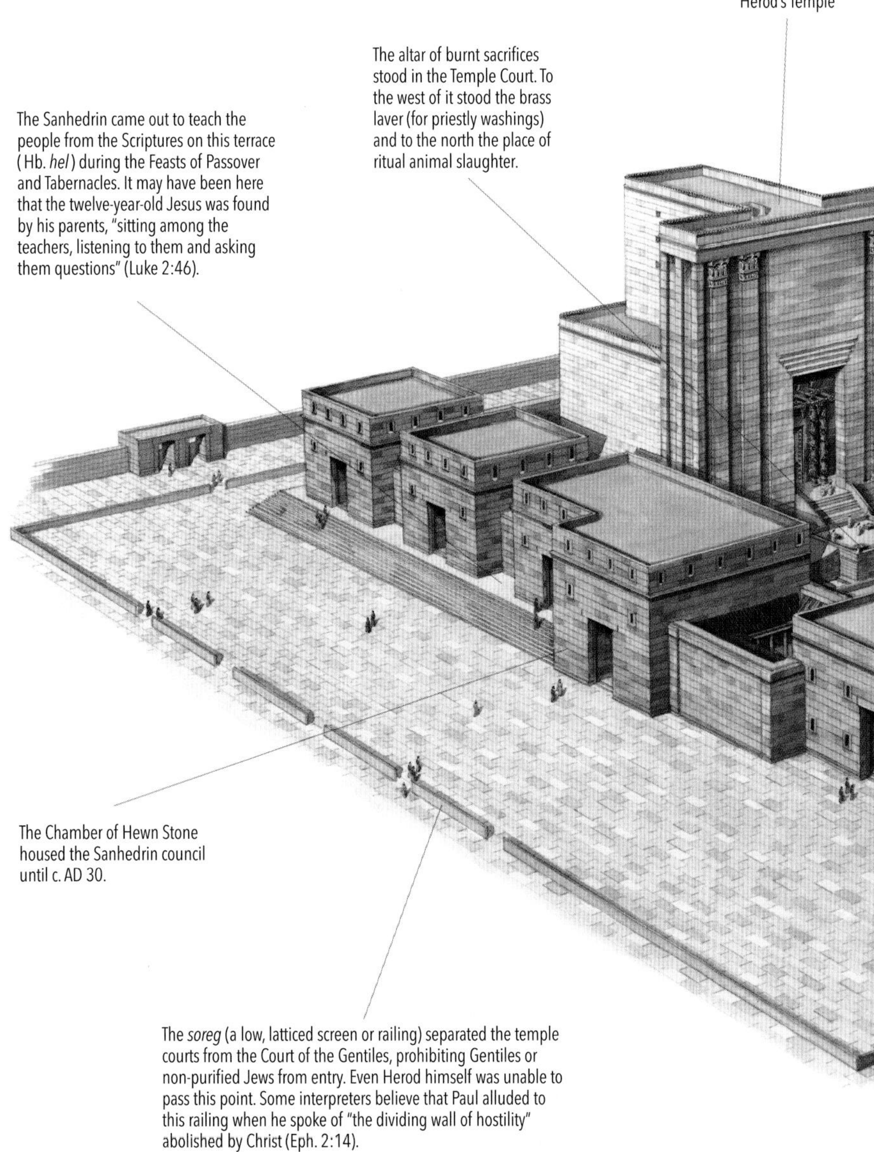

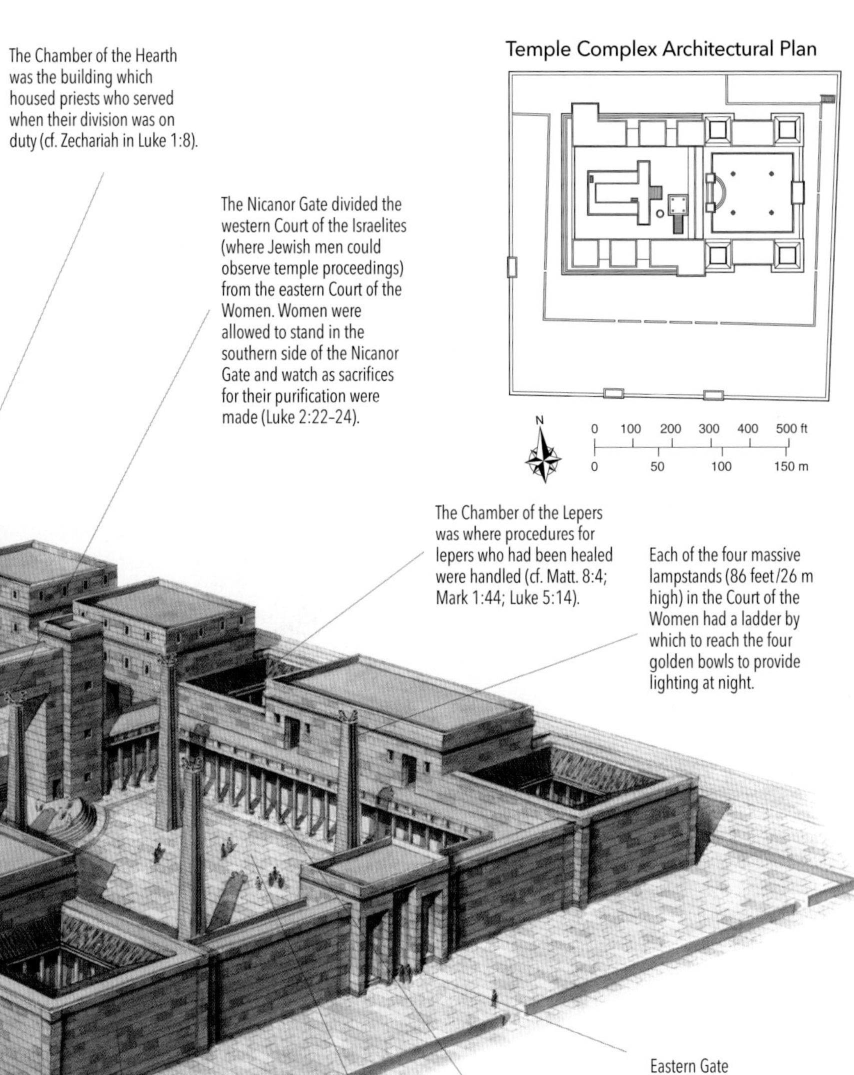

The Chamber of the Hearth was the building which housed priests who served when their division was on duty (cf. Zechariah in Luke 1:8).

The Nicanor Gate divided the western Court of the Israelites (where Jewish men could observe temple proceedings) from the eastern Court of the Women. Women were allowed to stand in the southern side of the Nicanor Gate and watch as sacrifices for their purification were made (Luke 2:22–24).

The Chamber of the Lepers was where procedures for lepers who had been healed were handled (cf. Matt. 8:4; Mark 1:44; Luke 5:14).

Each of the four massive lampstands (86 feet/26 m high) in the Court of the Women had a ladder by which to reach the four golden bowls to provide lighting at night.

These colonnades contained thirteen trumpet-shaped boxes into which people put their monetary offerings (cf. Luke 21:1–4); this was called "the treasury" (see Mark 12:41; John 8:20). The chief priests did not allow Judas's blood money to be put in the treasury (Matt. 27:6).

The Chamber of the Nazirites was where a Nazirite would bring his sacrifices upon completion of his vow.

The Court of the Women was a 233 feet/71 m square courtyard, capable of holding up to six thousand worshipers at a time. Its name does not indicate that it was restricted to women, but that they were not permitted to enter further into the temple courts. Their presence was normally restricted to the balconies above the colonnades. In this court, the infant Jesus was met by Simeon and Anna the prophetess (Luke 2:25–38).

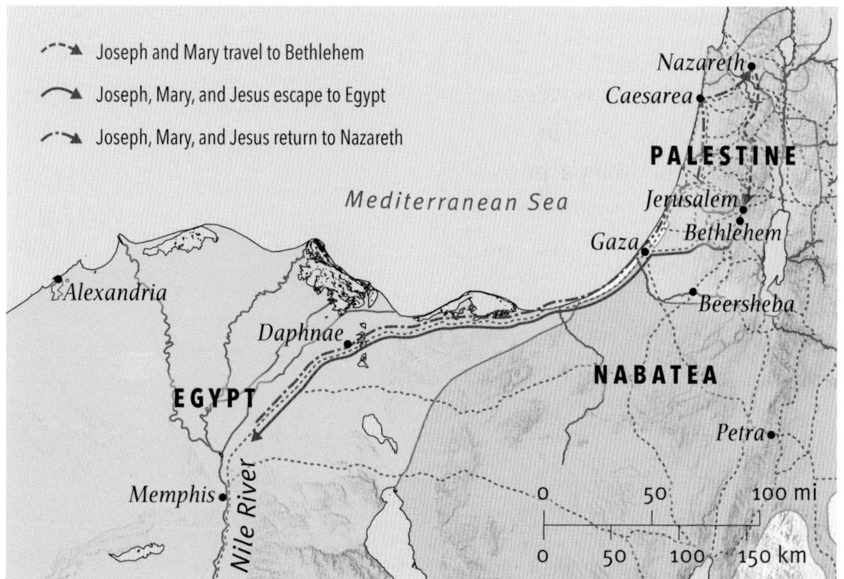

JESUS'S BIRTH AND FLIGHT TO EGYPT

As the time drew near for Jesus to be born, a mandatory Roman registration made it necessary for Joseph to return to his ancestral home of Bethlehem. There Mary gave birth to Jesus, and later, wise men from the East came to worship him. The wise men's recognition of a new king, however, troubled King Herod and the ruling establishment in Jerusalem, and Herod the Great sought to kill Jesus. Joseph and his family escaped to Egypt and stayed there until Herod died. When they returned to Palestine, they settled in the remote district of Galilee, where Jesus grew up in the village of Nazareth, to avoid the attention of the rulers in Jerusalem.

12/13 and the Passover on April 11.[5] This means that Jesus's birth took place before Herod's death in 4 BC.[6] The amount of time required for Mary's purification, the visit of the wise men, the family's flight to Egypt, and Herod's slaughter of the Bethlehem infants require at least three to four months, so the earliest Jesus could have been born is the month of December in 5 BC.[7] Most likely, therefore, Jesus was born sometime in the years 6 or 5 BC.

One other point is particularly important in determining the date of Jesus's birth. In the third chapter of his Gospel, Luke precisely dates the beginning of John the Baptist's ministry to the "fifteenth year of the reign of Tiberius Caesar," which would have been AD 28/29.[8] Later in the chapter, Luke states that Jesus began his public ministry when he was "about thirty years of age," most likely in the fall of AD 29.[9] The key word in Luke's statement is "about," which indicates his use of approximate or round numbers. Luke is not pinpointing Jesus's exact age but is rather giving a ballpark figure. Presumably, if Jesus had been over thirty-five years old at the start of his ministry, Luke would have rounded up to the next decade and would have stated that Jesus was about forty years of age. There was no year 0 between 1 BC and AD 1, so Luke's estimate of Jesus's age could not easily push his birth back farther than 6 or 7 BC at the most. On the other hand, Luke's comment allows us to date Jesus's birth late in 5 BC, making even a November or December birth possible.

Jesus was born near the end of Herod's long seventy-year life.

---

[5] Josephus, *Ant.* 17.167; 17.213.

[6] This also means that the AD sixth-century monk Dionysius Exiguus, who was responsible for dividing history between BC and AD based upon the birth of Christ, was off by a few years, which causes confusion today: How could Jesus have been *born* in 6 or 5 *BC* ("before Christ")?

[7] See the very helpful discussion of the date of Jesus's birth in Paul Maier, "The Date of the Nativity and the Chronology of Jesus' Life," in *Chronos, Kairos, Christos: Nativity and Chronological Studies Presented to Paul Finegan*, ed. Jerry Vardaman and Edwin M. Yamauchi (Winona Lake, IN: Eisenbrauns, 1989), 113–130; also available online at Biblical Foundations (blog), http://www.biblicalfoundations.org/wp-content/uploads/2014/03/MaierDateNativity.pdf (accessed April 14, 2014). See also Paul Maier, *In the Fullness of Time: A Historian Looks at Christmas, Easter, and the Early Church* (Grand Rapids, MI: Kregel, 1997); and Maier's children's book *The Very First Christmas* (St. Louis, MO: Concordia, 1998).

[8] Luke 3:1. See Andreas J. Köstenberger and Justin Taylor, "April 3, AD 33: Why We Believe We Can Know the Exact Date Jesus Died," *First Things*, April 3, 2013, http://www.firstthings.com/web-exclusives/2014/04/april-3-ad-33.

[9] Luke 3:23.

Herod had survived decades of palace intrigue and plots on his life by being more crafty and cruel than his opponents. In the words of Josephus quoted above, he never "failed to get the better of those whom he considered his enemies." It was after many years of survival by outfoxing and out-killing his opponents that Herod heard news from the wise men about the birth of a rival king. This historical background about Herod goes a long way in explaining his paranoia and cruel actions recorded in Matthew's second chapter.

MAGOI: WISE MEN FROM THE EAST

Matthew's account of the coming of the wise men has fascinated readers over the centuries, not least because of the wise men's dependence upon a star for guidance. Their arrival "from the east," their identification as *magoi*,[10] and their astronomical observations help us identify these mysterious visitors. Jews generally viewed *magoi* negatively because of their association with magic, but depending on the context, the *magoi* could represent wise men, priests, interpreters of dreams, astrologers, or sorcerers. They would have likely been held in high esteem in their home country for their learning and influence, and their association with the star in Matthew's account might suggest that these men should be viewed as astrologers. "From the east" indicates a homeland in either Persia, Babylon, or Arabia, most likely Babylon because the Babylonians had a great interest in astrology and a large Jewish community lived there as a result of the exile. However, the nature of the gifts—gold, frankincense, and myrrh—seems to indicate Arabia, while some have suggested Persia because the term *magoi* was originally associated with the Medes and Persians.[11]

In an intriguing antecedent account, 1 Kings 10:1–10 (cf. 2 Chron. 9:1–9) narrates the visit of the Queen of Sheba, which foreshadows the visit of the *magoi*. This royal figure came to Jerusalem to pay homage to Solomon, the son of David, and brought

[10] The plural Greek form of *magos*.

[11] Justin Martyr, writing in the mid-second century, reveals an early Christian tradition that the *magoi* were from Arabia. *Dialogue with Trypho* 77–78.

gifts of gold, spices, and precious stones (vv. 2, 10). This story reminds us that the *magoi* stand within a biblical trajectory in which Gentile dignitaries come to Jerusalem with valuable gifts to pay homage to the son of David.[12] A later commentary on the Queen of Sheba story even includes a miraculous star. Matthew thus may tell the story of the wise men to identify Jesus as the greater Son of David whom even Gentiles worship; in fact, he relays Jesus's statement later in his Gospel that the Queen of Sheba, who came "from the ends of the earth" to pay homage to Solomon, will "rise up" in judgment against those who in his day rejected Jesus as Messiah.[13] The message is unmistakable: even if Israel won't worship her long-awaited Messiah, Gentiles will.

How did these Gentiles come to know of Jesus's uniqueness and birth? In the case of the *magoi*'s visit, the star played a key role in the narrative, and many have attempted to identify the star with known astronomical events.[14] Halley's comet would have been too early (12 BC), and for ancient astrologers, comets normally indicated the death, not the birth, of a ruler. Chinese astronomers observed a nova or supernova for seventy days in 5–4 BC.[15] A triple conjunction of Jupiter and Saturn took place in 7 BC during May/June, September/October, and December in the zodiacal constellation of Pisces. Raymond Brown summarizes the potential significance of these conjunctions:

> Pisces is a constellation sometimes associated with the last days and with the Hebrews, while Jupiter . . . was associated with the world ruler and Saturn was identified as the star of the Amorites of the Syria-Palestine region. The claim has been made that this conjunction might lead Parthian astrologers to predict that there would appear in Palestine among the Hebrews a world ruler of the last days.[16]

---

[12] Cf. Ps. 72:10–11; Isa. 60:3–6. See also Song 3:6; 4:6.

[13] Matt. 12:41–42.

[14] See especially Konradin Ferrari-D'Occhieppo, "The Star of the Magi and Babylonian Astronomy," in Vardaman and Yamauchi, *Chronos, Kairos, Christos*, 41–54.

[15] Craig Keener, *A Commentary on the Gospel of Matthew* (Grand Rapids, MI: Eerdmans, 1999), 102.

[16] Raymond Brown, *The Birth of the Messiah*, rev. ed. (New York: Doubleday, 1993), 172–73.

These astronomical events would certainly have led Eastern astrologers to the conclusion that something unusual was happening in the world. Those in the ancient world commonly connected such astrological events with the birth of kings or other significant worldwide events, and it is historically plausible that the conjunction of planets noted above would have led Eastern astrologers to expect the birth of a king in Palestine. Because of the influence of exiled Jews throughout Babylon, the *magoi* may have been familiar with the prophecy from Balaam that "a star shall come out of Jacob, and a scepter shall rise out of Israel."[17] If so, they may have naturally connected this prophecy with the unusual astronomical phenomena they were observing.

Such considerations potentially provide important background information regarding the arrival of the *magoi* in Jerusalem in search of a newborn king. These astrological events, however, have a harder time explaining Matthew 2:9: "And behold, the star that they had seen when it rose went before them until it came to rest over the place where the child was." Simo Parpola provides a clear explanation of how the triple conjunction of Jupiter and Saturn could be described as rising, moving through the sky, and coming to rest for a period of time in the night sky.[18] The manner in which Matthew describes the movement of the star (or planet) is compatible with how contemporaries could have described either of these planets at that time. In a general way, the *magoi* could have set their course in the direction of a bright star on the horizon until they reached the house. Only an overly literal reading of Matthew's language could refuse this possibility, as if the star acted as a spotlight to illuminate the exact spot.

In any case, our belief in the truthfulness of Matthew's narrative depends not on adopting any particular explanation of his

[17] Num. 24:17. Although Num. 24:17 may possibly connect to Matthew's account of the *magoi*, Matthew does not establish a link. This silence is all the more remarkable since Matthew elsewhere explicitly indicates prophetic fulfillments by using formulaic language when introducing Old Testament quotations. The lack of any explicit citation of Num. 24:17 in Matthew's account should caution interpreters against making this text the key to understanding Matt. 2:1–12.

[18] Simo Parpola, "The Magi and the Star: Babylonian Astronomy Dates Jesus' Birth," *Bible Review* 17, no. 6 (2001): 17–23. See also Ferrari-D'Occhieppo, "Star of the Magi and Babylonian Astronomy."

account of the star of Bethlehem. Real danger lies in refusing to accept a miraculous or supernatural explanation. God somehow showed the *magoi* the way from Jerusalem to Jesus's home in Bethlehem in a way that can best be described as supernatural—whether through the triple conjunction of Jupiter and Saturn in the constellation of Pisces (an event that occurs once every eight hundred years), the appearance of an angel, or some other miraculous occurrence. Modern readers must beware of grasping for natural explanations too quickly when reading a narration of supernatural events. God quite possibly could have sent an angel to guide the *magoi* in a way that ancient people may have described as a moving star. The star's movement from Jerusalem to Jesus's home in Bethlehem (about six miles away) is a Christmas mystery that is ultimately above and beyond scientific verification or falsification.

THE CONFLICT OF KINGS

Now that we have introduced the main characters, it will be easy to understand the flow of the narrative. Matthew records that wise men from the East arrived in Jerusalem in search of a newly born king of the Jews. They claimed their astrological observations as the source of their knowledge and indicated that they had come to worship the new king. "Worship" in this context would likely indicate awarding honor and respect and a pledge of future allegiance and friendship. These men desired to ally themselves with this new king and the kingdom that he would rule. While Matthew does not indicate the size of their entourage or caravan, it would have needed to be large enough to provide protection and carry supplies during the long journey. Their journey would have lasted at least one to two months depending upon their exact place of origin (Arabia, Babylon, or Persia).

Matthew proceeds to note that this report from the *magoi* troubled Herod and with him all Jerusalem. Herod would have certainly been perturbed by the report of a rival king's birth and by the attempt of Eastern *magoi* to ally with him. The Parthian Empire to the East ruled the territory of ancient Persia and Babylon, and the Parthians were often at war with Rome. When Rome appointed Herod, an Idumaean, king of Judea in 40 BC, the Parthians controlled Judea and appointed Antigonus, the last rightfully born king in the Hasmonean line, king of Judea. By right of birth, Antigonus had a much stronger claim to the throne than Herod did. Between 40 and 37 BC, Herod and Rome fought a three-year war with Antigonus and Parthia. Herod won, the Parthians were driven out, and Antigonus was killed.[19] Josephus concludes by noting that Herod bribed a man named Antony to kill Antigonus because he feared that the Romans could eventually favor Antigonus or his descendants in light of their royal lineage.[20]

These events at the beginning of Herod's reign likely affected his response to the news of a newborn king. Three decades later, Eastern *magoi*—who were possibly connected to the Parthians, or at least their representatives—were again seeking, at some level, to ally with a rightfully born king of Judea. Herod had seen to it that the last man who lodged that claim, Antigonus, was killed, and although the Romans and Parthians were not waging open war at this point, they certainly did not trust each other. Herod's history with rival kings claiming Eastern Parthian support explains why he was disturbed by the arrival of the *magoi* and why he so quickly determined to kill the rival king despite the *magoi*'s astrological claims and the chief priests and scribes' biblical evidence. The statement that "all Jerusalem" was also troubled could indicate messianic hope for the overthrow of Herod, but more likely suggests general apprehension and fear at the possibility of political upheaval.

While the astronomical events convinced the *magoi* that a new

---

[19] A fuller account of these events can be found in Josephus, *Ant.* 14.381–491.

[20] Josephus records: "But Herod feared that if Antigonus were kept under guard by Antony and brought to Rome by him, he might plead the justice of his cause before the Senate and show that he was descended from kings while Herod was a commoner, and that his sons ought to reign by virtue of their lineage, even though he himself had committed offences against the Romans; and because of this fear Herod gave Antony a large bribe and persuaded him to put Antigonus out of the way. And when this was done, Herod was freed of his fear, and at the same time the rule of the Asamonaean [i.e., Hasmonean] line came to an end after a hundred and twenty-six years. Theirs was a splendid and renowned house because of both their lineage and their priestly office, as well as the things which its founders achieved on behalf of the nation. But they lost their royal power through internal strife, and it passed to Herod, the son of Antipater, who came from a house of common people and from a private family that was subject to the kings." Josephus, *Ant.* 14.489–491.

king had been born in Judea, they did not clearly pinpoint the location of his birth, thus explaining their arrival in Jerusalem. It would only be natural for a king to be born in the capital city. The narrative makes an implicit point here: the highest learning of humankind through general revelation and nature (the star) is not enough: humanity needs special revelation from God through his Word to find the truth. That revelation came through the chief priests and scribes. Although Herod did not have control over the Jewish religious leaders, some, if not many, would have been willing (for various possible motivations) to help him in his scriptural search for the location of this baby's birth.

The Jewish leaders pointed Herod to Bethlehem on the basis of a prophecy in the book of Micah.[21] Bethlehem was a small town with a rich history as the hometown of David.[22] Although there are several minor differences between Matthew's quotation and the Hebrew text of the Old Testament we possess (the Masoretic text), two differences stand out. First, Matthew highlights the significance of the quotation by adding the phrase "by no means."[23] The passage in Micah seems to mean that although the village of Bethlehem was little or insignificant, a ruler in Israel would come out of it. There's no way to know at what point the expression "by no means" entered the interpretive tradition that Matthew cites, but the addition of the phrase brings out the implicit point in the Hebrew text that because the ruler would come out of Bethlehem, the village would no longer be considered insignificant.

Second, the final line that Matthew quotes, "who will shepherd my people Israel," seems to reflect Micah 5:4 ("And he shall stand and shepherd his flock in the strength of the Lord") while quoting God's promise to David in 2 Samuel 5:2 ("You shall be shepherd of my people Israel"). This final line strengthens the connection between the messianic expectation expressed in Micah and a descendent of David while also commenting on the character of the Davidic messianic King. A shepherd-king would behave very

[21] Mic. 5:2.
[22] Ruth 1:1, 19; 2:4; 1 Sam. 17:12, 15.
[23] Just one word in the Greek, *oudamōs*.

differently than the murderous and cruel Herod. The quotation from Micah constitutes a straightforward prediction-fulfillment prophecy: Micah prophesied that the Messiah would be born in Bethlehem, and Jesus was in fact born there.

Armed with this new information, Herod secretly met with the *magoi* to determine the time at which the star appeared and sent them on a mission to find the child in Bethlehem, with orders to report back to him so he could worship the child as well. Herod apparently did not feel the need to search for the child personally, likely because he was quite sick in his later years and preoccupied with many pressing concerns related to his family and the nation. He evidently trusted that through his cunning he could get the information he needed from the *magoi* and dispense with this problem easily and quietly.

THE WORSHIP OF THE GENTILES

The *magoi* continued on their journey and were filled with joy as they saw the star's movement confirm their trip. That they found Mary and Jesus in a house indicates that this meeting took place not on the night of Jesus's birth but rather at some later time after Joseph had been able to secure more suitable lodging for his family. Perhaps they arrived while Joseph and Mary waited for the required forty days to elapse before Mary could be purified at the Jerusalem temple. (See the drawings of Herod's temple on the insert following page 64.)

Even though it is doubtful that the worship and gifts from these *magoi* indicate their recognition of Jesus's divinity, they are highly significant for at least two reasons. First, looking backward, they serve as an initial fulfillment of prophecies concerning the restoration of Israel. Ancient prophets had told of a day when the nations of the world would respond to God's light and glory by giving their wealth and glory:

> Arise, shine, for your light has come,
> and the glory of the LORD has risen upon you.

> For behold, darkness shall cover the earth,
> and thick darkness the peoples;
> but the LORD will arise upon you,
> and his glory will be seen upon you.
> And nations shall come to your light,
> and kings to the brightness of your rising. . . .
>
> Then you shall see and be radiant;
> your heart shall thrill and exult,
> because the abundance of the sea shall be turned to you,
> the wealth of the nations shall come to you.
> A multitude of camels shall cover you,
> the young camels of Midian and Ephah;
> all those from Sheba shall come.
> They shall bring gold and frankincense,
> and shall bring good news, the praises of the LORD.[24]

The gifts of the wise men also partially and symbolically point forward to the complete fulfillment of this prophecy in the New Jerusalem in God's future new creation as presented in the book of Revelation: "By its light will the nations walk, and the kings of the earth will bring their glory into it, and its gates will never be shut by day—and there will be no night there. They will bring into it the glory and the honor of the nations."[25] In Jesus's birth, the light and glory of God had already begun to dispel the darkness and produce the new creation!

Second, the gifts and worship of the *magoi* point forward to the inclusion of the Gentiles among God's people. The Jews at that time were primarily expecting the Messiah to deliver and restore the Jewish nation while judging, destroying, or subduing all others by force. The worship of the *magoi* pictures the willing submission of the Gentile nations without military action. It portrays their inclusion within the scope of God's kingdom and plan. The kingdom of this King would not be limited to Palestine

[24] Isa. 60:1–3, 5–6; cf. Ps. 72:10–11, 15.
[25] Rev. 21:24–26.

but would expand to encompass the entire world. Throughout his Gospel Matthew hints at this theme of God's kingdom extending throughout the entire world via the Gentile mission.[26] It culminates in Jesus's final words of the Gospel where he, as the conquering King ("all authority in heaven and on earth has been given to me"), instructs his followers to extend his kingdom throughout the entire world by making disciples of all the nations.[27]

Matthew concludes his account of the *magoi* by noting that they were warned in a dream not to return to Herod and departed to their country by another way. Given that in each of the three dreams an angel appeared to Joseph, we can probably safely assume that an angel appeared to at least one of the *magoi*, even though Matthew omits any reference to an angel. We are not told how long it took for Herod to determine that the *magoi* had sided with the new king and rejected his authority, but the final three episodes in chapter 2 likely occurred fairly quickly after their departure. The gifts and recognition of the *magoi* certainly provided Jesus no physical safety, and as a rival king, his life was in imminent danger. The silence of the *magoi* would only buy him so much time.

TWO RESPONSES

Moving beyond the facts and flow of the narrative, we may ask what the narrative was intended to accomplish. Few, if any, passages in Scripture are included simply to give information for the intellectually astute or historically curious. Most biblical narratives demand some kind of response, and the story of Herod and the *magoi* is no different.

Matthew seems intentionally to contrast two responses to Jesus's birth. On the one hand, Herod, with the (perhaps unwitting) aid of the Jewish religious leaders, rejected God's appointed King, while, on the other hand, Gentiles, with little knowledge of the

[26] Matt. 3:9; 4:15; 8:10–12.
[27] Matt. 28:18–19.

true God, recognized God's King and responded with submission, allegiance, and worship. The narrative pushes us, its readers, to consider our response to Jesus. With whom are you identifying, Herod or the *magoi*?

Take care not to answer too quickly. Herod would have self-identified as a religiously observant Jew. He consistently presented himself in this way and viewed his project to rebuild the temple as a powerful example of his commitment to Israel's God.[28] (See again the drawings of Herod's temple on the insert following page 64.) He intensified his guilt, however, by using Scripture to locate the child. This act confirmed his knowledge that he was setting himself against God and his purposes in order to maintain his own rule and dynasty. His knowledge of God and Scripture led him not to submission and worship; instead, he prized self-preservation and self-rule above anything else, even God. He would not bow to the authority of a different Judean king, whether that king had God's approval or not. Herod chose resistance and opposition to Jesus and God's plan.

Herod powerfully illustrates the fact that it's not enough to identify outwardly with God's people. It's not enough to give sacrificially of your funds and energy to build God's house (or temple) and to help others worship. It's not enough to learn about God and his plan through his Scriptures. Every one of us is confronted daily with a choice of our will: Whom will we serve? For whom will we live? This is not the kind of decision that can be made once and for all ("I gave my life to God when I was a child") or that can be

[28]Josephus states that Herod spent an incalculable sum in building the temple, a measure that resulted from his ambition "to godliness" (*eis eusebeian*). *J.W.* 1.400–401. Although Herod also funded temples to Roma and Augustus in support of the imperial cult and other non-Jewish cults, he primarily thought of himself as an observant Jew committed to the Jerusalem temple. This attitude is quite clear in Josephus's record of Herod's speech at the beginning of the temple project: "But that the enterprise which I now propose to undertake is the most pious and beautiful one of our time I will now make clear. For this was the temple which our fathers built to the most Great God after their return from Babylon, but it lacks sixty cubits in height, the amount by which the first temple, built by Solomon, exceeded it. . . . But since, by the will of God, I am now ruler and there continues to be a long period of peace and an abundance of wealth and great revenues, and—what is of most importance—the Romans, who are, so to speak, the masters of the world, are (my) loyal friends, I will try to remedy the oversight caused by the necessity and subjection of that earlier time, and by this act of piety make full return to God for the gift of this kingdom." *Ant.* 15.384–387.

determined by past or even present performance ("I have gone to church every Sunday for the last twenty years and regularly give money to the church"). It's the kind of decision we must make afresh *every day*, and that entails more (but not less) than mere outward actions. For whom are you living today?

4

EXILE, HOLOCAUST, AND NAZARETH

PROPHECIES FULFILLED

MATTHEW 2:13-23

Now when they had departed, behold, an angel of the Lord appeared to Joseph in a dream and said, "Rise, take the child and his mother, and flee to Egypt, and remain there until I tell you, for Herod is about to search for the child, to destroy him." And he rose and took the child and his mother by night and departed to Egypt and remained there until the death of Herod. This was to fulfill what the Lord had spoken by the prophet, "Out of Egypt I called my son."

Then Herod, when he saw that he had been tricked by the wise men, became furious, and he sent and killed all the male children in Bethlehem and in all that region who were two years old or under, according to the time that he had ascertained from the wise men. Then was fulfilled what was spoken by the prophet Jeremiah:

> "A voice was heard in Ramah,
> weeping and loud lamentation,
> Rachel weeping for her children;
> she refused to be comforted, because they are no more."

> But when Herod died, behold, an angel of the Lord appeared in a dream to Joseph in Egypt, saying, "Rise, take the child and his mother and go to the land of Israel, for those who sought the child's life are dead." And he rose and took the child and his mother and went to the land of Israel. But when he heard that Archelaus was reigning over Judea in place of his father Herod, he was afraid to go there, and being warned in a dream he withdrew to the district of Galilee. And he went and lived in a city called Nazareth, that what was spoken by the prophets might be fulfilled: "He shall be called a Nazarene."

C. 5 BC

The Wise Men Depart

The *magoi* were safely on their way to their homeland with their unusual story of the birth of a Judean king unassociated with the Herodian family, but all was not well back in Bethlehem. The second half of Matthew 2 is composed of three separate episodes. Each of these is relatively short and is based upon a specific instance of scriptural fulfillment. The episodes together explain how Jesus escaped Herod's attempt on his life and grew up in the obscure and ignominious northern town of Nazareth. The three related biblical citations that Matthew provides also offer a fascinating window into the way in which the earliest Christians interpreted the Hebrew Scriptures (i.e., the Old Testament).

NO LATER THAN MARCH–APRIL 4 BC

Refugees

After the *magoi* departed, an angel from God appeared to Joseph again in a dream. The first appearance of an angel to Joseph had occurred when he was preparing to divorce Mary secretly.[1] This time the angel instructed Joseph to flee with his family to Egypt to protect Jesus from Herod's murderous designs. As with his earlier dream, Joseph discreetly and quickly obeyed the instructions he received. While a large and prosperous Jewish community had

---

[1] Matt. 1:20.

established itself in Egypt by this point in history, Joseph and his family would have been little more than refugees in search of safety and anonymity. God had prepared in advance for their needs: the expensive gifts from the *magoi* would have likely provided sufficient means for them to start over in a foreign country.

"Out of Egypt I Called My Son"

Matthew concludes this brief episode by pointing to the way in which this event fulfilled Old Testament Scripture: "Out of Egypt I called my son."[2] This is a very important fulfillment quotation, not only because it is somewhat unconventional, but also because it requires an explanation for why an event that seems so unpleasant and inconvenient, to say the least, can in fact reflect God's will for his messianic child. In addition to helping us understand one of the ways in which the earliest Christians interpreted the Old Testament, it helps us grasp the mission and purpose of Jesus.

The first obvious point to make is that this fulfillment lies outside the contours of what we normally understand as prediction-fulfillment. The original prophecy comes from Hosea 11:1–3:

> When Israel was a child, I loved him,
> and out of Egypt I called my son.
> The more they were called,
> the more they went away;
> they kept sacrificing to the Baals
> and burning offerings to idols.
> Yet it was I who taught Ephraim to walk;
> I took them up by their arms,
> but they did not know that I healed them.

In and of itself, this passage is not forward-looking. Rather, it looks backward to Israel's history to make the painful point that even though God had called and treated Israel as a son, the people rejected him and worshiped idols instead. How can Matthew argue that Jesus's early life in Egypt fulfilled a prophecy that was not

---

[2] Hos. 11:1.

even a prophecy in the conventional sense (i.e., it lacked a future prediction)? The key to answering this question lies in the ancient interpretive method known as *typology*. How are we to understand this approach?

> As it is used in the scholarly discussion, it [typology] refers to events, institutions, or people [from the Old Testament] that foreshadow future things. The earlier thing is called the "type," and the correspondingly later thing, the "antitype." Typology is grounded in three assumptions that guide the authors of the biblical text: (1) God is sovereign over history and is directing it in ways that reveal his unchanging character; (2) historical patterns that pertain to significant events, institutions, and people theologically foreshadow later recurrences of similar things; and (3) the final historical fulfillments will eclipse their prior counterparts, since God's explicit expressions of his ultimate purpose outstrip what has already occurred.[3]

Essentially, typology is bound up with *correspondence in history*, that is, with a pattern in history that recurs, usually in escalated form. Underlying this view of history is the premise that the Jewish people, as well as the earliest Christians, looked to see how God had worked in Old Testament times to understand how he was working in the present and would work in the future.

Matthew's use of Hosea draws a strong connection between Jesus and Israel. Both play key roles in the history of redemption and share similar narratival patterns, with Israel's history foreshadowing the life of Jesus. What is the significance of this typological relationship?

Israel's purpose in the Old Testament was to mediate God's blessing, presence, and glory to the nations.[4] Reflecting on Jeremiah's letter to the exiles in Babylon, Christopher Wright aptly notes

[3]Jonathan Lunde, "An Introduction to Central Questions in the New Testament Use of the Old Testament," in *Three Views on the New Testament Use of the Old Testament*, ed. Kenneth Berding and Jonathan Lunde (Grand Rapids, MI: Zondervan, 2007), 18–19.

[4]Gen. 12:3; Pss. 67:1–7; 96:1–10; 145:10–12; Isa. 2:1–4; 56:7; 66:19; Zech. 8:23. For a much fuller and more detailed discussion of this theme, see Christopher Wright, *The Mission of God: Unlocking the Bible's Grand Narrative* (Downers Grove, IL: InterVarsity, 2006), 467–500.

that "they were not only to be the *beneficiaries* of God's promise to Abraham (in that they would not die out but increase), they were also to be the *agents* of God's promise to Abraham that through his descendants the nations would be blessed."[5] As we saw in chapter 2 above, God planned that the seed of Abraham would mediate his blessing to the nations.[6] Israel failed in this purpose by rejecting God in favor of idolatry, but God's purpose and plan would not be thwarted.[7]

In Matthew's view, God restarted Israel in her Messiah, Jesus. Jesus relived the history of Israel, but, instead of failing in the purpose to mediate God's blessings to the nations, Jesus succeeded in his sinless life and atoning death. You may not be familiar with thinking about Jesus as a "second Israel," but this is surely how Matthew understood him.[8] Consider the following points.

1. Why did Jesus choose *twelve* disciples?[9] Why not eleven or thirteen? Jesus was intentionally reconstituting the twelve tribes of Israel with allegiance to himself as the foundational criterion.

2. Why did Jesus fast and undergo *forty* days of temptation in the wilderness?[10] Couldn't he have accomplished the same thing in ten or twenty days? And why did he need to be *tempted* during this time? Again, Jesus was reliving the history of Israel. Israel was tempted for forty years in the wilderness with food serving as a focal point of temptation.[11] Israel failed to trust God and complained and grumbled, but Jesus determined to depend upon God's promises instead of taking the easy way out and thus passed the test.

3. Why did Jesus need to be baptized since he was sinless?[12] He needed to identify fully and completely with his people as their representative, the waters of baptism likely corresponding to

[5] Wright, *Mission of God*, 100 (emphasis original). See Jer. 29:1–14.
[6] Gen. 12:3.
[7] Hos. 11:2–7.
[8] For a fuller discussion of Jesus's solidarity with Israel, see William L. Kynes, *A Christology of Solidarity: Jesus as the Representative of His People in Matthew* (Lanham, MD: University Press of America, 1991), 9–36.
[9] See, e.g., Matt. 10:1.
[10] Matt. 4:1–11.
[11] Deut. 8:2–3; cf. Ex. 16:2–3; Ps. 78:17–32.
[12] Matt. 3:13–17.

the waters of the Red Sea. God confirmed Jesus's role as the new Israel when the voice from heaven declared, "This is my beloved Son, with whom I am well pleased."[13] The Old Testament clearly indicates that Israel was God's chosen son,[14] but at the baptism God declared that Jesus would take upon himself Israel's identity and mission.

Jesus's identity as the new Israel brings us back to Matthew's statement that Hosea's prophecy was fulfilled typologically in Jesus's Herod-induced exile in Egypt. While not prophetic or messianic in any straightforward or literal sense, Hosea's statement takes on a typological dimension by setting the event into the larger context of Israel's history. On the basis of the understanding that history unfolds in recurring, escalating patterns characteristic of God's supernatural divine intervention, Jesus "the Son" becomes the antitype for the type, Israel God's "son," and his "exile" in Egypt corresponds to Israel's similar exile to Egypt prior to the exodus.[15]

The passage in Hosea is a particularly useful summary of this stage of Israel's history because it speaks of Israel as a child and calls Israel God's "son." Jesus, as God's Son representing the new Israel, relived Israel's history in miniature and reconstituted the new people of God. The typological pattern would continue with the twelve disciples, who would bear witness to Jesus based on their allegiance to him as God's Son and Israel's true King. Matthew can thus accurately write, "This was to fulfill what the Lord had spoken by the prophet, 'Out of Egypt I called my son.'"[16]

A King's Fury

Matthew does not indicate how much time passed between Joseph's escape to Egypt with his family and Herod's realization that the

[13] Matt. 3:17.

[14] Ex. 4:22, 23; Jer. 31:9, 20; Hos. 11:1.

[15] The notion that Jesus leads a "new exodus" appears in all four New Testament Gospels and the book of Acts. Representative works on this topic include Rikki E. Watts, *Isaiah's New Exodus in Mark*, Biblical Studies Library (Grand Rapids, MI: Baker Academic, 2001); and David W. Pao, *Acts and the Isaianic New Exodus*, Biblical Studies Library (Grand Rapids, MI: Baker Academic, 2002).

[16] Matt. 2:15b.

magoi had tricked him, but it was unlikely very long. Accustomed to outsmarting everyone else, Herod was furious at the realization that the *magoi* had outfoxed the fox. He thus proceeded to have all the male children in and around Bethlehem under two years of age killed, a decision based upon the time of the star's appearance.

Why was Herod unable to investigate and determine the exact identity of the child? Why such an excessive response? Surely the other inhabitants of Bethlehem would have known whom the *magoi* visited. Several explanations are possible. Perhaps Herod suspected that if the *magoi* had allied with this rival king, then the villagers may have also allied with him and would have lied to protect him. Herod, or his representatives, may have distrusted their claim that the family and child had disappeared in the middle of the night. So Herod took the path of "better safe than sorry." This tyrannical response completely accords with what we know about Herod's cruel and paranoid character near the end of his life.

While such an action is exactly what we would expect Herod to do, critics of Matthew's historical reliability like to point out that we have no witness to this slaughter outside of his Gospel. Josephus provides a wealth of information concerning Herod's final years but makes no mention of this episode. We should bear in mind that Bethlehem was a small and relatively obscure town at this point in history, and the number of victims in Bethlehem and its vicinity could have been relatively low (perhaps one to two dozen). On the scale of atrocities committed in the ancient world, Herod's act would have been despicable but perhaps not of a sufficiently large scale to merit wide attention.

Nevertheless, the deaths of these infants and the mourning associated with them would have reverberated. If Josephus had known about the episode, he may well have commented on it. However, he completed his *Antiquities of the Jews* around AD 94, nearly one hundred years after the event, and, although he had good sources, his knowledge was not exhaustive. Matthew likely wrote a generation or two earlier and would have had access to oral traditions stemming directly from Jesus's family. The silence of our other sources therefore does not give us sufficient reason to distrust the historicity of Matthew's account.

One possible extrabiblical reference to this massacre survives that does not depend on Matthew's account. Macrobius, an early fifth-century (likely pagan) philosopher, recorded a quip attributed to Caesar Augustus: "When he heard that Herod king of the Jews had ordered boys in Syria under the age of two years to be put to death and that the king's son was among those killed, he said: 'I'd rather be Herod's pig than Herod's son.'"[17] Many assume that this comment relies on Matthew's Gospel because it postdates it by several centuries, but Macrobius, a Neoplatonist, displays no explicit knowledge of Christianity in his writings. The author obviously mixes up historical events as he locates the massacre in Syria (the Romans would have viewed Judea as part of the larger province of Syria) and includes Herod's own son in the slaughter (Herod killed his son around the same time period). But these very errors may indicate that Macrobius derived his information from the same Roman sources from which he drew all his other information about Caesar.[18] What is more, he could not have discovered the information about Herod's son, the main point of his comment, from Matthew's Gospel. Thus, this reference may well indicate knowledge of Herod's slaughter of the Bethlehem infants rooted in the non-Christian Roman world.

Rachel Weeps for Her Children

Matthew indicates that Herod's murderous actions unwittingly fulfilled Jeremiah's words: "A voice is heard in Ramah, lamentation and bitter weeping. Rachel is weeping for her children; she refuses to be comforted for her children, because they are no more."[19] Matthew's use of this passage is very similar to what we saw above with Hosea 11:1. Jesus is typologically reliving the history of Israel.

---

[17] *Macrobius: The Saturnalia: Translated with an Introduction and Notes*, trans. Percival Vaughan Davies (New York: Columbia University Press, 1969), 171 (*Sat.* 2.4.11).
[18] See Barry Beitzel, "Herod the Great: Another Snapshot of His Treachery?," *Journal of the Evangelical Theological Society* 57, no. 3 (2014):309–22.
[19] Jer. 31:15.

Within its original context in the book of Jeremiah, the passage Matthew cites is reflecting on the sorrow of the Babylonian exile. Ramah was a town about five miles north of Jerusalem that lay along the route the exiles were forced to travel between Jerusalem and Babylon.[20] Rachel was buried near Bethlehem,[21] and this Jeremiah passage poetically describes her as weeping over the loss and suffering of her descendants. Remarkably, the entirety of Jeremiah 31 focuses not on sorrow but on the joy and happiness that will fill God's people during his future restoration and salvation.[22] The prophet recalls the sorrow of exile to highlight, in contrast, the joy of the coming healing. In light of Matthew's use of Hosea's prophecy discussed above, it seems hardly coincidental that Jeremiah 31 twice describes Israel as God's son.[23]

Matthew notes that Israel went into exile in Babylon by way of a painful process that involved suffering and loss but would eventually lead to the restoration of the entire nation. In the same way, Jesus went into exile in Egypt in a painful process that again brought suffering and loss to Rachel's descendants but would lead

---

[20] Jer. 40:1.
[21] Gen. 35:19–20.
[22] Consider these excerpts from Jeremiah 31:

> "I have loved you with an everlasting love;
> therefore I have continued my faithfulness to you.
> Again I will build you, and you shall be built. . . .
>
> "for I am a father to Israel,
> and Ephraim is my firstborn. . . .
>
> "say, 'He who scattered Israel will gather him,
> and will keep him as a shepherd keeps his flock.'
> For the Lord has ransomed Jacob
> and has redeemed him from hands too strong for him.
> They shall come and sing aloud on the heights of Zion,
> and they shall be radiant over the goodness of the LORD. . . .
>
> I will turn their mourning into joy;
> I will comfort them, and give them gladness for sorrow.
> I will feast the soul of the priests with abundance,
> and my people shall be satisfied with my goodness, declares the LORD. . . .
>
> "There is hope for your future, declares the LORD. . . .
>
> "For I will satisfy the weary soul, and every languishing soul I will replenish." (Jer. 31:3b–4a, 9c, 10b–12a, 13b–14, 17a, 25)

Even more significantly, Jeremiah 31 concludes with God's promise of the new covenant (Jer. 31:31–40).
[23] Jer. 31:9, 20.

to the complete fulfillment of the restoration, healing, and salvation prophesied by Jeremiah.

Even though Matthew's quotations of Hosea 11:1 and Jeremiah 31:15 presuppose and support a typological relationship between *Jesus* and *Israel*, the narrative itself also points to a typological relationship between *Jesus* and *Moses*, the man who led Israel out of slavery into freedom. Moses's life was threatened as a baby when Pharaoh determined to kill all the male Hebrew babies.[24] As an adult, Moses fled into exile and didn't return to Egypt until those who were seeking his life were dead.[25] Josephus recounts Jewish traditions that also exhibit remarkable parallels with Jesus's birth. As the story goes, Pharaoh was warned in advance by a sacred scribe that an Israelite would be born who would "abase the sovereignty of the Egyptians and exalt the Israelites" and that God told Moses's father in a dream that Moses would "escape those who are watching to destroy him, and . . . deliver the Hebrew race from their bondage in Egypt."[26] Matthew's infancy narrative thus explicitly presents Jesus as the new Israel who would fulfill Israel's purpose for existence as a nation and implicitly presents Jesus as the new Moses who would lead God's people from slavery to salvation.

SOMETIME AFTER MARCH OR APRIL 4 BC

"He Shall Be Called a Nazarene"

Matthew concludes his narrative of Jesus's infancy by noting one final fulfillment of the Old Testament Scriptures. After Herod died, an angel appeared to Joseph in a dream for the third time to instruct him that he and his family could return safely to Israel. This message fulfilled the prior angelic promise and command to remain in Egypt "until I tell you."[27] Joseph continued his pattern

[24] Ex. 1:15.
[25] Ex. 2:15; 4:19; cf. Matt. 2:20.
[26] Josephus, *Ant.* 2.205, 215–16. See the fuller chart of parallels in Charles H. Talbert, *Matthew*, Paideia: Commentaries on the New Testament (Grand Rapids, MI: Baker Academic, 2010), 37–38.
[27] Matt. 2:13.

of obedience even though it meant that he would once again have to uproot and relocate his family.

In his return from Egypt, Joseph was faced with a choice. Where should they resettle? While deliberating, Joseph received instructions in a fourth and final dream not to return to Judea. This confirmed his own fears, which arose from the knowledge that Herod's son Archelaus was ruling there. Archelaus followed in the cruel and tyrannical footsteps of his father, and after just ten years of his reign, Caesar exiled him to Gaul, seized his property, and converted Judea into a Roman province.[28]

Joseph heeded this warning and, instead of resettling near Bethlehem, moved to the city of Nazareth in the district of Galilee. We know from Luke's account that Joseph and Mary had originally lived in Nazareth,[29] so it would have been quite natural for Joseph to return there after a few years of living abroad. Matthew does not mention that Mary and Joseph lived in Nazareth before the birth of Jesus, either because he did not know this or because it would have made no difference in his recounting of Jesus's infancy. All that mattered to Matthew was that Jesus had been born in Bethlehem but grew up in Nazareth, where his family resettled after their return from Egypt.

This leads to Matthew's fifth and final fulfillment quotation in the infancy narrative: "And he went and lived in a city called Nazareth, so that what was spoken by the prophets might be fulfilled, that he would be called a Nazarene."[30] This fulfillment quotation is instantly complicated by our inability to locate the source of the quotation in the Old Testament.[31]

Several considerations come into play as we try to understand retrospectively how this made sense to Matthew and the earliest Christians. First, Matthew alerts us to the fact that this may not be an exact quotation of a single specific text by saying that it "was

---

[28] Josephus, *Ant.* 311–313; 342–344, 355.
[29] Luke 1:26; 2:4.
[30] Matt. 2:23.
[31] The quotation itself is only two words in Greek: *Nazōraios klēthēsetai* ("He shall be called a Nazarene").

spoken by the prophets [plural]."[32] This opens up the possibility that Matthew is referring to a theme found in multiple prophets that can best be captured with the words "he shall be called a Nazarene."

As we develop further in the appendix, a prophetic theme immediately comes to mind, that of the "branch," from the Hebrew word *netzer* (or *ntzr* in its consonantal form). Isaiah 11:1 states, "There shall come forth a shoot from the stump of Jesse, and a branch [*ntzr*] from his roots shall bear fruit." By the first century, Jews and Christians had gathered a whole cluster of messianic texts related to a branch that, although using different Hebrew words, would have been associated with the branch (*ntzr*) of Isaiah 11:1.[33] Although it is impossible to know with certainty the original meaning of the Hebrew name Nazareth (likely *ntzrt*), it likely was quite closely related to "branch" (*ntzr*), and an English translation might very well render it "Branchville" or "Branchtown."[34]

Matthew is thus making the following point with this final fulfillment quotation: far from an accident, Jesus's association with Nazareth was planned by God in order that Jesus would be called a Nazarene, a confirmation of his identity as the prophesied and messianic Davidic branch of Isaiah 11:1. This connection is further strengthened by the proximity of Isaiah 11:1 to Isaiah 7:14, the first fulfillment of Scripture cited by Matthew in Jesus's infancy narrative.[35] Matthew would have easily connected the promised branch of Isaiah 11:1 with the promised birth of a son in Isaiah 7:14 and 9:6. Nazareth was a small, obscure town (likely consisting of around five hundred people), and no one at the beginning of the first century associated it with the Messiah.[36] Looking back

---

[32] Matt. 2:23.

[33] Isa. 4:2; 53:2; Jer. 23:5; 33:15; Zech. 3:8; 6:12.

[34] This is a complicated discussion in scholarly circles. For more details, see Raymond Brown, *The Birth of the Messiah: A Commentary on the Infancy Narratives in the Gospels of Matthew and Luke*, 2nd ed. (Garden City, NY: Doubleday, 1993), 207–13; and Craig Keener, *A Commentary on the Gospel of Matthew* (Grand Rapids, MI: Eerdmans, 1999), 113–15. Both discuss other possible Old Testament allusions, such as a relationship to the terms "Nazirite" (*nezer*) or "to watch" (*natzar*), but neither of these options would have been as obviously messianic to Matthew and his first readers as Jesus's designation as the branch of Isa. 11:1.

[35] Matt. 1:23.

[36] See Nathanael's dismissive remark in John 1:46.

after the fact, however, Matthew and the other earliest Christians recognized God's providential care in causing the messianic branch to grow up in "Branchville."

REFLECTIONS ON MATTHEW

We have finished walking through Matthew's infancy narrative, but before moving on to the Gospel of Luke, it will be beneficial to review some of Matthew's main themes.

First and foremost, Matthew aims to demonstrate Jesus's connection to the Old Testament. *Jesus was the long-awaited and long-expected Messiah who would fulfill God's promises and rescue his people.* God had not forgotten his people or his creation despite centuries of exile, foreign domination, suffering, and apparent nonfulfillment. From the very first verse of his Gospel, Matthew stresses Jesus's link to the Old Testament. The genealogy presents Jesus as the culmination of the entire Old Testament narrative. As the "son of Abraham" and the "son of David," Jesus was the promised "seed" who would bring blessing to the nations and extend God's rule throughout creation as the heir to David's throne.

Following the genealogy, Matthew's infancy narrative is structured in five episodes surrounding five scriptural quotations, the latter four of which center on geographical locations (Bethlehem, Egypt, Ramah, and Nazareth):

1. *Matthew 1:18–25* highlights the fulfillment of Isaiah 7:14 and focuses on Jesus's identity and purpose. He was Immanuel, God with us, and he would save his people from their sins.

2. *Matthew 2:1–12* emphasizes the fulfillment of Micah 5:2 in Jesus's birth in Bethlehem. In addition, the *magoi's* worship points forward to Jesus's universal kingship, and the conflict with Herod reveals the incompatibility of Jesus's kingdom with the kingdoms of this world. There is room for only one king in individual lives and in the cosmos as a whole. The *magoi* recognize and submit to the legitimate King, while King Herod epitomizes rejection and opposition to God's King.

3. *Matthew 2:13–15* points to the fulfillment of Hosea 11:1 in

Jesus's escape to and return from Egypt. As the new Israel, Jesus relived the history of the nation, but instead of failing where Israel had failed, Jesus succeeded and brought to completion God's purpose and plan for the nation of Israel and the world.

4. *Matthew 2:16–18* notes the fulfillment of Jeremiah 31:15 in Herod's slaughter of the children of Bethlehem. This painful development further deepens Jesus's solidarity with Israel as he relives the exile, and, as the broader context of Jeremiah 31 makes clear, the final word lies not with exile, suffering, and loss but with God, who will replace sorrow with joy when he brings final and full restoration.

5. *Matthew 2:19–23* draws attention to Jesus's fulfillment of the messianic "branch" prophecies found in the Old Testament Prophets through the providential connection between the Branch (*ntzr*) and Nazareth (*ntzrt*). Jesus was the promised Messiah—or Davidic branch—who would rescue his people and fulfill God's promises.

Second, Matthew's birth narrative prepares the reader for what follows in Matthew's Gospel. We come away with a strong sense of who Jesus is. *He is the Son of David, the Son of Abraham, the Son of God, Immanuel, a new Israel, and a new Moses.* We also come away from the birth narrative with a great deal of curiosity, expectation, and anticipation. How will Jesus fulfill all that was said about him at his birth? How will he fulfill the promises to David and reestablish David's kingdom? How will he extend God's blessing to the nations as the Son of Abraham? How will he live up to the title "Immanuel"? How will he save his people from their sins? How will he, as the embodiment of a new Israel, fulfill God's original plans and purposes for Israel? How will he transform sorrow and death into joy, restoration, and salvation? You will have to read the rest of Matthew's Gospel to find the answers to these questions. Jesus's fulfillment is both different from and superior to anything that could have been guessed by most people at the beginning of the first century and, for that matter, the twenty-first.

TWO KINGDOMS

Before moving on to the Gospel of Luke, we should briefly reflect upon Matthew's contrast between two kings and two kingdoms. The apostle Paul develops this contrast further in Colossians, where he speaks of "giving thanks to the Father, who has qualified you to share in the inheritance of the saints in light. He has delivered us from the domain of darkness and transferred us to the kingdom of his beloved Son, in whom we have redemption, the forgiveness of sins."[37]

Paul paints salvation in these verses as a transfer of dominion and allegiance. At one time, we were under the dominion of darkness and sin, but God has graciously transferred us into the kingdom of his Son, Jesus. This kingdom transfer is linked to redemption and forgiveness of sins.

These verses also paint a very spiritual picture of the world, a picture that our current materialistic and naturalistic culture rarely considers. Ultimately, there are only two kingdoms, and every human being belongs to one of them. This is the reality whether a person wants to believe it or not. Every human being is either serving in slavery under the dominion of sin and darkness or serving with allegiance and submission in God's kingdom of righteousness, peace, and joy. No third option or neutral ground exists. Thanks be to God who has rescued us and transferred us into the kingdom of his Son!

[37] Col. 1:12–14.

PART 2

LIGHT OF THE NATIONS

5

TWO MIRACULOUS CONCEPTIONS

LUKE 1:5-38

In the days of Herod, king of Judea, there was a priest named Zechariah, of the division of Abijah. And he had a wife from the daughters of Aaron, and her name was Elizabeth. And they were both righteous before God, walking blamelessly in all the commandments and statutes of the Lord. But they had no child, because Elizabeth was barren, and both were advanced in years.

Now while he was serving as priest before God when his division was on duty, according to the custom of the priesthood, he was chosen by lot to enter the temple of the Lord and burn incense. And the whole multitude of the people were praying outside at the hour of incense. And there appeared to him an angel of the Lord standing on the right side of the altar of incense. And Zechariah was troubled when he saw him, and fear fell upon him. But the angel said to him, "Do not be afraid, Zechariah, for your prayer has been heard, and your wife Elizabeth will bear you a son, and you shall call his name John. And you will have joy and gladness, and many will rejoice at his birth, for he will be great before the Lord. And he must not drink wine or strong drink, and he will be filled with the Holy Spirit, even from his mother's womb. And he will turn many of the children of Israel to the Lord their God, and he will go before him in the spirit and power of Elijah, to turn the hearts of the fathers to the children, and the disobedient to the wisdom of the just, to make ready for the Lord a people prepared."

And Zechariah said to the angel, "How shall I know this? For I am an old man, and my wife is advanced in years." And the angel answered him, "I am Gabriel. I stand in the presence of God, and I was sent to speak to you and to bring you this good news. And behold, you will be silent and unable to speak until the day that these things take place, because you did not believe my words, which will be fulfilled in their time." And the people were waiting for Zechariah, and they were wondering at his delay in the temple. And when he came out, he was unable to speak to them, and they realized that he had seen a vision in the temple. And he kept making signs to them and remained mute. And when his time of service was ended, he went to his home.

After these days his wife Elizabeth conceived, and for five months she kept herself hidden, saying, "Thus the Lord has done for me in the days when he looked on me, to take away my reproach among people."

In the sixth month the angel Gabriel was sent from God to a city of Galilee named Nazareth, to a virgin betrothed to a man whose name was Joseph, of the house of David. And the virgin's name was Mary. And he came to her and said, "Greetings, O favored one, the Lord is with you!" But she was greatly troubled at the saying, and tried to discern what sort of greeting this might be. And the angel said to her, "Do not be afraid, Mary, for you have found favor with God. And behold, you will conceive in your womb and bear a son, and you shall call his name Jesus. He will be great and will be called the Son of the Most High. And the Lord God will give to him the throne of his father David, and he will reign over the house of Jacob forever, and of his kingdom there will be no end."

And Mary said to the angel, "How will this be, since I am a virgin?"

And the angel answered her, "The Holy Spirit will come upon you, and the power of the Most High will overshadow you; therefore the child to be born will be called holy—the Son of God. And behold, your relative Elizabeth in her old age has also conceived a son, and this is the sixth month with her who was called barren. For nothing will be impossible with God." And Mary said,

"Behold, I am the servant of the Lord; let it be to me according to your word." And the angel departed from her.

LUKE AS HISTORIAN

Luke explicitly opens his Gospel in the manner of an ancient historian. In contrast to Matthew, who begins his Gospel with a genealogy, Luke commences with a discussion of his historiographic approach to investigating and verifying the contents of his account:

> Inasmuch as many have undertaken to compile a narrative of the things that have been accomplished among us, just as those who from the beginning were eyewitnesses[1] and ministers of the word have delivered them to us, it seemed good to me also, having followed all things closely for some time past, to write an orderly account for you, most excellent Theophilus, that you may have certainty concerning the things you have been taught.[2]

Luke makes two critical points in this opening statement. First, he expresses awareness of prior narratives of Jesus's life based directly upon eyewitness testimony. This likely would have included the Gospel of Mark along with a number of other sources. Critical scholars often downplay the significance of the eyewitness character of the Gospels and assume that various Christian communities existed in relative isolation from each other. On the contrary, the earliest Christian communities were in regular contact with each other (they were, as one writer remarked, a "holy Internet"!),[3] and the existence and testimony of living eyewitnesses would have safeguarded the truthfulness of the stories of Jesus's life well into the period in which our four Evangelists wrote their Gospels.[4]

---

[1] The word "eyewitnesses" is *autoptai* in the original Greek, which is a composite of *autos* ("themselves") and *optai* ("those who saw").

[2] Luke 1:1–4.

[3] Michael B. Thompson, "The Holy Internet: Communication Between Churches in the First Christian Generation," in *The Gospels for All Christians: Rethinking the Gospel Audiences*, ed. Richard Bauckham (Grand Rapids, MI: Eerdmans, 1998), 49–70.

[4] For an excellent discussion of these issues, see Richard Bauckham, *Jesus and the Eyewitnesses: The Gospels as Eyewitness Testimony* (Grand Rapids, MI: Eerdmans, 2006); and Richard Bauckham, ed., *The Gospels for All Christians.* On the strong arguments in support of dating the composition of Luke's Gospel to around AD 58–60, see Andreas J. Köstenberger, L. Scott Kellum, and Charles L.

Second, Luke affirms that he had personally followed and investigated these events for some time and was writing an orderly account so that Theophilus (to whom the Gospel was dedicated) would have certainty in regard to what he had been taught about Jesus. Theophilus (who may or may not have been a Christian) was probably the literary patron who financed Luke's two-volume work on Christianity (Luke-Acts).

Although neither Luke nor Acts explicitly identifies its author, the surviving evidence from the New Testament and the apostolic Fathers (including the ancient title of Luke's Gospel, "According to Luke") strongly points to the Luke we know from the pages of the New Testament.[5] Throughout his travels with Paul, particularly while Paul spent two years in prison in Caesarea (AD 55–57),[6] Luke would have had ample time and opportunity to interview Palestinian eyewitnesses.

While Luke's use of Mark is evident throughout most of the Gospel, Mark omits an infancy narrative, so Luke must have drawn this information from different oral or written sources. The infancy narratives hold several clues within themselves. First, the accounts in Luke are told from Mary's perspective with details that could have come only from Mary herself (particularly the initial visit of Gabriel to Mary).[7] Luke explicitly mentions that Mary "treasured up all these things, pondering them in her heart."[8] This statement strongly suggests that Mary was the source of the information about Jesus's infancy preserved in Luke's Gospel. This maternal viewpoint also nicely complements Matthew's infancy narrative, which, as mentioned, reflects Joseph's perspective. We cannot verify if Luke ever met Mary personally, but even if not, he may have had access to her memories of the events through James or Jude, Jesus's half-brothers who in due course became leaders

---

Quarles, *The Cradle, the Cross, and the Crown: An Introduction to the New Testament* (Nashville, TN: B&H Academic, 2009), 261–64.

[5] Col. 4:14; 2 Tim. 4:11; Philem. 24; and the "we" passages in Acts 16:10–17; 20:5–15; 21:1–18; 27:1–28:16.

[6] Acts 21:17–27:1.

[7] See Luke 1:26–38.

[8] Luke 2:19.

in the Jerusalem church; John, who helped take care of Mary after Jesus's death;[9] or some other unnamed family member(s).

Second, Luke is the only source of information about John the Baptist's parents and birth. Since Mary and Elizabeth were relatives,[10] the unusual circumstances surrounding the birth of John the Baptist may have been preserved within family circles alongside the information about Jesus's birth. Luke may have also gained access to this information from some original disciples of John the Baptist who later became followers of Jesus.

Third, Luke's infancy narrative, particularly the hymns or canticles, reflects Semitic Greek and may have been translated from an original Aramaic or Hebrew source.[11] In any case, the theological content of the hymns, Mary's *Magnificat* and Zechariah's *Benedictus*, conveys exactly what we would expect at this point in salvation history. These portions reflect Jewish expectations of God's salvation based on the Old Testament with little evidence of later Christian developments. They express Second Temple Jewish hopes in God's salvation without betraying knowledge of what that salvation would look like in Jesus's death and resurrection. The expectations in these hymns support Luke's claim to have drawn on sources based on the eyewitnesses and original participants themselves.

BRIDGING THE OLD AND NEW TESTAMENTS

We saw in Matthew's Gospel that he used a genealogy along with five strategic Old Testament quotations to bridge the gap between the Old Testament and Jesus's birth. Both Matthew and Luke use the infancy narratives to bridge this gap between the Testaments, but Luke takes a different approach than Matthew. Old Testament allusions saturate his narrative, but rather than explicitly quote Old Testament prophecies, Luke instead focuses on the birth of Jesus's forerunner, John the Baptist, the final representative of

[9] John 19:26–27.

[10] Luke 1:36.

[11] There is no way to know with certainty if these sources were primarily oral or written or whether they were translated into Greek by Luke or others before him. Luke, of course, would have adapted the material in order to produce a coherent narrative.

the Old Testament era. Luke makes this point explicit later in his narrative:

> When John's messengers had gone, Jesus began to speak to the crowds concerning John: "What did you go out into the wilderness to see? A reed shaken by the wind? What then did you go out to see? A man dressed in soft clothing? Behold, those who are dressed in splendid clothing and live in luxury are in kings' courts. What then did you go out to see? A prophet? Yes, I tell you, and more than a prophet. This is he of whom it is written,
>
> > 'Behold, I send my messenger before your face,
> > who will prepare your way before you.'
>
> I tell you, among those born of women none is greater than John. Yet the one who is least in the kingdom of God is greater than he."[12]

John was the greatest of the Old Testament prophets because he was the forerunner of the Messiah. Despite John's greatness, he was still living in the time of nonfulfillment, so that the least in the kingdom of God—that is, the least of the ones living under the new covenant in the time of fulfillment—would be greater than John. Luke thus presents John as the final prophetic representative of the Old Testament era while Jesus inaugurated a new stage of fulfillment in salvation history.

Luke strengthens this point in the way he presents John the Baptist's parents. The description of Zechariah and Elizabeth along with their supernatural conception fits right in with other Old Testament narratives.[13] Zechariah was a priest, and Elizabeth, too, was of priestly descent. They both were righteous and fulfilled all of God's ritual and moral commandments. They were, however, old and childless, and in first-century Jewish culture, many viewed barrenness as shameful, a sign of God's displeasure and judgment. Yet as Luke describes the couple, he emphasizes that their barren-

[12] Luke 7:24–28.

[13] See Abraham and Sarah, Jacob and Rachel, Samson's parents, and Samuel's parents.

ness arose not from sin; it instead served a key purpose in God's plan of salvation history.

7 OR 6 BC

Zechariah's division of priests (Abijah) served semiannually in the Jerusalem temple. During the week of service, these priests conducted daily rituals in the temple, including the offering of sacrifices and the burning of incense inside the Holy Place. The priests divided responsibility by way of lots, and during this particular week of service the lot fell to Zechariah, who was to offer incense on one of the days. This incense symbolized prayer, and while Zechariah offered the incense, the people who gathered outside the temple prayed, likely for God's mercy and favor and for the fulfillment of God's promises to Israel. Because of the large number of priests, each priest was allowed this honor only once in a lifetime, making this an incredibly special moment for Zechariah.

In the Spirit and Power of Elijah

Zechariah was unexpectedly interrupted right in the midst of this solemn moment. The appearance of an angel, standing on the right side of the altar of incense, filled Zechariah with fear. Fear is the natural and expected response to unexpected supernatural appearances and events. The angel quickly spoke to alleviate his fear and assured Zechariah that God had heard his prayer and that Elizabeth would bear a son, who was to be named John.

The angel proceeded to make several unexpected and amazing predictions concerning this son. The promise of miraculous conception would have been wonderful enough to fill Zechariah with unspeakable joy without these additional pronouncements.

First, John would be great in the sight of the Lord.

Second, he must abstain from wine and strong drink. This statement could indicate that John would identify as an Old Testament Nazirite.[14] However, while he certainly kept an ascetic

[14] Num. 6:1–3.

lifestyle, no evidence suggests that John followed all the requirements of a Nazirite.[15]

Third, and perhaps most remarkable, the boy would be filled with the Holy Spirit from his mother's womb. This prophecy strongly conveyed God's choice of John; from the very moment of conception, God would be preparing John for his prophetic task.

Fourth, John would turn many Israelites back to God. This purpose characterized John's ministry of calling people to a baptism of repentance and is mentioned twice by the angel.[16] The goal of turning people back to God was "to make ready for the Lord a people prepared."[17] The people were not yet ready for God's acts of restoration and salvation and had to be prepared through repentance.

Fifth, John would "go before him in the spirit and power of Elijah."[18] Although not a word-for-word quotation, this reference would draw any observant reader back to the book of Malachi, particularly the final two verses of the Old Testament (in the Christian ordering of the books): "Behold, I will send you Elijah the prophet before the great and awesome day of the Lord comes. And he will turn the hearts of fathers to their children and the hearts of children to their fathers, lest I come and strike the land with a decree of utter destruction."[19] This prophecy led many Second Temple Jews to expect Elijah to return before God's final judgment and restoration.[20] The angel does not here identify John as the literal Elijah himself but indicates that John would operate in the *spirit and power* of Elijah to fulfill Malachi's prophecy.

Zechariah's Response

In response to these incredible claims, Zechariah shifted from fear to doubt, or at least uncertainty, and he asked the angel for tan-

---

[15] Luke 7:33.
[16] Luke 1:16, 17.
[17] Luke 1:17.
[18] Luke 1:17.
[19] Mal. 4:5–6; cf. Mal. 3:1.
[20] Mark 9:11–13; Matt. 17:10–13. Sirach 48:10 similarly states, "At the appointed time, it is written, you [Elijah] are destined to calm the wrath of God before it breaks out in fury, to turn the hearts of parents to their children, and to restore the tribes of Jacob." Bruce Metzger and Roland Murphy, eds., *The New Oxford Annotated Apocrypha* (New York: Oxford University Press, 1991), 154.

gible proof or reassurance: "How shall I know this?"[21] Throughout Scripture, the biblical narratives indicate that believers may sometimes rightly ask God for a sign, and God occasionally does provide signs and confirmation to his people.[22] In this case, however, the angel's response makes clear that Zechariah had received sufficient revelation to warrant belief and that his desire for a sign arose because of doubt. We might note that on some occasions God chooses to confirm things beyond any possible doubt, while at other times he expects us to act upon the truth that we know without supernatural confirmation.

The angel answered Zechariah's question by first identifying himself and his role. The angel was Gabriel, apparently an angel of high rank (standing "in the presence of God") who was first encountered by name in the book of Daniel.[23] The Bible itself reveals relatively little information about the angelic realm, but during the Second Temple period, Jewish speculation about angels abounded.[24] Gabriel explicitly identified Zechariah's lack of faith and pronounced immediate consequences: Zechariah would lose his ability to speak until Gabriel's words were fulfilled.[25] That people "made signs" to communicate with Zechariah indicates that he became both mute and deaf.[26]

The scene now shifts to the people anxiously waiting and praying outside the temple. It was customary for the priest to offer

[21] Luke 1:18.

[22] Ex. 3:12; Judg. 6:36–40; 1 Sam. 10:2; 2 Kings 20:8–11; Isa. 7:11–14.

[23] Dan. 8:16 and 9:21.

[24] See *1 Enoch* 9:1; 10:9; 20:7; 40:9; 54:6; *2 Enoch* 21:3, 5; 24:1; *Apocalypse of Moses* 40:1. *1 Enoch* 20:1–8 is worth quoting in full to give readers a taste of Second Temple Jewish speculation about angels: "And these are the names of the holy angels who watch: Suru'el, one of the holy angels—for (he is) of eternity and of trembling. Raphael, one of the holy angels, for (he is) of the spirits of man. Raguel, one of the holy angels who take vengeance for the world and for the luminaries. Michael, one of the holy angels, for (he is) obedient in his benevolence over the people and the nations. Saraqa'el, one of the holy angels who are (set) over the spirits of mankind who sin in the spirit. Gabriel, one of the holy angels who oversee the garden of Eden, and the serpents, and the cherubim." *1 Enoch* 40:9–10 assigns different functions: "And he said to me, 'The first one is the merciful and forbearing Michael; the second one, who is set over all disease and every wound of the children of the people, is Raphael; the third, who is set over all exercise of strength is Gabriel; and the fourth, who is set over all actions of repentance unto the hope of those who would inherit eternal life, is Phanuel by name.' (So) these are his four angels: they are of the Lord of the Spirits, and the four voices which I heard in those days." E. Isaac, trans., "1 [Ethiopic Apocalypse of] Enoch: A New Translation and Introduction," in *The Old Testament Pseudepigrapha*, ed. James H. Charlesworth (New York: Doubleday, 1983): 1:23–24, 32.

[25] Luke 1:20.

[26] Luke 1:62.

incense and then to stand outside and pronounce the Aaronic blessing upon the people: "The Lord bless you and keep you; the Lord make his face to shine upon you and be gracious to you; the Lord lift up his countenance upon you and give you peace."[27] When Zechariah finally appeared yet could not speak, the people rightly concluded that he had seen some kind of vision in the temple.

Since Zechariah's priestly division served in the temple only two weeks per year, he would have supported himself and his wife with some other job throughout the year. Luke recounts that after Zechariah returned home, Elizabeth conceived. Elizabeth could not easily communicate with her husband (though he doubtless shared with her what the boy's name should be; Luke 1:60, 63), but she assumed that the pregnancy was an answer to their prayers and was God's way of taking away her reproach among the people for being childless. What is more, Elizabeth kept the pregnancy a secret for five months, likely to avoid ridicule from those who would have laughed at her claims to be pregnant until it was obvious that she was.

C. 7, 6, OR 5 BC

The Annunciation

Luke's infancy narrative weaves back and forth between John the Baptist and Jesus; he tells a story of two miraculous conceptions and births. The accounts are intentionally parallel. In both cases, Gabriel announces the birth in advance to a parent,[28] the births are described,[29] the boys are named,[30] and a prophecy indicates the future significance and ministry of the child.[31] The parallel nature of the accounts highlights the close relationship these two men would share with each other in God's plan. The accounts also clearly communicate the superiority of Jesus. John would be a

[27] Num. 6:24–26.
[28] Luke 1:5–25; 26–38.
[29] Luke 1:57–58; 2:1–20.
[30] Luke 1:59–66; 2:21.
[31] Luke 1:67–79; 2:28–32.

prophet of God to prepare the way for God's coming to his people,[32] while Jesus would be called the "Son of the Most High."[33] To apply a certain designation to someone was to draw attention to that person's identity. John would *prepare the way* for the coming of the Lord, while Jesus himself *was* the Lord, the Son of the Most High, who was coming to his people.

In the sixth month of Elizabeth's pregnancy, God sent Gabriel to a virgin named Mary in Nazareth, who was betrothed to a man "of the house of David" named Joseph.[34] This betrothal represented a legally binding contract that could be broken only by divorce, and at this time in Galilee, it was culturally unacceptable to consummate the marriage during the period of betrothal. Gabriel greeted Mary with high praise: "Greetings, O favored one, the Lord is with you!"[35] Mary, however, was troubled by the unexpected appearance of the angel with his unusual greeting. Gabriel responded by calming Mary and moving quickly to the announcement:

> Do not be afraid, Mary, for you have found favor with God. And behold, you will conceive in your womb and bear a son, and you shall call his name Jesus. He will be great and will be called the Son of the Most High. And the Lord God will give to him the throne of his father David, and he will reign over the house of Jacob forever, and of his kingdom there will be no end.[36]

This announcement far surpasses all that Gabriel declared concerning John the Baptist. Jesus would be called the Son of the Most High and would receive David's throne and reign over a kingdom that would never end. This pronouncement connects back to God's promise to David that "your house and your kingdom shall be made sure forever before me. Your throne shall be established forever."[37] Other Old Testament writers echoed this expectation

[32] Luke 1:15–17, 76.
[33] Luke 1:32.
[34] Luke 1:27.
[35] Luke 1:28.
[36] Luke 1:30–33.
[37] 2 Sam. 7:16.

concerning the eternal nature of David's throne.[38] Gabriel thus clearly declared that Jesus would bring this promise made to David to final fulfillment.

Gabriel's choice of words, "you will conceive in your womb and bear a son, and you shall call his name Jesus," also seems to intentionally parallel the wording of Isaiah 7:14, "the virgin shall conceive and bear a son, and shall call his name Immanuel." Gabriel's very words imply fulfillment, even though Luke does not explicitly identify Jesus's birth as the realization of this passage in Isaiah.[39]

Mary's Response

Mary was likely in awe concerning Gabriel's amazing pronouncement regarding Jesus's identity, but she initially expressed a logistical concern: "How will this be, since I am a virgin?"[40] This question suggests that Mary assumed a virginal conception before her marriage to Joseph. How would she conceive a child before consummating her marriage to Joseph? In contrast to Zechariah's earlier reaction, Mary's question indicated not a lack of faith but rather an uncertainty regarding the means of fulfillment. How could this be possible?

Gabriel responded by drawing attention to the supernatural nature of the conception. This event would be completely out of the ordinary. *John's* conception was miraculous in the sense that an old barren couple would conceive, but *Jesus's* conception would be miraculous in an entirely different way. The Holy Spirit and God's power would overshadow Mary and produce the conception so that the child would truly be called "holy—the Son of God."[41] Luke often combined the Spirit with power, and the parallelism of the construction suggests a single idea and should not be pressed to

---

[38] Pss. 89:3–4; 132:11–12; Isa. 9:7; Mic. 4:7; Dan. 7:14.

[39] Raymond Brown points out that we cannot be sure that Luke is alluding to Isa. 7:14 because an angel uses similar wording in the birth announcement to Hagar in Gen. 16:11: "Behold, you are pregnant and shall bear a son. You shall call his name Ishmael, because the Lord has listened to your affliction." *The Birth of the Messiah*, rev. ed. (New York: Doubleday, 1993), 300.

[40] Luke 1:34.

[41] Luke 1:35.

make a Trinitarian point about the relationship between God the Father, God the Son, and God the Holy Spirit.[42] The language of the Holy Spirit "overshadowing" Mary recalls God's original creative work in Genesis 1:2, which depicts "the Spirit of God" as "hovering over the face of the waters." The coming of Jesus into the world would mark the beginning of God's work of new creation. The Greeks had many tales of their gods impregnating human women through intercourse, but the angel's words dismiss any possibility of such a process—the conception was supernaturally accomplished while Mary was still a virgin.[43]

Unlike Zechariah, Mary did not ask Gabriel for a sign. Nevertheless, Gabriel proceeded to provide one: "your relative Elizabeth in her old age has also conceived a son, and this is the sixth month with her who was called barren."[44] Luke does not specify what kind of relative Elizabeth was, so while John could have been Jesus's cousin, the two may have been more distantly related. The provision of this sign implies that, since Elizabeth had kept her pregnancy secret, the news from Judah had not yet reached Mary in Nazareth. Mary first heard of Elizabeth's pregnancy from Gabriel.

Gabriel's final statement reminded Mary, and powerfully reminds us today, of the extent of God's power: "For nothing will be impossible with God."[45] This idea, expressed throughout the Old Testament,[46] fills us today with hope. God is not limited by our limitations, discouraged by our discouragements, or hindered by our shortcomings. He is sovereign over all things! In the hands of a tyrant such as Herod, this kind of power could terrify and devastate, but when combined with God's covenantal love and care for his creation and image bearers, it can fill us with hope and peace,

---

[42] See Luke 1:17; 4:14; Acts 1:8; 6:5–8; 10:38. But note that Luke 1:17 refers to "spirit and power" in reference to the spirit of Elijah and not explicitly to the Holy Spirit.

[43] See I. Howard Marshall's discussion of proposed pagan parallels in *The Gospel of Luke*, New International Greek Testament Commentary (Grand Rapids, MI: Eerdmans, 1978), 73–76. Luke's narrative is saturated with allusions to the Old Testament and lacks any hint of dependence upon Greco-Roman or Egyptian parallels. First-century Jews and Christians would have found such a thought abhorrent.

[44] Luke 1:36.

[45] Luke 1:37.

[46] See, for example, Gen. 18:14; Job 42:2.

no matter what the circumstances. Certainly, Mary's knowledge of God's covenant love comforted her when the angel asserted God's limitless power.

Mary's final response to Gabriel epitomizes the response of a true disciple: "Behold, I am the servant of the Lord; let it be to me according to your word."[47] Mary's world was about to be turned upside down; everything was about to change. She had no way of knowing the future repercussions of the angel's announcement or how she might explain the pregnancy to Joseph and her family. Despite all the uncertainties and potential disasters, she chose to submit willingly to God's plan. She committed herself to God and his design for her life no matter what the personal sacrifice or cost. Nothing in the narrative suggests that believers should pray to Mary or that Mary gives grace from heaven, but the account unequivocally presents this young Jewish girl's complete commitment and fearless submission as a model for all who consider themselves Christians to follow.

ANSWERING GOD'S CALL

How have you responded to God's call on your life, whatever it might be? Or have you withdrawn in fear of the uncertainties of the future and settled for a safe form of Christianity that requires little or no faith and entails hardly any risk? That form of Christianity is both rampant and lifeless. What would it look like for you to step out in fearless faith in response to what you know to be God's plan for your life? Consider Mary, a young, vulnerable Jewish girl whose entire future and hope for a normal life were jeopardized by God's plan for her life. Mary did not draw back in order to protect herself and her future. She embraced God's future and desire for her life. What about you?

Even if you desire to live with Mary's courage, you may be unsure about God's plan for your life. "Yes," you say, "I want to follow God wherever he is leading, but I don't know where that might be." This uncertainty often paralyzes Christians with fear. What is

[47] Luke 1:38.

God's will for my life? While we don't have space to discuss this matter in detail here, let us share a few thoughts that may help you navigate these waters.

First, start with what God makes clear concerning his will for your character. The following two verses plainly state God's will for your life: "Rejoice always, pray without ceasing, give thanks in all circumstances; for this is the will of God in Christ Jesus for you"; and "For this is the will of God, your sanctification: that you abstain from sexual immorality."[48] Be thankful and abstain from sexual immorality. These issues have to do with the kind of person you are, your character. We often get the cart before the horse by trying to do "great" things for God while neglecting the "small" things of our character, the "small" choices we make when nobody is watching. Jesus made it quite clear that the small things *are* the great things: "One who is faithful in a very little is also faithful in much, and one who is dishonest in a very little is also dishonest in much."[49]

Second, start with what God makes clear concerning the big picture of what all Christians should do. Jesus addressed every Christian with the closing words in the Gospel of Matthew: "Go therefore and make disciples of all nations, baptizing them in the name of the Father and of the Son and of the Holy Spirit, teaching them to observe all that I have commanded you. And behold, I am with you always, to the end of the age."[50] Does this mean that every Christian should become a missionary? These verses have motivated and guided many missionaries through the centuries, but no, God does not call every Christian to move cross-culturally as a vocational missionary. God does, however, call every Christian to be actively involved in God's mission to the world.

If you are seeking God's will for your vocational life, start with your involvement in God's mission to the world. Based upon what you know of your gifts, skills, desires, and abilities, how could you best impact the world in a positive way for God and his kingdom?

---

[48] 1 Thess. 5:16–18; 4:3.
[49] Luke 16:10.
[50] Matt. 28:19–20.

For many Christians, this will involve not moving to a different country but rather being the best mechanic, lawyer, housewife, accountant, or construction worker possible in the power of God's Spirit and for his glory.

The power of the gospel to transform society and the world does not lie in every Christian becoming a vocational missionary or pastor but in every Christian experiencing the transforming power of the gospel and living out that power at their work site, in their office building, and in their home. What do you enjoy? What do you do best? Do it with all your strength for God's glory and kingdom. And allow Mary's model to be your guide. As Mary gave herself fully to God's call on her life, give yourself fully to his call on yours!

6

GOD AT WORK AGAIN AT LAST!

DELIVERANCE FOR ISRAEL

LUKE 1:39-56

In those days Mary arose and went with haste into the hill country, to a town in Judah, and she entered the house of Zechariah and greeted Elizabeth. And when Elizabeth heard the greeting of Mary, the baby leaped in her womb. And Elizabeth was filled with the Holy Spirit, and she exclaimed with a loud cry, "Blessed are you among women, and blessed is the fruit of your womb! And why is this granted to me that the mother of my Lord should come to me? For behold, when the sound of your greeting came to my ears, the baby in my womb leaped for joy. And blessed is she who believed that there would be a fulfillment of what was spoken to her from the Lord."

And Mary said,

"My soul magnifies the Lord,
and my spirit rejoices in God my Savior,
for he has looked on the humble estate of his servant.
For behold, from now on all generations will call me blessed;
for he who is mighty has done great things for me,

and holy is his name.
And his mercy is for those who fear him
from generation to generation.
He has shown strength with his arm;
he has scattered the proud in the thoughts
of their hearts;
he has brought down the mighty from their thrones
and exalted those of humble estate;
he has filled the hungry with good things,
and the rich he has sent away empty.
He has helped his servant Israel,
in remembrance of his mercy,
as he spoke to our fathers,
to Abraham and to his offspring forever."

And Mary remained with her about three months and returned to her home.

JOHN AND JESUS MEET

We have noted how Luke structures his infancy narrative around the parallel announcements, conceptions, and births of John the Baptist and Jesus. Despite the parallel structures of the accounts, only in this brief section (Luke 1:39–56) do they intersect.[1] Without this meeting of John and Jesus *in utero* through Mary and Elizabeth, their respective birth narratives would be parallel but unrelated.

The angel Gabriel had given Mary a sign to confirm his message, and Mary wasted no time seeking proof of the angel's word. Luke states that Mary "went with haste" to the hill country of Judah to meet with Elizabeth.[2] Elizabeth had kept her pregnancy secret, so Mary went in person to confirm the angel's prediction that Elizabeth had conceived a son in her old age. Luke remains fairly vague about the exact location of Elizabeth's home, but the hill country of Judah would have required a journey of a few days for Mary, traveling anywhere from sixty to one hundred miles, depending upon the exact destination.

[1] Luke 1:39–56.
[2] Luke 1:39.

Upon Mary's greeting, John, in his prenatal state, provided his first prophecy and bore witness to Jesus's identity by leaping in his mother's womb. Elizabeth, also "filled with the Holy Spirit," gave voice to John's message: "Blessed are you among women, and blessed is the fruit of your womb!"[3] The parallelism of Elizabeth's statement indicates that Mary was blessed because of the identity of the child she was carrying, the "Lord" himself.[4] John the Baptist's later ministry would largely serve to prepare the way for Jesus and to point people to Jesus;[5] he began this ministry even before he was born!

Elizabeth uttered an additional blessing on Mary for believing that the Lord's word spoken to her would be fulfilled. Mary's faith was demonstrated and proved by her visit to Elizabeth. She had not merely assented intellectually to the angel's words but had put her faith into practice by her actions. God had declared the impossible, and Mary had believed.

THE *MAGNIFICAT*: SOURCE

We discussed Luke's sources in the previous chapter, but it is worth giving a bit more attention to this issue as it relates to the hymns. Critical scholars, for the most part, doubt that the hymns or canticles contained in Luke's infancy narrative were written by the people to whom Luke attributes them, both because the content of these hymns is rather general and because they think it unlikely that the speakers composed them on the spot.[6] Raymond Brown argues that "the most satisfactory solution is that the canticles were composed in a non-Lucan circle and that originally they praised the salvific action of God without any precise reference to the events that Luke was narrating in the infancy narrative."[7] In other words, Luke came across these hymns somewhere and

[3] Luke 1:41–42.
[4] Luke 1:43.
[5] Luke 3:4, 15–16; John 1:29–34.
[6] For a summary of the general historical-critical approach to Luke's canticles, see Raymond Brown's lengthy discussion in *The Birth of the Messiah*, rev. ed. (New York: Doubleday, 1993), 346–65.
[7] Ibid., 349.

thought they would make good additions to the infancy narratives of John and Jesus even though they originally had nothing to do with Mary, Zechariah, the angels, or Simeon. Since the latter two hymns are rather short, most of the attention focuses on Mary's *Magnificat* and Zechariah's *Benedictus*.[8] Such skepticism, however, does not hold up against the evidence.

We must keep several points in mind. First, the hymns employ Hebrew poetic parallelism and, in view of the Semitic nature of the Greek, are likely based on Hebrew originals. Second, the hymns' poetic nature admittedly suggests that their composers did not likely create them out of nothing on the spot. Luke, however, does not claim that Mary or Zechariah produced the material completely on their own; he rather records what they said or, in the case of Zechariah, prophesied. This detail opens up options in two directions. On the one hand, Mary and Zechariah may have used existing Jewish hymns or poems that they already knew by heart and adapted to give voice to their thoughts and emotions. The hymns are thoroughly based on Old Testament words and motifs and parallel the content of other hymns in Second Temple Jewish literature. On the other hand, the speakers or family members could have polished and improved this modified hymn after the moment of utterance.

Such a proposal maintains that the oral or written family traditions Luke received from his eyewitness sources already associated these hymns with their respective speakers. It also does justice to the content of the hymns, which reflect the hopes and expectations that Jews would have naturally expressed in hearing Gabriel's two announcements while showing no dependence upon later Christian theology or beliefs. These canticles fit their surrounding contexts because both Zechariah and Mary believed that the claims of these modified Jewish hymns were being fulfilled in the events surrounding the respective births of John and Jesus.

This approach to the issue fits well with the historical, liter-

[8] The title *Magnificat* comes from the first word of the Latin text, which is translated in English as "magnifies" from the Greek *megalunō*. Zechariah's hymn, likewise, has traditionally been labeled the *Benedictus* based upon the first word of the Latin translation of the hymn, translated in English as "blessed" from the Greek *eulogētos*.

ary, and linguistic evidence unless one is already committed to the presupposition that Luke had no access to reliable family traditions concerning the births of John and Jesus. Yet nothing in the hymns themselves undermines the scenario presented above. Rather, this proposal corresponds better with Luke's claim in his preface to have accessed and investigated the sources and traditions based on eyewitness testimony.

THE *MAGNIFICAT*: CONTENT

Mary's hymn should be categorized as a hymn of praise or thanksgiving and as such has many parallels in the book of Psalms. Hymns of praise begin by praising or extolling God and proceed by giving reasons for the praise, reasons often introduced with the words "for" or "because." Psalm 117 illustrates this pattern well: "Praise the Lord, all nations! Extol him, all peoples! *For* great is his steadfast love toward us, and the faithfulness of the Lord endures forever. Praise the Lord!"[9]

The *Magnificat* perhaps finds its most substantial parallel in Hannah's hymn following her dedication of Samuel to the Lord:

> My heart exults in the Lord;
>   my horn is exalted in the Lord.
> My mouth derides my enemies,
>   because I rejoice in your salvation.
>
> There is none holy like the Lord;
>   for there is none besides you;
>   there is no rock like our God.
> Talk no more so very proudly,
>   let not arrogance come from your mouth;
> for the Lord is a God of knowledge,
>   and by him actions are weighed.
> The bows of the mighty are broken,
>   but the feeble bind on strength.
> Those who were full have hired themselves out for bread,

[9] Ps. 117:1–2. Other examples include Psalms 8, 33, 100, 103, 104, 111, 113, 135, 136, and 145–150.

but those who were hungry have ceased to hunger.
The barren has borne seven,
but she who has many children is forlorn.
The Lord kills and brings to life;
he brings down to Sheol and raises up.
The Lord makes poor and makes rich;
he brings low and he exalts.
He raises up the poor from the dust;
he lifts the needy from the ash heap
to make them sit with princes
and inherit a seat of honor.
For the pillars of the earth are the Lord's,
and on them he has set the world.

He will guard the feet of his faithful ones,
but the wicked shall be cut off in darkness,
for not by might shall a man prevail.
The adversaries of the Lord shall be broken to pieces;
against them he will thunder in heaven.
The Lord will judge the ends of the earth;
he will give strength to his king
and exalt the horn of his anointed.[10]

Both the *Magnificat* and Hannah's hymn speak about rejoicing in God's salvation and in the great reversal that God will bring about as he humbles the mighty while exalting the lowly and fills the hungry while sending away the rich empty-handed.

Mary begins her hymn by praising God: "My soul magnifies the Lord, and my spirit rejoices in God my Savior."[11] The Greek word translated "magnifies" (*megalunō*) expresses the idea of making or declaring something or someone great. By extension, it expresses praise, glory, and high honor. At the outset of the hymn, Mary expresses her joy in God's actions as her Savior and praises him accordingly.

Following this introduction of praise, the rest of the *Magnificat*

[10] 1 Sam. 2:1–10.
[11] Luke 1:46.

provides the reasons for Mary's praise of God.[12] The first three reasons concern Mary's personal situation,[13] while the remaining reasons focus on what God is accomplishing through the birth of her child.[14] She points briefly to God's attributes—his might, holiness, and mercy—but primarily highlights God's actions, centering on the help he was about to provide Israel in response to the promises he had made to Abraham and his offspring.[15]

In reflecting on her personal situation, Mary notes that God has done mighty things for her and that despite her humble estate, all generations will call her blessed. Mary knows that God has chosen her through no merit of her own. She knows that God has no obvious reason to select her for the task of bearing his Son. She knows that she has no claim upon this privilege but that God has nonetheless chosen her. Because of God's choice, all future generations will call her blessed just as Elizabeth had done. This is not pride or arrogance but worship of a God who can transform individuals and reverse circumstances. The *Magnificat* serves to transfer any praise directed at Mary to God.

The *Magnificat* proceeds by focusing on God's attributes.[16] His name is holy, and his mercy is available to endless generations of those who fear him. Those who fear God revere and serve him with humble allegiance and obedience. God's mercy is the divine attribute that binds together the *Magnificat*, occurring here and at the end of the song.[17] Mary highlights how God is demonstrating his mercy through the deliverance of his people in response to the promises he had made to Abraham concerning his offspring.[18]

The remainder of the *Magnificat* is structured around seven verbs that all denote completed actions.[19] God is the subject of each of these actions, and the seven actions provide seven more reasons for Mary's praise. Instead of focusing on what God has done for

[12] See the use of "for" in Luke 1:48, 49.
[13] Luke 1:48–49.
[14] Luke 1:50–55.
[15] Luke 1:54–55.
[16] Luke 1:49b–50.
[17] Luke 1:50, 54.
[18] Luke 1:54–55.
[19] Luke 1:51–54a.

her personally, these seven actions focus on what God has done for his people by sending Jesus. These actions had not yet occurred in time, but the way in which Mary words her praise conveys her certainty that God will accomplish them through her Son. With the conception of Jesus, the fulfillment of God's promises to his people is a *fait accompli.*

In Jesus, God would:

1. Show strength with his arm – positive
2. Scatter the proud – negative
3. Bring down the mighty – negative
4. Exalt the humble – positive
5. Fill the hungry – positive
6. Send away the rich – negative
7. Help Israel – positive (summary)

The ancient Greek (Septuagint) translation of Psalm 89:10 combines the first three of these actions: "You yourself brought down the proud one as a wounded man and with your strong arm you scattered your enemies."[20] This is highly significant, because while Psalm 89 focuses on celebrating God's promises to David, it also mourns the lack of fulfillment and calls upon God to remember his steadfast love or mercy (as the Septuagint renders the term in Ps. 89:49). Mary likely had this psalm in mind—probably in its Aramaic or Hebrew form—from the moment Gabriel announced to her that God would give to her Son the throne of his father David and that he would reign over Jacob forever.[21] *Gabriel's announcement to Mary functions as God's answer to the plea of Psalm 89.* Each of the seven actions highlighted in the *Magnificat* draws attention to the anticipated reversal by which God would restore and help Israel (show strength, exalt, fill the hungry) while opposing (scattering, bringing down, sending away) her enemies and oppressors.

The *Magnificat* concludes by emphasizing that God will per-

[20] Authors' translation of the Septuagint.
[21] Luke 1:33.

form these things on account of his mercy in fulfillment of his promises to Abraham.[22] The Old Testament contains many expressions of expectation that God would deal mercifully with Israel in accordance with his ancient promises,[23] and Mary's song communicates her belief that in her soon-to-be-born Son, Jesus, God was in fact acting at last in mercy to make good on his ancient promises.

Mary does not, at this point, display any awareness of how God was actually going to fulfill these long-standing promises to Abraham and his offspring through her Son. She seems to share the same picture of a militaristic political messiah common at the time.[24] This argument again favors the hymn's authenticity. Mary seems oblivious to the fact that the complete fulfillment of these prophecies would be delayed until the second coming of Christ. In the first coming, Jesus would fulfill the promises to Abraham as indicated in the book of Micah:

> Who is a God like you, pardoning iniquity
>   and passing over transgression
>   for the remnant of his inheritance?
> He does not retain his anger forever,
>   because he delights in steadfast love.
> *He will again have compassion on us;*
>   *he will tread our iniquities underfoot.*
> *You will cast all our sins*
>   *into the depths of the sea.*
> *You will show faithfulness to Jacob*
>   *and steadfast love to Abraham,*
> *as you have sworn to our fathers*
>   *from the days of old.*[25]

Jesus's first coming would decisively deal with his people's sin problem while his second coming would set things straight politically and economically in his creation once and for all.

---

[22] Luke 1:54b–55.
[23] 2 Sam. 22:51; Ps. 98:3; Mic. 7:18–20.
[24] For more on this widespread view, see the appendix.
[25] Mic. 7:18–20.

Luke concludes this section by noting briefly Mary's return to her home in Nazareth after staying with Elizabeth for three months. Based on a lunar calendar, a pregnancy would last ten months, so this timetable would place Mary's return to Nazareth a month before the birth of John. Mary's home going marks the point where Luke's narrative begins to intersect with Matthew's. Once Mary returned, her pregnancy would become known, and Joseph would have to make the difficult choice of what to do with his apparently unfaithful "wife"/fiancée.[26]

THE *MAGNIFICAT*: REFLECTION

We saw in the previous chapter that Mary's response to Gabriel's message could serve as a strong model of committed discipleship: "let it be to me according to your word." The *Magnificat* also provides us with a model of praise and worship. What would it look like for you to compose a similar hymn? How would you express your praise and thanks to God for sending Jesus and bringing salvation through him, and what reasons would you give for your praise (using "for" or "because")? What attributes or actions of God would you highlight?

[26] Matt. 1:18–25. Note that in Matt. 1:19, Joseph is called Mary's "husband" even during the betrothal period, which indicates how ancient Jews considered the betrothal period to be akin to marriage in many ways. This view, of course, differs from contemporary culture where engagement is often considered much less permanent than marriage.

7

ISRAEL'S RESTORATION

LUKE 1:57-80

Now the time came for Elizabeth to give birth, and she bore a son. And her neighbors and relatives heard that the Lord had shown great mercy to her, and they rejoiced with her. And on the eighth day they came to circumcise the child. And they would have called him Zechariah after his father, but his mother answered, "No; he shall be called John." And they said to her, "None of your relatives is called by this name." And they made signs to his father, inquiring what he wanted him to be called. And he asked for a writing tablet and wrote, "His name is John." And they all wondered. And immediately his mouth was opened and his tongue loosed, and he spoke, blessing God. And fear came on all their neighbors. And all these things were talked about through all the hill country of Judea, and all who heard them laid them up in their hearts, saying, "What then will this child be?" For the hand of the Lord was with him.

And his father Zechariah was filled with the Holy Spirit and prophesied, saying,

"Blessed be the Lord God of Israel,
  for he has visited and redeemed his people
and has raised up a horn of salvation for us
  in the house of his servant David,
as he spoke by the mouth of his holy prophets from of old,
that we should be saved from our enemies
  and from the hand of all who hate us;

to show the mercy promised to our fathers
and to remember his holy covenant,
the oath that he swore to our father Abraham, to grant us
that we, being delivered from the hand of our enemies,
might serve him without fear,
in holiness and righteousness before him all our days.
And you, child, will be called the prophet of the
Most High;
for you will go before the Lord to prepare his ways,
to give knowledge of salvation to his people
in the forgiveness of their sins,
because of the tender mercy of our God,
whereby the sunrise shall visit us from on high
to give light to those who sit in darkness and in the
shadow of death,
to guide our feet into the way of peace."

And the child grew and became strong in spirit, and he was in the wilderness until the day of his public appearance to Israel.

C. 7, 6, OR 5 BC

The Birth of John the Baptist

Joy. Pure, overwhelming, exuberant joy. This theme runs through the first chapter of Luke's Gospel. It is joy over God's mercy, promises, and actions. It is joy in the birth of a son to an old couple who had longed for a child their entire married lives but had given up hope. It is joy in the activity of God among his people again to bring help, restoration, and deliverance through his Messiah after centuries of nonfulfillment, oppression, poverty, and warfare.

The note of joy first sounded when Gabriel promised Zechariah that he would have "joy and gladness" and that "many [would] rejoice" at John's birth.[1] Joy was implicit in Elizabeth's declaration that the Lord had acted "to take away my reproach among people."[2] John "leaped for joy" in Elizabeth's womb upon Mary's greeting

[1] Luke 1:14.
[2] Luke 1:25.

and the presence of Jesus.[3] Mary's hymn, the *Magnificat*, listed various reasons why Mary's "spirit rejoice[d] in God my Savior."[4] Finally, Gabriel's initial words came true following the birth of John when Elizabeth's neighbors and relatives "rejoiced with her."[5]

The joy that Luke narrates offered but a small foretaste of the joy that would surround the birth of the child who would be called "Wonderful Counselor, Mighty God, Everlasting Father, Prince of Peace":[6]

> The people who walked in darkness
> have seen a great light;
> those who dwelt in a land of deep darkness,
> on them has light shone.
> You have multiplied the nation;
> you have increased its joy;
> they rejoice before you
> as with joy at the harvest,
> as they are glad when they divide the spoil. . . .
> For to us a child is born,
> to us a son is given."[7]

The messianic child was on his way, and the land was being filled with joy.

The account of John's birth is fairly straightforward and focuses particularly on the naming of the child. On the eighth day following the birth, Zechariah and Elizabeth circumcised and named the child.[8] Neighbors and relatives came to witness this important event, assuming that they would name the child Zechariah after his father or possibly after a grandfather. Elizabeth objected and emphatically declared that the boy would be called John. This highly unusual turn of events led those gathered to seek confirmation from Zechariah.

[3] Luke 1:44.
[4] Luke 1:47.
[5] Luke 1:58.
[6] Isa. 9:6c.
[7] Isa. 9:2–3, 6a.
[8] For this practice, see Gen. 17:12–14; 21:4; Lev. 12:3; Phil. 3:5.

Luke does not mention whether Elizabeth and Zechariah had conferred about the name in writing, but the neighbors and relatives assumed that Elizabeth was acting independently. They were sure that Zechariah would set things straight and give a proper family name to the child and were therefore quite amazed when Zechariah wrote on a tablet that the boy's name would in fact be John. While a common enough name in first-century Palestine, John[9] was not the name of Zechariah or an immediate ancestor. The wonder and amazement of those present came from the apparently independent confirmation of this unexpected name. The neighbors and relatives were further filled with awe and fear when Zechariah miraculously recovered after naming John and began to bless God.

Luke concludes the narrative of John's birth by noting that "fear came on all their neighbors. And all these things were talked about through all the hill country of Judea, and all who heard them laid them up in their hearts, saying, 'What then will this child be?' For the hand of the Lord was with him."[10] The birth of John was the talk of the town, and for good reason! Zechariah had returned from his service in the temple both deaf and mute. Shortly thereafter Elizabeth isolated herself from the community in seclusion. Forty weeks (ten lunar months) later, it was announced that she, an old barren woman, had borne a son, and both Elizabeth and Zechariah, apparently independently, chose an unexpected name. To top it all off, as soon as Zechariah confirmed the name, he miraculously regained his hearing and speech. This was definitely no ordinary birth! We might also note that those who treasured the memory of these events in their hearts may have preserved John's birth narrative in enough detail for Luke to incorporate it into his Gospel.

The *Benedictus*: Introduction

The amazed relatives and neighbors had asked, "What then will this child be?"[11] They knew who he was, the only son of an aged

[9] The name means "Yahweh has given grace" or "Yahweh is gracious."
[10] Luke 1:65–66.
[11] Luke 1:66.

priestly couple, but the incredible circumstances surrounding his birth led them to expect that the boy would not simply follow in the footsteps of his father. There was something unusual and special about his boy. What would he become?

Zechariah's prophetic hymn of praise, the *Benedictus*, answers this question. Grammatically, the hymn is divided into two sentences. The first sentence[12] focuses on Jesus as the fulfillment of God's promises to David and Abraham. Zechariah was prophesying under the inspiration of the Holy Spirit, but this does not preclude the likelihood that Elizabeth had discussed Mary's visit with him. The second sentence[13] explores John's identity and mission and concludes by again pointing to Jesus. The hymn as a whole gives a voice to Zechariah, who had been silent from the beginning of the narrative,[14] and identifies John's role in relation to Jesus, the main figure in the fulfillment of God's plan for the restoration of Israel.

The *Benedictus*: Part 1

The *Benedictus*, like the *Magnificat*, begins with a declaration of praise to God, followed by the word "for" to indicate the reason for the praise: "Blessed be the Lord God of Israel, for he has visited and redeemed his people and has raised up a horn of salvation for us in the house of his servant David."[15] The phrase "Blessed be the Lord, the God of Israel" occurs as a refrain throughout the book of Psalms.[16] More importantly, Zechariah seems to be drawing on David's praise upon Solomon's succession to the throne. "Blessed be the LORD, the God of Israel, who has granted someone to sit on my throne this day, my own eyes seeing it."[17] Just as David praised God because he saw that his dynasty would continue through his heir, Zechariah praises God for having raised up a "horn" of salvation

[12] Luke 1:68–75.
[13] Luke 1:76–79.
[14] Luke 1:20.
[15] Luke 1:68–69.
[16] Pss. 41:13; 72:18; 106:48.
[17] 1 Kings 1:48.

in the house of David—David's dynasty would continue through his heir.[18]

Zechariah outlines the reasons for his praise (the "for") using three verbs that describe God's actions. He has visited his people, redeemed his people, and raised up the Davidic Messiah. Each of these actions fits with Zechariah's blessing of the Lord as the God "of Israel." He gives no hint here of a Gentile mission or of the expansion of the Messiah's kingdom to encompass all the nations of the world. Zechariah understands the coming of Jesus prophetically in terms of God's promises to Israel. Similar to the *Magnificat*, each of these three main verbs indicates the certainty of their completion. God had sent the Messiah, a baby in Mary's womb at this point, and God's Messiah would surely not fail to accomplish God's mission to redeem his people. The bullet had been fired and would hit its mark; God's action could not be hindered or undone.

The *Benedictus* proceeds by indicating that these three actions (visiting, redeeming, raising up the Davidic Messiah) accorded with (1) the "holy prophets from of old"[19]; and (2) his "holy covenant" and "oath" to Abraham.[20] The goal of the prophetic promises and the covenant with Abraham was that God's people would be saved from their enemies[21] and enabled to serve God without fear in righteousness all their days.[22] As with the *Magnificat*, God's mercy drives these three divine actions as God remembers his promises to Abraham.[23] Without naming Jesus or Mary, Zechariah uses the first sentence of the *Benedictus* to praise God for raising up the Davidic Messiah to deliver his people in fulfillment of his ancient promises.

The *Benedictus*: Part 2

The second sentence of the *Benedictus* switches the focus to John. Technically, we could label the second part "a hymn in honour of

[18] The "horn" is an Old Testament symbol for strength that pointed toward the coming of a Davidic messianic king. This designation clearly indicates that Zechariah is not here referring to his own son, who was of Aaronic descent.
[19] Luke 1:70.
[20] Luke 1:72–73.
[21] Luke 1:71, 74.
[22] Luke 1:74–75.
[23] Luke 1:54–55, 72–73.

a child at his birth."[24] The *Benedictus* proper would then end with the first sentence. The material devoted to John, however, is short[25] and quickly returns to conclude the entire hymn by focusing on the Messiah.[26] So it is better to view the *Benedictus* as a unity with two parts rather than two different hymns.

The second part of the *Benedictus* hangs on one main verb in the future tense: "And you, child, *will be called* the prophet of the Most High."[27] This statement parallels Gabriel's pronouncement concerning Jesus that he "will be called the Son of the Most High."[28] As mentioned with regard to Jesus, to call someone something is to speak of that person's identity, so these statements indicate that Jesus is the Son and John is the prophet of the Most High.

The next line gives the reason that John would be God's prophet: "for you will go before the Lord to prepare his ways, to give knowledge of salvation to his people in the forgiveness of their sins."[29] It is impossible to know from the hymn itself if Zechariah intended the epithet "Lord" to refer to Jesus or God. Elizabeth had earlier called Jesus "Lord,"[30] so we might expect Zechariah to do the same. Jesus, as God's Son and divinely appointed representative, would be equivalent to God himself, so the ambiguity here causes no problem. In Jesus, God himself was coming to his people. Old Testament prophets had prophesied of a future day when someone would prepare the way for God to come to his people,[31] and Zechariah here identifies John as this individual.

John would prepare the way by giving people the knowledge of salvation in the forgiveness of their sins. This expectation corresponds well to the message of repentance from sin that charac-

[24] Greek *genethliakon*. I. Howard Marshall, *The Gospel of Luke*, New International Greek Testament Commentary (Grand Rapids, MI: Eerdmans, 1978), 86.
[25] Luke 1:76–77.
[26] Luke 1:78–79.
[27] Luke 1:76.
[28] Luke 1:32.
[29] Luke 1:76b–77.
[30] Luke 1:43.
[31] Isa. 40:3; Mal. 3:1; 4:5.

terized John's ministry.[32] Zechariah rightly recognized that Israel could not experience political, militaristic, social, and economic deliverance[33] until God had first saved his people by forgiving their sins. This is a powerful truth. All mankind's best attempts to maintain world peace and eliminate poverty, oppression, and tyranny falter at this point. The destructive presence of sin derails the best intentions and efforts of the human will. Only by decisively dealing with the sin problem can salvation spread to all the other dimensions of human life and society.

The *Benedictus* concludes by again highlighting God's mercy as the motivation behind God's actions and by focusing again on the Messiah, the "sunrise" who "shall visit us from on high to give light to those who sit in darkness and in the shadow of death, to guide our feet into the way of peace."[34] The Greek word translated "sunrise"[35] carried messianic overtones in two ways. First, the translators of the Greek version of the Old Testament used this word to translate the obvious messianic Davidic term for "branch."[36] Thus for some Jews, "sunrise" referred clearly to the Davidic Messiah.

Second, the more basic meaning of the word has to do with a rising light, whether a star or the sun at dawn. This second interpretation fits the context better and also carries clear messianic meaning. Balaam had prophesied that "a star shall come out of Jacob, and a scepter shall rise out of Israel."[37] Other messianically significant texts also use the language of light and darkness: "The people who walked in darkness have seen a great light; those who dwelt in a land of deep darkness, on them has light shined."[38] John would prepare the way for Jesus,[39] while Jesus would be the light that would give light to those in darkness and death, the light that would guide his people to the path of peace.[40]

---

[32] Luke 3:3.
[33] Luke 1:71, 74.
[34] Luke 1:78–79.
[35] I.e., *anatolē*.
[36] Zech. 3:8; 6:12.
[37] Num. 24:17b.
[38] Isa. 9:2; cf. 42:6–7.
[39] He would be a "lamp" that would shine "for a while" (John 5:35).
[40] John 1:9–11; 8:12; 9:5.

JOHN'S EXIT FROM THE SCENE

Luke concludes chapter 1 by noting briefly that John "grew and became strong in spirit" and "was in the wilderness until the day of his public appearance to Israel."[41] The narrative picks up John's story again in chapter 3 by noting that the word of God came to John "in the wilderness" and that "he went into all the region around the Jordan, proclaiming a baptism of repentance for the forgiveness of sins" in fulfillment of Isaiah's prophecy.[42] Some have proposed that John spent his time in the wilderness with the Qumran community, but no direct available evidence supports this suggestion. Also, John's close ties to the Jerusalem priesthood through his father make it unlikely that he would have found refuge in a group that existed in opposition to the Jerusalem priesthood. Any possible ties between John and the Dead Sea community, of course, remain inconclusive, and we cannot completely rule out some interaction between John and the Qumran sectaries.

Ultimately, Luke's brief comment on John's growth into adulthood in Luke 1:80 functions to move John off the scene in order to focus solely and exclusively on Jesus in Luke's second chapter. The births of John and Jesus are parallel in Luke's infancy narrative, but Luke consistently presents Jesus as the more significant of the two, with John playing the role of prophet and forerunner. By devoting a large section of his narrative (all of chapter 2) to Jesus, Luke makes this point emphatically. John's role is essential and fulfills prophecy, but his ultimate purpose is to prepare people for the coming of Jesus. The birth of Jesus is the pinnacle of Luke's infancy narrative and the climax of everything presented in chapter 1. The "Son of the Most High" was about to be born to restore and reign over Israel forever.[43]

THE WORLD'S GREATEST NEED

What is wrong with the world, and how do we fix it? Most people recognize that something is wrong with the world, that things are

---

[41] Luke 1:80.
[42] Luke 3:2–6; cf. Isa. 40:3–5.
[43] Luke 1:32–33.

not as they should be. The Bible explains this brokenness in terms of sin, our rejection of God's rule. This explanation, of course, deeply offends people because we do not like to think of ourselves as sinners. We might make the occasional bad decision, but we do not like the idea that we might be the problem. If we reject the biblical explanation for the brokenness of the world, what other explanation makes sense? What is wrong, and how do we fix it?

Perhaps education is the answer. If only we could make sure that everyone has access to better education, the world would become a better place. This solution, however, is hollow because even our best-educated citizens lie, steal, and oppress others to get ahead. Education cannot change the brokenness of the human heart.

Perhaps we can work together to eliminate poverty. This would surely make the world better. We should definitely seek to help the poor, but few can agree on the best way to do so, and our best attempts get derailed by greed and corruption. Even if we could raise everybody's standard of living, would economic prosperity fix human brokenness?

Perhaps world peace is the answer. Wasn't this the goal of the League of Nations? Wasn't World War I the war to end all wars? The sad history of human civilization would lead an objective observer to assume that war and conflict are inevitable. Human beings cannot seem to stop oppressing and conquering each other for selfish reasons.

The world is a broken place filled with broken people, and we cannot fix ourselves with better education, economic mobility, or peaceful relationships. This brings us back to the biblical explanation and solution. The world is broken because of sin, and we need a supernatural solution to the problem.

As we have seen, Zechariah prophesied that the Lord would "give knowledge of salvation to his people in the forgiveness of their sins."[44] This is very close to the angel's words in Matthew that Jesus "will save his people from their sins."[45] Both Matthew

[44] Luke 1:77.
[45] Matt. 1:21.

and Luke celebrate the coming of Jesus to this world as God's solution to the problem of sin. Because of sin, each one of us needs to be rescued by God's dramatic rescue operation (Jesus's death on the cross) and spiritually reborn, not merely improved—you can't improve the sin nature! The cure starts with salvation and forgiveness, but that is not where it ends. God's plan is to completely transform humanity, to fix what has broken us, and to restore his image in us so we will once again reflect his glory.

As Christians, we find ourselves in this process of transformation. We are far from perfect, but we are moving in the right direction. We are "being renewed in knowledge in the image of [our] creator,"[46] and we are "being transformed into the same image from one degree of glory to another."[47] Wherever you are today in this process of transformation, we encourage you to take a step in the right direction, a step toward God in prayer and faith. God will respond with forgiveness of sins and power for transformation. This is what the world needs and what God has promised to provide.

---

[46] Col. 3:10.

[47] 1 Cor. 3:18.

8

THE HUMBLE KING IS LAID IN A MANGER

LUKE 2:1-7

In those days a decree went out from Caesar Augustus that all the world should be registered. This was the first registration when Quirinius was governor of Syria. And all went to be registered, each to his own town. And Joseph also went up from Galilee, from the town of Nazareth, to Judea, to the city of David, which is called Bethlehem, because he was of the house and lineage of David, to be registered with Mary, his betrothed, who was with child. And while they were there, the time came for her to give birth. And she gave birth to her firstborn son and wrapped him in swaddling cloths and laid him in a manger, because there was no place for them in the inn.

JANUARY 16, 27 BC–AUGUST 19, AD 14

Reign of Caesar Augustus: Worldwide Scope

As Luke prepared to narrate an event that would impact the entire world and change the course of history, he drew attention to the ruler of the "entire" world, Caesar Augustus. "All the world"[1] refers to the administrative extent of the Roman Empire despite the fact that there were other lands outside of Roman rule. Most

[1] Luke 2:1.

people in the Mediterranean world would have thought of Caesar as the ruler of enough of the world to consider it "all." The ruler of the world was busy governing his subjects and expanding the boundaries of his empire, while, without his knowledge, the true and rightful ruler of the world was being born in a tiny village at the eastern end of the empire.

Luke explicitly contrasts the two rulers by mentioning Augustus at the outset of Jesus's birth narrative. This reference to Augustus also draws attention to the fact that God is sovereign over the affairs of all people. Even without realizing it, human rulers do God's bidding, and God used Roman administrative policy to fulfill Micah's prophecy that the Messiah would be born in Bethlehem.[2]

6 OR 5 BC

The Census

The census is a central plot element in Luke's narrative because it explains how Joseph and Mary ended up in Bethlehem for Jesus's birth.[3] Luke's reference to this census has become the single most-discussed historical issue in Luke's entire Gospel. Critics are quick to claim that Luke's reference to this census represents a historical error, but such hasty claims go beyond the historical evidence. The main critiques of Luke's historical accuracy (or lack thereof) in portraying the census under Quirinius were enumerated by Emil Schürer over a century ago and can be summarized as follows:[4]

1. No evidence points to an empire-wide census in the time of Augustus.

[2] Mic. 5:2.
[3] Luke 2:2.
[4] See Emil Schürer's discussion in *A History of the Jewish People in the Age of Jesus Christ*, ed. Geza Vermes and Fergus Miller, rev. ed. (Edinburgh: T&T Clark, 1973), 1:399–427. See also able responses to these objections in Harold Hoehner, *Chronological Aspects of the Life of Christ* (Grand Rapids, MI: Zondervan, 1977), 13–23; and Darrell Bock, *Luke 1:1–9:50*, Baker Exegetical Commentary on the New Testament (Grand Rapids, MI: Baker, 1994), 903–9. Cf. I. Howard Marshall, *The Gospel of Luke*, New International Greek Testament Commentary (Grand Rapids, MI: Eerdmans, 1978), 97–104.

2. A Roman census would not have required Joseph and Mary to return to Bethlehem; they could have been counted in Nazareth.
3. No Roman census occurred in Palestine during the reign of Herod the Great.
4. Josephus does not record any census before Quirinius's famous census in AD 6, which caused a revolt.[5]
5. Quirinius was governor of Syria in AD 6–7, a full decade after the death of Herod the Great in 4 BC. Neither Tacitus[6] nor Josephus mentions Quirinius holding a governorship of Syria during the reign of Herod the Great.

However, the inferences and conclusions in these objections go beyond the actual historical evidence and can be addressed as follows.

1. Augustus was very concerned with census taking, and his rule was marked by a great increase in census activity. This involved at least three censuses of Roman citizens in 28 BC, 8 BC, and AD 14, along with various censuses of all inhabitants (citizens and noncitizens) in the provinces.[7] Since Judea was a client kingdom of Rome, Herod was responsible for collecting his own taxes and paying tribute to Rome. Nevertheless, Rome could still require censuses in client kingdoms.[8] Luke's opening statement thus accurately summarizes the situation: Augustus's focus on census taking throughout the empire also affected client kingdoms such as Judea.[9]

2. While we cannot know for certain, Herod may have modified a Roman-style census in an effort to avoid offending the Jewish population. He quite plausibly could have fulfilled the census

---

[5]Josephus, *Ant.* 17.355; 18.1–10, 26.
[6]Tacitus, *Ann.* 3.48.
[7]*Res gest. divi Aug.* 8; Suetonius, *Aug.* 27.5, 37; Tacitus, *Ann.* 1.11; Dio Cassius, *Romaika* 53.1.3; 53.22.5; Livy, *Per.* 134, 138. For later evidence from Egypt, see OxyP 2.254–256.
[8]Tacitus, *Ann.* 4.41.
[9]Roman interference in Judea may likely have begun near the end of Herod's reign seeing that Augustus and Herod's relationship cooled in 8 BC. Josephus records Caesar's words to Herod that, "whereas formerly he had treated him as a friend, he would now treat him as a subject." *Ant.* 16.291. Although Caesar did not carry out his threat, Herod as a client king depended completely on Rome, and Roman imperial policies affecting the empire as a whole would have influenced and impacted Herod's leadership.

requirement by allowing Jews to follow their tradition of associating with their tribe, which would explain why Mary and Joseph traveled to Bethlehem.[10]

3. This argument is from silence. We actually possess only a quite fragmentary record of Palestinian history during the time of Herod. Josephus provides most of the extant information, but he published his main work almost a century after the events and was quite selective and far from exhaustive in the information he included. Herod would certainly have employed some form of census and record keeping in order to facilitate accurate taxation. In fact, Josephus indicates that Herod had excellent records for this purpose, records that required some kind of census activity.[11] Herod likely based such census activity on Roman precedent, modifying it to fit Jewish culture and expectations.

Josephus's use of the word translated "village clerk" (Greek, *kōmogrammateus*) is quite significant.[12] Brook Pearson discusses how this word is used in over two hundred papyri and that the office of the village clerk or scribe was primarily concerned with census information and statistics about property and taxation.[13] According to Pearson, "It seems fairly clear, then, that, at least in Egypt, the office of *kōmogrammateus* was intricately tied to the census. It is difficult to believe that this office, so casually mentioned in the threats that Bernice reports to her mother [in Josephus], was drastically different in Herod's kingdom."[14]

4. This objection echoes the previous claim and assumes that Josephus wrote an exhaustive account of this period. But if Herod had modified the basic Roman census format to avoid offending

[10] Other circumstances could also have motivated their journey. Parallels with Egyptian and Arabian census and property returns indicate that one could live away from one's legal place of registration and would need to return there for either the census, a property return (if either Mary or Joseph owned or inherited property near Bethlehem), or both. Stanley Porter, "The Reasons for the Lukan Census," in *Paul, Luke and the Graeco-Roman World: Essays in Honour of Alexander J. M. Wedderburn*, ed. Alf Christopherson et al., Library of New Testament Studies 217 (London: Sheffield Academic Press, 2002), 165–88, 181–82.

[11] Josephus, *Ant.* 15.365; 16.64; 17.229, 319. See the discussion of the significance of these texts in Brook W. R. Pearson, "The Lucan Censuses, Revisited," *CBQ* 61 (1999): 262–82, 265–66.

[12] See Josephus, *Ant.* 16.203 and *J.W.* 1.479.

[13] The most important papyri include *POxy.* 79, 240, 251, 252, 254, 255, 288, 488. Pearson, "Lucan Censuses," 271.

[14] Pearson, "Lucan Censuses," 271.

his Jewish subjects and thus dodged a revolt, Josephus would have had no reason to comment on it. The silence of a historical source does not sufficiently compel us to doubt Luke's claim, especially if the historical sources overwhelmingly support many of Luke's other historical pieces of information. In contrast, Quirinius's census in AD 6 was so memorable because it marked the transfer of Judea to direct Roman governance after the exile of Herod's son Archelaus and led to a bloody revolt. The nature and manner of this census would have differed quite significantly from the way in which Herod had conducted his census(es).

5. The previous four points all concern the probability and nature of Roman-influenced census activity in Palestine during the latter years of Herod's rule. This final point concerns the reference to Quirinius, who conducted his infamous census in AD 6, which marks a fixed historical point that leaves a decade between the death of Herod in 4 BC and Quirinius's census. Historians have proposed various theories to suggest that Quirinius held some leadership position in Syria and was involved in census activity in Judea before the famous census of AD 6, and although this is certainly possible, no real corroborating historical evidence supports this claim, making it impossible to prove or falsify.

The grammar of Luke's reference only complicates the matter.[15] Instead of translating the phrase, "This was the first registration when Quirinius was governor of Syria," we could translate it, "This was the registration before Quirinius was governor of Syria" (ESV footnote). The difference hinges on how one renders the Greek word *prōtos*, which can mean "first (in a series)," "foremost," "earlier," or "before." The grammar is not decisive, so we need to take other contextual and historical factors into account.[16]

First, historically, as far as we know from the surviving sources, no second registration or census occurred under Quirinius that we might compare the two. This reality makes it difficult for *prōtos* to refer to the "first" registration, unless it is pointing to a registra-

[15] Luke 2:2.

[16] Pearson, "Lucan Censuses," 278–82; Porter, "Reasons for the Lukan Census," 173–76.

tion associated with Quirinius's name that predated his famous census in AD 6.

Second, Luke clearly knew that Quirinius's infamous census in AD 6 had led to a revolt.[17] Yet Luke and Matthew make no reference to a revolt or to social upheaval in the context of Jesus's birth narratives.

Third, since Quirinius's census and the resulting upheaval were so well known, if Luke was referring to a prior census, the translation of *prōtos* as "before" makes perfect sense. Luke also clearly knew that Jesus's birth took place during the reign of Herod,[18] so he could not have meant that Jesus was born during Quirinius's census of AD 6. If he had, it would have made Jesus about twenty years old at the start of his ministry instead of "about thirty years of age," as Luke claimed.[19] These contextual historical factors support the translation of Luke's reference as, "This was the registration before Quirinius governed Syria." Alternatively, the perhaps more natural grammatical translation of *prōtos* in the Greek, "This was the first registration when Quirinius was governor of Syria," makes a similar point by distinguishing this otherwise unattested registration associated with Quirinius from the second more famous one in AD 6. Either way, Luke would have wanted to make this point, since the mention of a census would have immediately brought Quirinius and his infamous census to the minds of his earliest readers.

In summary, all five above-mentioned objections have reasonable answers. The grammar of Luke's reference could legitimately point to a census before the famous census and governorship of Quirinius, and the other aspects of Luke's account all have parallels in nearby provinces. Readers can find further discussion of this complicated historical issue in the scholarly literature. Yet one thing is for sure: the fragmentary nature of the historical evidence for this time period makes unjustifiable the dogmatic claims of

[17] Acts 5:37.
[18] Luke 1:5; 3:1, 23.
[19] Luke 3:23.

critics that Luke *must* be in error.[20] Pearson's conclusion to the matter is worth quoting:

> Translated out of its context, this verse makes very little sense and creates a plethora of problems. However, in the face of the evidence (1) that Herod must have kept accurate records of census and taxation, (2) that he most likely used the census in ways very similar to those of his Roman overlords, both to collect taxes and to exercise strict social control over an unruly people, (3) that many indirect statements in Josephus square with what we know of the census process in other Roman territories, (4) that one of the offices of the census process is mentioned by Josephus in such a way as to assume that the process was a part of everyday life, and (5) that each and every aspect of the census as it is described by Luke has close parallels in other parts of the Roman Empire, we would do better to take a plausible grammatical solution which accords with the evidence rather than to ignore the evidence on the basis of shaky grammar. The meaning suggested for this verse—"this registration was earlier than when (or before) Quirinius governed Syria"—works in terms of context, rather than in terms of a predetermined prejudice to find contradictions in the narrative.[21]

We have focused this discussion on historical data and historical plausibility and probability because Christianity is solidly grounded in history. This focus on history, however, must not distract from what we know about the nature of Scripture as the Word of God. Paul clearly states that "[a]ll Scripture is breathed out by God and profitable for teaching, for reproof, for correction, and for training in righteousness."[22]

We trust the Bible ultimately because it has been inspired by God. Our faith does not rest on Josephus, Tacitus, Suetonius, or

---

[20] If someone *must* be in error, it comes down to Luke versus Josephus, and there is widespread awareness that Josephus made historical mistakes. A neutral historiographic approach would not automatically favor Josephus over Luke. See the discussion of errors in Josephus in J. H. Rhoads, "Josephus Misdated the Census of Quirinius," *Journal of the Evangelical Theological Society* 54, no. 1 (2011): 65–87; Craig S. Keener, *Acts: An Exegetical Commentary*, vol. 2, *3:1–14:28* (Grand Rapids, MI: Baker Academic, 2013), 1233.

[21] Pearson, "Lucan Censuses," 282.

[22] 2 Tim. 3:16.

some yet-to-be-discovered Judean census return from the time of Herod. Our faith rests on the God who raised Jesus from the dead and who, through the Holy Spirit, inspired Jesus's earliest followers to pass on and record the stories of Jesus's life and teaching accurately.

The Journey to Bethlehem

Joseph's journey to Bethlehem to register lawfully and possibly pay taxes matches Matthew's description of him as a righteous man.[23] Jews living in Galilee would have made this three-day journey (90–120 miles depending on the route chosen) annually to attend Passover in Jerusalem, so it would have been a trek. Luke makes no mention of Mary and Joseph having a donkey, and it is equally (if not more) plausible that they walked the entire way. The notion that Mary rode a donkey actually stems from a mid-second-century Christian tradition.[24] It would not have been unreasonable for a pregnant woman in antiquity with a more active lifestyle and less concern for potential medical problems to walk on such a journey.

Luke does not make clear why Mary joined Joseph on the journey. She may have needed to register herself (or any property she may have owned). Joseph may have wanted her to come with him so that he would not miss the birth. Or some other combination of reasons may have motivated her decision. Regardless, Luke assumes that it was quite natural for Mary to travel with Joseph and that this detail required no additional comment.

Joseph had to go to Bethlehem because "he was of the house and lineage of David."[25] The trip may have been motivated by other factors such as religious festivals, business, or extended family situations, but Luke only draws explicit attention to the census and Joseph's ancestry. We know from Matthew's account that the birth in Bethlehem fulfilled Micah's prophecy, but Luke seems mainly

[23] Matt. 1:19.
[24] *Prot. Jas.* 17.
[25] Luke 2:4.

concerned with Joseph's legal descent from David, because this established Jesus as a legal Davidic heir.

The Birth

While Joseph and Mary were in Bethlehem, Mary went into labor and bore Jesus, her firstborn son (implying that she had later sons as well). While completely speculative, the journey may have induced labor or at least sped up the delivery. Luke's account is amazingly brief in light of the way succeeding generations have expanded it. It may come as a surprise, but Scripture mentions neither the presence of animals, a stable, nor even an innkeeper (whether mean and coldhearted or regretful at the lack of space). The narrative does discuss three things: swaddling cloths (not *clothes*); a manger; and an inn with no vacancies.

The swaddling cloths simply indicate that Mary was taking care of Jesus in the same way that any other responsible woman at that time would have taken care of a newborn child. The strips of cloth indicate neither poverty nor any other spiritual significance but were the common means by which mothers kept newborn babies warm.[26] It has also been argued that the strips of cloth were "wrapped around young infants to keep their limbs straight."[27] The swaddling cloths, along with the manger, would have identified Jesus as a newborn to the searching shepherds later that evening.[28]

While the mention of swaddling cloths would have been quite normal, the choice to lay the child in a manger (a feeding trough for animals) seems out of the ordinary. We could translate the word for manger[29] as "feeding stall," but Luke seems to indicate that it functioned as some kind of crib or cradle, so "manger" or "feeding trough" is a better rendering. With no mention of a stable, the manger could have been in the open air, in an animal pen near the house, in a small cave, or in the area of a house used for animals. Luke provides insufficient details to determine the setting

[26] Ezek. 16:4; Wisd. of Sol. 7:4.
[27] Marshall, *Gospel of Luke*, 106.
[28] Luke 2:12.
[29] Greek *phatnē*.

with precision, although the earliest extrabiblical Christian traditions from the mid-second century describe the setting as a cave.[30]

Luke provides the reason that Mary was forced to lay Jesus in an animal feeding trough: "there was no place for them in the inn."[31] The word for "inn"[32] could likewise point to different settings depending upon the context, and Luke provides too little contextual information to arrive at a definitive determination. It may point to an ancient inn that would have consisted of a large room in which everyone found a place to lie down wherever they could or to the guest room in a private residence (possibly that of relatives). Either way, there was no room for a birth in the normal place where Joseph and Mary would have expected to find lodging.

These two details—the necessity of a manger and the lack of room with normal society—are both significant and unexpected. Why would God's own Son, the expected Davidic Messiah, be born in such a way? This scandalous set of circumstances points forward to Jesus's future rejection by his own people[33] and the shame and embarrassment of death on a cross. The unexpected setting of Jesus's birth also anticipates the unexpected way in which Jesus would go about putting things right in God's creation. His life and death did not match people's expectations. He wasn't born like a king; he didn't live like a king; and he certainly didn't die like a king. He was nonetheless God's promised and long-awaited King.

REFLECTIONS ON JESUS'S BIRTH

Luke's narrative of Jesus's birth is tantalizingly brief but makes some significant points. First, the worldwide scope reflected in the reference to Caesar Augustus and the Roman Empire indicates that Jesus would have importance on a global scale. Second, this grand opening sharply contrasts with the humble and ignoble setting of the birth. God was going to turn the world upside down, but not in the way people were expecting. All of the birth announcements

---

[30] *Prot. Jas.* 18:1; Justin, *Dial.* 78.4.

[31] Luke 2:7.

[32] Greek *kataluma*.

[33] Cf. John 1:10–11.

and hymns in the first chapter of Luke's Gospel are characterized by anticipation, the anticipation that God was finally going to fulfill his promises given throughout the Old Testament and act in and through the coming of Jesus to establish his rule over his people. The messianic Son had finally been born, but the setting of the birth gives Luke's readers the first real hint that this King may not fit everyone's expectations.

We will come back to this issue of expectations later, but for now it is worth reflecting on our expectations of God, his character, and his actions. Wrong expectations are a key source of disillusionment and disappointment. A cynical person might argue that we should never expect anything from anyone in order to avoid being let down. Such an approach to people and God, however, will surely lead to a bitter and lonely life. We need each other, and we need God. What happens, then, when God fails to meet our expectations or to act in the way that we thought, hoped, and prayed that he would?

In such instances, we need to reevaluate our expectations to make sure they align with the promises of God. God has not promised us that we will be free from all sickness and have lots of money in this lifetime. He has not promised that bad things will not happen to good people. He has not promised that we and our loved ones will never die. In this present age life is fatal; no one gets out alive. He has promised that he will be with us no matter what and that nothing can ever separate us from his love.[34] He has promised that resurrection will triumph over death and that there will be a future day when he will personally wipe every tear from every eye and remove sickness and death from his creation forever.[35] We will not always understand why things happen, but we can trust that God will fulfill his promises. He is faithful.[36]

---

[34] Rom. 8:38–39.

[35] Rev. 21:1–7.

[36] See Andreas J. Köstenberger, Darrell L. Bock, and Josh D. Chatraw, "Is God Immoral Because He Allows Suffering?," chap. 1 in *Truth in a Culture of Doubt: Engaging Skeptical Challenges to the Bible* (Nashville, TN: B&H Academic, 2014).

9

THE FIRST WITNESSES: SHEPHERDS

LUKE 2:8-20

And in the same region there were shepherds out in the field, keeping watch over their flock by night. And an angel of the Lord appeared to them, and the glory of the Lord shone around them, and they were filled with fear. And the angel said to them, "Fear not, for behold, I bring you good news of great joy that will be for all the people. For unto you is born this day in the city of David a Savior, who is Christ the Lord. And this will be a sign for you: you will find a baby wrapped in swaddling cloths and lying in a manger." And suddenly there was with the angel a multitude of the heavenly host praising God and saying,

> "Glory to God in the highest,
> and on earth peace among those with whom he is pleased!"

When the angels went away from them into heaven, the shepherds said to one another, "Let us go over to Bethlehem and see this thing that has happened, which the Lord has made known to us." And they went with haste and found Mary and Joseph, and the baby lying in a manger. And when they saw it, they made known the saying that had been told them concerning this child. And all who heard it wondered at what the shepherds told

> them. But Mary treasured up all these things, pondering them in her heart. And the shepherds returned, glorifying and praising God for all they had heard and seen, as it had been told them.

6 OR 5 BC

The Setting

The child had finally been born! All of history had been marching forward to this one moment, the moment at which God would come to live physically within his creation in order to defeat Satan, sin, and death. God had come, but not in the way everyone expected. It was not like the time when God drew near to his people at Sinai.[1] God's visit at Sinai was terrifying:

> a blazing fire and darkness and gloom and a tempest and the sound of a trumpet and a voice whose words made the hearers beg that no further messages be spoken to them. For they could not endure the order that was given, "If even a beast touches the mountain, it shall be stoned." Indeed, so terrifying was the sight that Moses said, "I tremble with fear."[2]

There was no earthquake, fire, or smoke the night Jesus took his first breath and cried for the first time. The night didn't pass, however, without a witness. Luke notes that shepherds were watching their sheep at night in that region. Rather than comment on the exact number of shepherds, Luke simply uses the plural to indicate that there were multiple shepherds. Shepherds had to keep a night watch in order to protect the flock from thieves or wild animals. This detail has led some to date Jesus's birth somewhere between April and November, given the claim that shepherds normally only kept their flocks out in the fields in this manner during those months. But shepherds near Bethlehem may very well have kept their flocks out year-round, so this detail by itself cannot pinpoint the exact month conclusively.[3]

---

[1] Ex. 19:9–25; 20:18–21.

[2] Heb. 12:18–21.

[3] I. Howard Marshall, *The Gospel of Luke*, New International Greek Testament Commentary (Grand Rapids, MI: Eerdmans, 1978), 108.

The shepherds most likely were having an uneventful night until the appearance of an angel of the Lord filled them with fear. Fear is the normal response to supernatural and angelic appearances, but Luke describes this appearance in greater detail, for "the glory of the Lord shone around them."[4] Here the "glory" points toward the visible and manifest divine presence—visible perhaps in intense brightness or color.[5] While Luke describes the fear-inspiring appearance of the angel Gabriel to Zechariah and Mary with more subtlety,[6] the shepherds were enveloped with the powerfully and brilliantly visible glory of God. The narrative gives no hint that only the shepherds could see this luminous display, but as far as we know, the shepherds were the sole observers because of the late hour and distance from the town.

Why shepherds? Interpreters have long puzzled over the significance of this angelic appearance to shepherds. The only point necessary on a narrative level is the fact that the shepherds were nearby and awake at that point in the night, but there's likely more to it. Because of their proximity to Jerusalem, the sheep may have been used for sacrifices in the temple, thus foreshadowing Jesus's sacrificial death. David was a shepherd before becoming a king, so the shepherds may also carry some Davidic symbolism. Because of their work, shepherds were almost always ceremonially unclean, and, although Luke makes no mention of it, later Jewish texts indicate that shepherds were generally distrusted and viewed negatively.

Most likely, the revelation to shepherds parallels and reinforces the lowly circumstances of the birth and the manger with no room in normal human habitation.[7] The angel appeared not to the rich and powerful or to the particularly righteous and religious, but to lowly shepherds, to average people who would be receptive to the message. Paul's later words to the well-off Corinthians ring true in this regard:

---

[4] Luke 2:9.

[5] Rev. 21:23.

[6] Luke 1:11, 28.

[7] On the back end of the story of Jesus, compare the fact that the first witnesses to the risen Jesus were women who likewise would have had a comparatively lower status in first-century Palestinian society.

> For consider your calling, brothers: not many of you were wise according to worldly standards, not many were powerful, not many were of noble birth. But God chose what is foolish in the world to shame the wise; God chose what is weak in the world to shame the strong; God chose what is low and despised in the world, even things that are not, to bring to nothing things that are, so that no human being might boast in the presence of God.[8]

Paul's words are a fitting commentary on the way God works in general, including the circumstances of the Messiah's birth. What is more, just as the worship of the *magoi* pointed forward to Jesus's ethnically universal rule (encompassing both Jew and Gentile), the message to the shepherds points forward to an accessibility that depends not upon one's status (religious or socioeconomic), position, wealth, or prestige. The birth of this child was good news for *all*!

The Message: A Savior, Christ the Lord

The angel makes this point explicit: "I bring you good news of great joy that will be for all the people."[9] The good news was for all the people. "People" (Greek *laos*) at this point likely points to the people of Israel, but the larger narrative of Luke-Acts indicates that God's people will expand to include all people regardless of nationality. James makes this point at the end of the Jerusalem council: "Simeon has related how God first visited the Gentiles, to take from them a people [*laos*] for his name."[10] As we saw in the hymns of Mary and Zechariah, the shepherds would have understood the angel to be speaking at this point in a more limited fashion about all the people of Israel.

Significantly, in declaring good news, the angel used the verb for the proclamation of the gospel.[11] We could alternately translate this phrase, "I *proclaim* or *announce the gospel* [good news] of great joy to you," or more woodenly, "I *gospel* great joy to you." The angel quickly provided the content of this gospel, announcement, or

[8] 1 Cor. 1:26–29.
[9] Luke 2:10.
[10] Acts 15:14.
[11] Greek *euangelizō*.

proclamation that would provide great joy to all the people: "For unto you is born this day in the city of David a Savior, who is Christ the Lord."[12] In this case, the gospel was a proclamation of the birth of Jesus that very day along with a clear indication of his identity as Savior, Christ, and Lord—all significant titles.

Luke had earlier featured the term "Savior" in Mary's *Magnificat*,[13] where she applied it directly to God, so its use here likely points back to Old Testament perceptions of God as Savior of his people.[14] The apostle Paul brought "God" and "Savior" together in Jesus when he powerfully declared that Christians were "waiting for our blessed hope, the appearing of the glory of our great God and Savior Jesus Christ."[15] Peter did the same when he wrote of "the righteousness of our God and Savior Jesus Christ."[16] Those in the Greco-Roman world also commonly spoke about the various gods and emperors as "saviors," so the first non-Jewish readers of Luke would have understood the term most likely against that background. The angel thus proclaimed Jesus to be *the* Savior in continuation of God's role as Savior in the past and in direct contrast to the various saviors of Greco-Roman religion and politics.

The angel's pronouncement bears some striking similarities to the way in which Augustus and other Roman emperors were discussed and worshiped in the imperial cult. Consider these statements from the 9 BC Priene Calendar Inscription:

> Since Providence, which has ordered all things and is deeply interested in our life, has set in most perfect order by giving us Augustus, whom she filled with virtue that he might benefit humankind, sending him as a *savior* [*sōtēr*], both for us and for our descendants, that he might end war and arrange all things, and since he, Caesar, by his appearance (excelled even our anticipations), surpassing all previous benefactors, and not even leaving to posterity any hope of surpassing what he has done, and since the birthday of the *god*

[12] Luke 2:11.
[13] "God my Savior" in Luke 1:47.
[14] Isa. 45:15, 21.
[15] Titus 2:13.
[16] 2 Pet. 1:1.

> Augustus was the beginning of the *good tidings* [*euangelion*; gospel, good news] for the world that came by reason of him.[17]

Providence had sent the "god" Augustus to be the savior of the Roman world, and his birth was the beginning of the gospel (good news). Such rhetoric pervaded the political and religious language of the first century. In contrast, the angel announced the gospel of God's Son, Jesus, who would be the true Savior of the world.

How would this baby save his people? And from what would he save them? Zechariah had praised God for raising up a "horn of salvation" to save and deliver his people from the hands of their enemies.[18] The angel's message to Joseph in Matthew's infancy narrative provides another perspective: "You shall call his name Jesus, for he will save his people from their sins."[19] Peter discusses Jesus as Savior in these terms: "God exalted him at his right hand as Leader and Savior, to give repentance to Israel and forgiveness of sins."[20] Salvation through the forgiveness of sins must precede political and economic salvation. The forgiveness of sins was accomplished through Jesus's death on the cross, while political and economic salvation will be established at his return.[21]

"Christ" translates the Hebrew word for "messiah." We discuss messianic expectation at length in the appendix, so we need not repeat that discussion here. It suffices to note that the angel indicated the Davidic nature of this Messiah by explicit reference to the "city of David."[22] According to the angel's gospel, this newly born Savior was the long-awaited Davidic Messiah who would rescue God's people and rule over them.

---

[17] Quoted in Craig Evans, "Mark's Incipit and the Priene Calendar Inscription: From Jewish Gospel to Greco-Roman Gospel," *Journal of Greco-Roman Christianity and Judaism* 1 (2000): 68–69 (emphasis added). For the Greek text, see W. Dittenberger, ed., *Orientis graeci inscriptiones selectae*, (Leipzig, 1903–1905), 458; for facsimiles of the original inscription from the pillar of the north hall of the market at Priene, see Adolf Deissmann, *Light from the Ancient East* (repr., Grand Rapids, MI: Baker, 1978), 366–67.

[18] Luke 1:69, 71, 74.

[19] Matt. 1:21.

[20] Acts 5:31.

[21] That said, Luke makes clear that the role reversal between rich and poor has already been inaugurated at Jesus's first coming. See Darrell L. Bock, *A Theology of Luke-Acts*, Biblical Theology of the New Testament (Grand Rapids, MI: Zondervan, 2012), chap. 17.

[22] Luke 2:11.

"The Lord" is an ambiguous term usually used to refer to either Yahweh[23] or Jesus.[24] As we saw earlier, it is occasionally hard to tell to whom the word refers. The ambiguity of the term caused no problem for the earliest Christians because Jesus was in fact God Incarnate. Jesus was God in the flesh, God visible to human eyes.[25]

The angel's gospel thus proclaimed that the Savior, the Christ, the Lord himself, had just been born. All three of these titles are again brought together in Paul's letter to the Philippians: "But our citizenship is in heaven, and from it we await a Savior, the Lord Jesus Christ."[26] The legitimacy of these titles declared at his birth will be demonstrated beyond all possible doubt when our Savior and Lord Jesus Christ returns "with the voice of an archangel, and with the sound of the trumpet of God."[27]

The angel proceeded to provide the shepherds with a sign to confirm the gospel. The shepherds would find a newborn baby wrapped in swaddling cloths lying in a manger. Presumably, under normal circumstances, the shepherds would not expect to find a newborn in an animal feeding trough. The strangeness of the sign would help the shepherds search and confirm the angelic message.

Without warning, the angel was joined by a multitude of angels praising God and singing the third hymn of Luke's infancy narrative. This hymn consists of just two lines and therefore doesn't require the kind of detailed commentary provided for the *Magnificat* and *Benedictus*. The angels worshiped by giving God glory in a shout of praise: "Glory to God in the highest!" The angels did not provide a reason for this worship since the reason had already been stated: the Savior, the Christ, the Lord had been born! Instead of providing another reason for glorifying God, they announced peace upon those with whom God was pleased or upon whom God's favor rested.[28]

---

[23] Luke 1:6, 9, 16, 32, 38, 46, 66; 10:21; see also Matt. 9:38; 1 Tim. 6:15; Rev. 4:11.
[24] Luke 2:11; Acts 2:36; Rom. 10:9; 1 Cor. 12:3; Phil. 2:11.
[25] We will discuss this theme in more detail in part 3, where we treat John's Gospel.
[26] Phil. 3:20.
[27] 1 Thess. 4:16.
[28] The text-critical issue related to this phrase presents itself as follows: Does the original text of Luke 2:14 read *eudokias* ("of good pleasure," genitive case) or *eudokia* ("good will," nominative case)? In Greek, the difference is only a single letter, a final sigma. A look at the oldest and most

Later in Luke's Gospel, Jesus himself echoes the thought of the second line of the hymn in a prayer to God. "In that same hour he rejoiced in the Holy Spirit and said, 'I thank you, Father, Lord of heaven and earth, that you have hidden these things from the wise and understanding and revealed them to little children; yes, Father, for such was your *gracious will* [*eudokia*].'"[29] The angels announced peace upon those with whom God was pleased, and Jesus thanked God that it was his pleasure to hide truth from the wise and reveal it to children. This revealed truth consisted of knowledge of the Son.[30] God's pleasure and peace rest on those to whom the truth of Jesus's identity is revealed, his identity as Savior, Christ, and Lord.

The Response

After the angelic host departed, the shepherds quickly went in search of the child and found Mary and Joseph with the baby Jesus, who was lying in a manger. The closing verses of this section record three different responses to the angelic announcement of the gospel of Jesus's birth.

First, the shepherds responded by glorifying and praising God and by telling other people about what they had heard and seen.[31] This is bearing witness at its best. The shepherds weren't embarrassed and didn't wait for further information or training; they simply passed on the amazing account of what they had seen and heard. Witnessing is as simple as sharing what you know to be true about God and what he has done for and in you. What have you heard and seen? The shepherds added to their witness their praise

---

reliable manuscripts makes clear that all three major codices—Sinaiticus, Alexandrinus, and Vaticanus—point to *eudokias* as the original wording. Interestingly, in both Sinaiticus and Vaticanus, later correctors erased the final sigma in order to change the harder genitive to the easier nominative reading, which subsequently found its way into many Byzantine manuscripts and writings by the church fathers. Later still, the King James Version based its rendering of Luke 2:14 on this textual tradition, issuing in the (most likely erroneous) translation, "on earth peace, *good will* toward men." More likely, the original reading was, "on earth peace toward men *of good will*." For more on this issue, see the introduction to chap. 3 in Andreas J. Köstenberger, Benjamin L. Merkle, and Robert L. Plummer, *Going Deeper with New Testament Greek: An Intermediate Study of the Grammar and Syntax of the New Testament* (Nashville, TN: B&H Academic, 2016).

[29] Luke 10:21.

[30] Luke 10:22.

[31] Luke 2:17, 20.

and worship as they reflected on what the angel had announced: the birth of a Savior, Christ, the Lord!

Second, the people who heard the shepherds were filled with wonder, amazement, and surprise at their report.[32] This is an acceptable initial response, but Luke gives no indication that those people acted on what they heard. Some may have surmised that it sounded like good news while others may have suspected the shepherds were crazy.

Third, Luke records that Mary "treasured up all these things, pondering them in her heart."[33] This comment is repeated later in the narrative: "And his mother treasured up all these things in her heart."[34] Mary's perspective pervades the infancy narrative in Luke, and these verses give a reasonable clue as to how Luke came upon this information. Mary would have remembered the details of the swaddling cloths, the manger, and the report of the shepherds and at some point would have shared these stories with other family members and friends. In this way, Luke would have gained access to Mary's eyewitness testimony, whether oral or written.

Even though this explanation is plausible, even probable, these verses cannot by themselves prove that Mary was the direct source of Luke's account. Luke may simply be asserting that Mary treasured and reflected on the significance of these events in a deeper way than the others. She would have shared their amazement but would also have carried a deeper level of insight and engaged in a deeper level of reflection than they did. After all, she was Jesus's mother and the recipient of the amazing angelic pronouncement regarding her Son!

The shepherds responded with praise, worship, and witness; the people who heard their report responded with amazement; and Mary responded with quiet reflection. How will you respond to the good news of the birth of Jesus, the Savior, the Christ, the Lord?

---

[32] Luke 2:18.
[33] Luke 2:19.
[34] Luke 2:51.

10

LIGHT OF REVELATION FOR THE GENTILES

FURTHER WITNESSES

LUKE 2:21–40

And at the end of eight days, when he was circumcised, he was called Jesus, the name given by the angel before he was conceived in the womb.

And when the time came for their purification according to the Law of Moses, they brought him up to Jerusalem to present him to the Lord (as it is written in the Law of the Lord, "Every male who first opens the womb shall be called holy to the Lord") and to offer a sacrifice according to what is said in the Law of the Lord, "a pair of turtledoves, or two young pigeons." Now there was a man in Jerusalem, whose name was Simeon, and this man was righteous and devout, waiting for the consolation of Israel, and the Holy Spirit was upon him. And it had been revealed to him by the Holy Spirit that he would not see death before he had seen the Lord's Christ. And he came in the Spirit into the temple, and when the parents brought in the child Jesus, to do for him according to the custom of the Law, he took him up in his arms and blessed God and said,

"Lord, now you are letting your servant depart in peace,
according to your word;

for my eyes have seen your salvation
that you have prepared in the presence of all peoples,
a light for revelation to the Gentiles,
and for glory to your people Israel."

And his father and his mother marveled at what was said about him. And Simeon blessed them and said to Mary his mother, "Behold, this child is appointed for the fall and rising of many in Israel, and for a sign that is opposed (and a sword will pierce through your own soul also), so that thoughts from many hearts may be revealed."

And there was a prophetess, Anna, the daughter of Phanuel, of the tribe of Asher. She was advanced in years, having lived with her husband seven years from when she was a virgin, and then as a widow until she was eighty-four. She did not depart from the temple, worshiping with fasting and prayer night and day. And coming up at that very hour she began to give thanks to God and to speak of him to all who were waiting for the redemption of Jerusalem.

And when they had performed everything according to the Law of the Lord, they returned into Galilee, to their own town of Nazareth. And the child grew and became strong, filled with wisdom. And the favor of God was upon him.

6 OR 5 BC

The First Glimpse of Suffering

Jesus has been born. The Davidic heir has arrived to rule over the house of Jacob and save his people from their enemies in fulfillment of God's promises to Abraham and David.[1] Gabriel's announcements to Zechariah and Mary and the hymns sung by Mary and Zechariah establish the birth of Jesus as the fulfillment of a host of Old Testament promises and expectations concerning how God would act in the future to rescue and restore his people.

Simeon and Anna take the prophetic stage in this final section of Luke's infancy narrative, and Simeon powerfully highlights

[1] Luke 1:33, 54–55, 69, 71–73; 2:11.

two ways in which God's fulfillment in Jesus would exceed and transform everyone's preconceived expectations. Yes, Jesus was the fulfillment of God's promises, God's salvation, and the consolation of Israel, but this fulfillment would expand to include the Gentiles and would result in suffering as it produced division and opposition within God's people Israel. Up to this point, Luke's infancy narrative has consisted entirely in an escalation of joy, praise, and happiness as births were announced, accomplished, and celebrated. Simeon's final prophecy introduces the first clear glimpse of the dark days that lay ahead. God's salvation had come, but it would not be accomplished without suffering.

Fulfilling the Law

Jesus came as the fulfillment of Old Testament promises, and Luke goes out of his way to highlight Joseph and Mary's obedience to the law. Jesus would save Israel as a law-observant Jew within Judaism. Joseph and Mary circumcised and named Jesus on the eighth day according to Jewish customs based upon Old Testament prescriptions,[2] but Luke presents the event primarily as an act of obedience to the angel's instructions. In both Matthew and Luke, it is clear that God chose the name Jesus specifically as a way to convey the nature of Jesus's mission. Unlike Matthew, Luke doesn't explicitly highlight the significance of Jesus's name ("Yahweh saves"); rather, he implicitly weaves the theme of Jesus as God's salvation throughout the narrative.[3]

In describing the reason for the family's journey to the temple in Jerusalem, Luke points to two practices mandated in the Pentateuch. First, the law required Mary to offer sacrifices for her purification forty days after the birth.[4] According to the law, the sacrifice would have been a lamb and a pigeon, but provision was made for poor families to offer "two turtledoves or two pigeons."[5] This may be a clue to Joseph and Mary's socioeconomic position,

---

[2] Gen. 17:12–14; Lev. 12:3.

[3] Luke 1:69, 71, 77; 2:11, 30; cf. Matt. 1:21.

[4] Lev. 12:1–8.

[5] Lev. 12:8.

but it is also possible that most people at this time offered the lesser sacrifice. It is not entirely clear why Luke refers to the time for "their" purification,[6] since the Levitical instructions concerned only the mother, but the couple may have believed that Mary's cultic impurity had been communicated to Joseph (following the position taken by the Pharisaic house of Shammai), thus demanding his purification as well.[7]

Second, the law required Mary and Joseph to present Jesus to God as the firstborn and redeem him back from God.[8] This practice was based on God's protection of the firstborn among his people during the deaths of the firstborn of Egypt.[9] They were to make the redemption payment at the temple[10] a month after birth,[11] but for practical reasons, families would likely have combined the redemption of the firstborn with the purification of the mother as described by Luke. The narrative makes no mention of Joseph and Mary paying the required amount of five shekels to redeem Jesus, so Luke may be suggesting that just as Hannah dedicated Samuel to God's service at the temple,[12] so Jesus was completely consecrated and set apart to God. More than likely, they paid the redemption price according to the law while Luke simply made no comment about it.

Luke goes out of his way to point out that Joseph and Mary followed the laws surrounding childbirth.[13] This argument connects with Paul's statement that "when the fullness of time had come, God sent forth his Son, born of woman, born under the law, to redeem those who were under the law, so that we might receive

---

[6] Luke 2:22.

[7] Richard Bauckham, "Luke's Infancy Narrative as Oral History in Scriptural Form," in *The Gospels: History and Christology: The Search of Joseph Ratzinger-Benedict XVI*, ed. Bernardo Estrada, Ermenegildo Manicardi, and Armand Puig I Tàrrech (Vatican City: Libreria Editrice Vaticana, 2013), 1:399–417.

[8] Ex. 13:2, 11–16; Num. 8:5–22; 18:15–18; Neh. 10:35–36.

[9] Ex. 13:15; Num. 8:17.

[10] Neh. 10:35–36.

[11] Num. 18:16.

[12] 1 Sam. 1:11, 22, 28.

[13] See especially the following references: "according to the Law of Moses" (Luke 2:22); "as it is written in the Law of the Lord" (Luke 2:23); "according to what is said in the Law of the Lord" (Luke 2:24); "to do for him according to the custom of the Law" (Luke 2:27); "they had performed everything according to the Law of the Lord" (Luke 2:39).

adoption as sons."[14] Being born "under the law" enabled Jesus to be "the end of the law for righteousness to everyone who believes."[15]

Simeon: A Light for the Gentiles

Luke proceeds to introduce a new character to the narrative. Simeon, like Zechariah and Joseph, was a righteous and religiously devout man.[16] He is described as waiting for the "consolation" (*paraklēsis*) of Israel. This language connects back to promises throughout Isaiah: "Comfort [*parakaleō*], comfort my people, says your God"; "Sing for joy, O heavens, and exult, O earth; break forth, O mountains, into singing! For the Lord has comforted [*parakaleō*] his people and will have compassion on his afflicted."[17]

While Simeon was waiting for the consolation of Israel, the Holy Spirit rested on him and revealed to him that he would not die until he saw "the Lord's Christ," Yahweh's Messiah.[18] The Holy Spirit had been active throughout Luke's infancy narrative,[19] and Luke mentions him three times in Simeon's brief introduction to stress the divine source of Simeon's knowledge and prophecy.[20]

When Simeon saw Jesus in the temple complex, he took the baby in his arms, blessed God, and uttered the fourth hymn of Luke's infancy narrative, known as the *Nunc Dimittis* (named after the first two words of the Latin translation, which mean "now dismiss"). Simeon blessed God for allowing him to depart in peace, having seen God's salvation in the form of the tiny baby. He was thus free to die knowing that he had seen God's fulfillment of his promises to his people with his own eyes.

Although the earlier mention of Caesar Augustus merely hinted at Jesus's universal significance,[21] Simeon's next words make this point directly. God's salvation prepared in the presence

[14] Gal. 4:3–4.
[15] Rom. 10:4.
[16] Matt. 1:19; Luke 1:6; 2:25.
[17] Isa. 40:1; 49:13 (from the Septuagint, the Greek translation of the Old Testament). Cf. 57:18; 61:2.
[18] Luke 2:26.
[19] Luke 1:35, 41, 67.
[20] Luke 2:25–27.
[21] Luke 2:1.

of all peoples (plural) included both Jews and Gentiles: "a light for revelation to the Gentiles, and for glory to your people Israel."[22] With these words, Simeon declared the fulfillment of several messianic servant prophecies in Isaiah: "he says: 'It is too light a thing that you should be my servant to raise up the tribes of Jacob and to bring back the preserved of Israel; I will make you as a *light for the nations*, that my *salvation* may reach to the end of the earth'"; "I am the Lord; I have called you in righteousness; I will take you by the hand and keep you; I will give you as a covenant for the people, a *light for the nations*."[23]

More significantly, right before the famous "suffering servant" passage of Isaiah,[24] we find these words:

> The voice of your *watchmen*—they lift up their voice;
> together they sing for joy;
> for eye to eye they see
> *the return of the Lord to Zion.*
> Break forth together into singing,
> you waste places of Jerusalem,
> for the Lord has *comforted* his people;
> he has *redeemed* Jerusalem.
> The Lord has bared his holy arm
> *before the eyes of all the nations,*
> and all the ends of the earth shall *see*
> the *salvation* of our God.[25]

Simeon and Anna function as watchmen who recognize and bear witness to Jesus as the fulfillment of these passages.

Everything in Luke's infancy narrative up to this point focuses on Jesus as the fulfillment of God's promises to Israel. Jesus would be Israel's Messiah and ruler. He would rescue Israel from her enemies. Simeon's statement affirms and expands this perspective. Yes, Jesus would bring God's salvation and glory to Israel,

[22] Luke 2:32.
[23] Isa. 49:6; 42:6.
[24] Isa. 52:13–53:12.
[25] Isa. 52:8–10.

but he would do this not by destroying or enslaving the Gentiles but by giving the light of revelation (originally reserved for Israel) to the Gentile nations as well. Jesus fulfills all the Old Testament promises concerning the restoration and redemption of Israel as he extends the light and rule of his kingdom over all the nations of the world. These nations are not to be subservient to Israel but co-members of the unified people of God. Simeon's words thus form a literary *inclusio* with Paul's final words at the end of Luke's two-volume work in Acts: "Therefore let it be known to you that this salvation of God has been sent to the Gentiles; they will listen."[26]

Simeon: Division, Opposition, and Suffering

Joseph and Mary were amazed by Simeon's unexpected actions and words, but Simeon was not finished. Simeon blessed them and proceeded to speak about the child's future. His words, however, stand in stark contrast to everything else that had been said up to this point in Luke's narrative. The angelic announcements concerning the births of John and Jesus and the four hymns of Luke's infancy narrative all gave the impression that, with the birth of Jesus, there was nothing to do but rejoice and bless God for his accomplished salvation and deliverance. The Son of the Most High, the Savior, the Christ, the Lord had come! Simeon's words provided the first real indication that God's plan for rescuing his people and the Gentile nations would not come without cost.

First, Simeon notes that Jesus was appointed for the falling and rising of many in Israel. Although the text could indicate that many would fall and then rise, it more likely points to two different responses to Jesus. Some would rise and experience God's salvation through his Messiah, while others in Israel would fall and fail to experience this long-awaited salvation. The New Testament repeatedly discusses this double response using the image of the rejected stone that becomes a stumbling stone to some while becoming the cor-

[26] Acts 28:28.

nerstone to others.[27] Simeon points forward to the reality that not all in Israel will rise to experience God's salvation in his Messiah.

Simeon's next line develops the theme of rejection and opposition. Jesus would be a "sign that is opposed."[28] The Savior, the Christ, the Lord had come but would be opposed and rejected. Simeon parenthetically adds a direct word to Mary that "a sword will pierce through your own soul also."[29] This foreboding prophecy likely includes Mary's sorrow at the cross but goes far beyond that moment. The angel had told Mary directly that her Son, as the Son of the Most High, would sit on the throne of David and rule over the house of Jacob forever.[30] Her sorrow would arise not just because her firstborn would die an excruciatingly painful death but also because God's promises would seem to have failed. How could a crucified Son rule over God's people? The "sword" that would pierce through Mary's soul likely relates to a whole host of shattered hopes, dreams, and expectations as she would watch her Son go up against the religious leaders of the Jerusalem temple and pay the ultimate price.

Simeon's final words also carry negative connotations: "so that thoughts [*dialogismos*] from many hearts may be revealed."[31] The word *dialogismos* is always used negatively in the New Testament.[32] The thoughts from many hearts that will be revealed are negative thoughts of opposition, hostility, and doubt. Simeon's final prophecy can be summarized as follows: the hostile thoughts of many will be revealed; a sword will pass through Mary's heart; Jesus will be opposed; and many will fall and rise in Israel. This is not the picture we get from the *Magnificat* or the *Benedictus*, but it is the final prophetic word of Luke's infancy narrative. It makes a solemn declaration that even as God's salvation was coming to his people to bring light to the Gentiles and glory to Israel, it would not come without conflict, suffering, and cost. It would not come the way

---

[27] Matt. 21:42; Mark 12:10–11; Luke 20:17–18; Acts 4:11–12; Rom. 9:30–33; 1 Pet. 2:4–8; drawn from Ps. 118:21–23; Isa. 8:14–15; 28:16.

[28] Luke 2:34.

[29] Luke 2:35.

[30] Luke 1:32–33.

[31] Luke 2:35.

[32] Matt. 15:19; Mark 7:21; Luke 5:22; 6:8; 9:46, 47; 24:38; Rom. 1:21; 14:1; 1 Cor. 3:20; Phil. 2:14; 1 Tim. 2:8; James 2:4.

most people were expecting. In retrospect, we know that it would not come without blood, sacrifice, and even death.

Anna

Simeon did not bear witness alone but was joined by Anna, an aged prophetess from the tribe of Asher, who confirmed his testimony as a second witness, a woman.[33] Luke notes that Anna began to give thanks to God and speak about Jesus to all who were waiting for the redemption of Jerusalem.[34] Despite the opposition and rejection that Simeon had just prophesied, Anna still declared Jesus to be the redemption of Jerusalem. God's purposes would not fail!

It is fascinating to note that Luke omits Anna's actual words. Perhaps they had been lost in the oral tradition or gone unrecorded in the written sources to which Luke had access. Luke does, however, include quite a bit of information about this woman. Anna's life spoke much louder than her words. She was from one of the ten tribes of Israel that was lost to history after the Assyrian exile and thus represented a foretaste of the restoration of *all* Israel. She had been widowed after only seven years of marriage and spent the ensuing decades through age eighty-four in regular faithful worship, fasting, and prayer, night and day, in the temple.[35] We need not assume that she had a bed somewhere in the temple complex; Luke's description rather makes the point that she spent every waking moment in prayer and worship in the temple complex, likely at the court of women.

In Luke's infancy narrative, Anna thus speaks with her life of devotion, worship, prayer, and fasting. This life recognized Jesus as the long-awaited redemption of Jerusalem. Those who, like Anna,

---

[33] Deut. 19:15; Matt. 18:16. See the discussion of male-female pairs in Luke-Acts in Andreas J. Köstenberger and Margaret E. Köstenberger, *God's Design for Man and Woman: A Biblical-Theological Survey* (Wheaton, IL: Crossway, 2014), chap. 3.

[34] Luke 2:38.

[35] The Greek could be translated to indicate that she lived as a widow for eighty-four years after her husband died. If Anna had been married at twelve years of age, she would have been approximately 103 years old at this point. Although highly unusual, such a lifespan is certainly not impossible and could explain why people remembered those details long after they forgot her exact words.

devoted their lives to God in genuine worship and service would recognize Jesus as God's salvation.

MATTHEW AND LUKE IN HARMONY

Luke notes that after their visit to the temple, Jesus's parents returned with their infant Son to their hometown of Nazareth in Galilee.[36] Luke omits any mention of the family's escape to Egypt to elude Herod's fury.[37] Up to this point, we have examined the infancy narratives in Matthew and Luke each in their own right (i.e., vertically), but it is also important to look at both narratives together (i.e., horizontally) because both record historical information about Jesus's birth. Do these accounts contradict each other, or can they be harmonized?

Raymond Brown notes the following points that Matthew and Luke share in common:

1. The parents to be are Mary and Joseph, who are legally engaged or married but have not yet come to live together or have sexual relations.[38]
2. Joseph is of Davidic descent.[39]
3. An angel announces the forthcoming birth of the child.[40]
4. The conception of the child by Mary is not through intercourse with her husband.[41]
5. The conception is through the Holy Spirit.[42]
6. The angel directs them to name the child Jesus.[43]
7. An angel states that Jesus is to be Savior.[44]
8. The birth of the child takes place after the parents have come to live together.[45]
9. The birth takes place in Bethlehem.[46]

---

[36] Luke 2:39.
[37] Matt. 2:13–23.
[38] Matt. 1:18; Luke 1:27, 34.
[39] Matt. 1:16, 20; Luke 1:27, 32; 2:4.
[40] Matt. 1:20–23; Luke 1:30–35.
[41] Matt. 1:20, 23, 25; Luke 1:34.
[42] Matt. 1:18, 20; Luke 1:35.
[43] Matt. 1:21; Luke 1:31.
[44] Matt. 1:21; Luke 2:11.
[45] Matt. 1:24–25; Luke 2:5–6.
[46] Matt. 2:1; Luke 2:4–6.

10. The birth is chronologically related to the reign (or days) of Herod the Great.[47]
11. The child is raised in Nazareth.[48]

Further smaller connections can be adduced, but these form the heart of the storyline in both Gospels.

What are the differences? Matthew contains no explicit reference to several events in Luke 1–2, while Luke contains no explicit reference to some of the major events in Matthew 2 (see chart below). Matthew is told from Joseph's perspective, while Luke is told from Mary's vantage point.

PARTS OF THE STORY ABSENT FROM MATTHEW	PARTS OF THE STORY ABSENT FROM LUKE
Angelic announcements to Zechariah, Mary	Visit of the *magoi*
Mary's visit to Elizabeth, song (*Magnificat*)	Herod's plot
Birth of John the Baptist	Escape to Egypt
Zechariah's song (*Benedictus*)	Slaughter of the innocents
Journey from Nazareth to Bethlehem	Joseph's decision as to where to resettle
The manger	
Lack of room in the inn/guest house	
Angelic announcement to the shepherds	
Presentation in the temple, Simeon, and Anna	

These differences, however, are not hard to harmonize. Matthew may not have known any of the events recorded in Luke 1 or,

[47] Matt. 2:1; Luke 1:5.
[48] Matt. 2:23; Luke 2:39. Raymond Brown, *The Birth of the Messiah*, rev. ed. (New York: Doubleday, 1993), 34–35.

if he did, chose to omit them. The wording of Matthew 2:22–23 suggests that Matthew may have been unaware that Joseph and Mary lived in Nazareth before the birth. He records nothing of the night of the birth or of the visit to the temple forty days later. The events he does record in Matthew 2 take place after Jesus's presentation at the temple. The lack of overlap between the events in the two accounts makes them easy to harmonize.

Raymond Brown, however, highlights two details that lead him to believe the accounts are "contrary to each other" and cannot both be historical.[49] First, Luke locates Mary in Nazareth[50] and uses the census to explain how the birth took place in Bethlehem, while Matthew indicates that the family lived in a house in Bethlehem[51] and spends time explaining why the family moved to Nazareth instead of resettling in Bethlehem.[52] Second, "Luke tells us that the family returned peaceably to Nazareth after the birth at Bethlehem (2:22, 39); this is irreconcilable with Matthew's implication (2:16) that the child was almost two years old when the family fled from Bethlehem to Egypt and even older when the family came back from Egypt and moved to Nazareth."[53]

However, Brown greatly overstates his claim of irreconcilability. First, nothing Matthew says actually contradicts Luke's account about Mary and Joseph being in Nazareth prior to the birth. Matthew is silent on the matter. Brown draws attention to Matthew's reference to the visit of the wise men at a house,[54] but this would have occurred after the night of the birth (anywhere from two months to two years), and we have every reason to believe that Joseph would have secured a legitimate habitation by that point. Matthew's silence about the life of Joseph and Mary in Nazareth before the birth simply indicates his ignorance of or lack of interest in these details for the purpose of his narrative and does not represent a contradiction. No biblical author omnisciently claims

[49] Brown, *Birth of the Messiah*, 36.
[50] Luke 1:26; 2:39.
[51] Matt. 2:11.
[52] Matt. 2:22–23.
[53] Brown, *Birth of the Messiah*, 34–35.
[54] Matt. 2:11.

to include every detail, nor would it be possible to do so given narrative purposes, space limitations, and costs of writing material.[55]

Second, narrators commonly compress time and omit details (either from ignorance or conscious choice). Luke's reference to the family's return to Nazareth after the presentation in the temple does not contradict the events recorded in Matthew 2; he just doesn't comment on them. Again, silence does not equal contradiction. Luke may not have known about the events of Matthew 2, but he also may have known about them and omitted reference to them because they did not contribute to the points he was trying to make in his infancy narrative. By the end of the presentation in the temple, Luke was ready to move on with the narrative and get to Jesus's adult ministry (though he does include the story of the twelve-year-old Jesus in the temple and, later, Jesus's genealogy). Perhaps Luke doubted that Matthew's use of the Old Testament would be meaningful to his Gentile audience. Perhaps most likely, Luke wrote independently at roughly the same time as Matthew and so was unaware of how Matthew was going to write his infancy narrative. Whatever the reason for the omission (whether ignorance or author's selectivity), it is illegitimate to construe silence necessarily as contradiction.

The lack of significant overlap between the infancy narratives in Matthew and Luke points to largely independent narratives instead of contradictory narratives. Apart from the one verse dedicated to the birth itself, the two Gospels record events from time periods and settings that complement rather than conflict with each other. Both Gospels are united on the main storyline,[56] and the differences reflect different sources, varying perspectives, and authorial selectivity.

FROM INFANCY TO ADULTHOOD

Luke concludes his infancy narrative by noting that Jesus "grew and became strong, filled with wisdom. And the favor of God was

[55] Cf. John 21:25.

[56] See the similarities noted above.

upon him."[57] This concluding summary indicates that the rest of Jesus's early years were consistent with early expectations and pointed forward to his future ministry.

The account of Jesus's visit to the temple for the Feast of Passover at the age of twelve provides a transition from the infancy narrative to Jesus's adult ministry.[58] Jesus's actions do not reflect youthful rebellion or disobedience. Rather, the narrative highlights the effects of Luke's prior statement. Jesus was indeed growing into maturity; he was filled with wisdom beyond his age, and God's favor rested upon him. In anticipation of his future ministry, the narrative also reflects Jesus's awareness of his relationship to God as his Father and his growing mastery of the Old Testament Scriptures.

Luke records the return of Jesus's family to Nazareth and later notes that "Jesus increased in wisdom and stature and in favor with God and man."[59] Jesus was ready for what lay ahead.

CONCLUSION

Luke's infancy narrative is infused with joy over the fulfillment of God's promises to his people. This joy bubbles over in the central hymns of the narrative, Mary's *Magnificat* and Zechariah's *Benedictus*, which both celebrate that God had remembered his promises and had acted in mercy to rescue his people. These hymns presuppose some things about God's character—attributes expressed in God's own description of himself in Exodus 34:6–7b: "a God merciful and gracious, slow to anger, and abounding in steadfast love and faithfulness, keeping steadfast love for thousands, forgiving iniquity and transgression and sin, but who will by no means clear the guilty."

This description of God became foundational for the way in which God was described and approached throughout the entire Old Testament.[60] Today it gives us confidence that God longs to

[57] Luke 2:40.
[58] Luke 2:41–52.
[59] Luke 2:52.
[60] Num. 14:18–19; Neh. 9:17; Pss. 86:15; 103:8; 145:8; Joel 2:13; Jonah 4:2; Mic. 7:18, 20.

forgive us because of his great love and mercy. It also reminds us, however, that sin must be punished—he will not clear the guilty. He will not just look the other way or wink at our sin. God is both loving and just. He longs to forgive but will punish the guilty. Some find these two attributes of God contradictory. How can a loving and forgiving God punish people? Jesus, of course, is the answer. God's justice required that sin be punished, but his love moved him to provide a means of forgiveness and salvation. Luke's infancy narrative celebrates the beginning of this salvation in the birth of our "Savior, who is Christ the Lord."[61]

With Luke's infancy narrative, the stage has been set. God's Savior has come. The rest of the Gospel describes how Jesus delivers his people and establishes his kingdom. It didn't happen in the way everyone was expecting, but that's a story for another day.[62]

---

[61] Luke 2:11b.

[62] And another book: see Andreas J. Köstenberger and Justin Taylor with Alexander Stewart, *The Final Days of Jesus: The Most Important Week of the Most Important Person Who Ever Lived* (Wheaton, IL: Crossway, 2014).

PART 3

INCARNATE WORD

11

PREEXISTENCE: THE WORD WAS GOD

JOHN 1:1–5, 18

In the beginning was the Word, and the Word was with God, and the Word was God. He was in the beginning with God. All things were made through him, and without him was not any thing made that was made. In him was life, and the life was the light of men. The light shines in the darkness, and the darkness has not overcome it.

No one has ever seen God; the only God, who is at the Father's side, he has made him known.

ETERNITY PAST

In the Beginning Was the Word

"In the beginning was the Word, and the Word was with God, and the Word was God." Even in English, these words resonate with cadence, redound with meaning, and are resplendent with majesty. "In the beginning" makes the reader go back all the way to creation, where it is said, "In the beginning, God created the heavens and the earth."[1] But wait! This is not the book of Genesis; instead, John's Gospel reads, "In the beginning was *the Word*"! Even this

[1] Gen. 1:1.

point reflects the creation narrative, which records that everything that was made came into being when God *spoke*:

> *And God said*, "Let there be light," and there was light. And God saw that the light was good. And God separated the light from the darkness. God called the light Day, and the darkness he called Night. And there was evening and there was morning, the first day.
>
> *And God said*, "Let there be an expanse in the midst of the waters, and let it separate the waters from the waters." And God made the expanse and separated the waters that were under the expanse from the waters that were above the expanse. And it was so. And God called the expanse Heaven. And there was evening and there was morning, the second day.
>
> *And God said*, "Let the waters under the heavens be gathered together into one place, and let the dry land appear." And it was so. God called the dry land Earth, and the waters that were gathered together he called Seas. And God saw that it was good.
>
> *And God said*, "Let the earth sprout vegetation, plants yielding seed, and fruit trees bearing fruit in which is their seed, each according to its kind, on the earth." And it was so. The earth brought forth vegetation, plants yielding seed according to their own kinds, and trees bearing fruit in which is their seed, each according to its kind. And God saw that it was good. And there was evening and there was morning, the third day.
>
> *And God said*, "Let there be lights in the expanse of the heavens to separate the day from the night. And let them be for signs and for seasons, and for days and years, and let them be lights in the expanse of the heavens to give light upon the earth." And it was so. And God made the two great lights—the greater light to rule the day and the lesser light to rule the night—and the stars. And God set them in the expanse of the heavens to give light on the earth, to rule over the day and over the night, and to separate the light from the darkness. And God saw that it was good. And there was evening and there was morning, the fourth day.
>
> *And God said*, "Let the waters swarm with swarms of living creatures, and let birds fly above the earth across the expanse of the heavens." So God created the great sea creatures and every living creature that moves, with which the waters swarm, accord-

ing to their kinds, and every winged bird according to its kind. And God saw that it was good. And God blessed them, saying, "Be fruitful and multiply and fill the waters in the seas, and let birds multiply on the earth." And there was evening and there was morning, the fifth day.

And God said, "Let the earth bring forth living creatures according to their kinds—livestock and creeping things and beasts of the earth according to their kinds." And it was so. And God made the beasts of the earth according to their kinds and the livestock according to their kinds, and everything that creeps on the ground according to its kind. And God saw that it was good.

Then God said, "Let us make man in our image, after our likeness. And let them have dominion over the fish of the sea and over the birds of the heavens and over the livestock and over all the earth and over every creeping thing that creeps on the earth."

> So God created man in his own image,
> in the image of God he created him;
> male and female he created them.

And God blessed them. And God said to them, "Be fruitful and multiply and fill the earth and subdue it, and have dominion over the fish of the sea and over the birds of the heavens and over every living thing that moves on the earth." And God said, "Behold, I have given you every plant yielding seed that is on the face of all the earth, and every tree with seed in its fruit. You shall have them for food. And to every beast of the earth and to every bird of the heavens and to everything that creeps on the earth, everything that has the breath of life, I have given every green plant for food." And it was so. And God saw everything that he had made, and behold, it was very good. And there was evening and there was morning, the sixth day.[2]

CREATION

"And God said . . . And God said . . . And God said. . . ." It is impossible to miss the recurring cadence in the creation narrative that God made everything there is—the entire universe and all

[2] Gen. 1:3–31.

that it contains—by the power of his spoken Word. God's Word is powerful! It is so powerful that nothing can resist it. In fact, God's Word has life-giving power. By it God spoke light into being and separated it from darkness. By it God created all living beings, including humanity, and he made humans, both male and female, in his image and likeness. In fact, the insight that the Word, or wisdom, was with God at creation was not new with John. A famous passage in the Old Testament book of Proverbs taught as much:

> "The Lord possessed me at the beginning of his work,
> the first of his acts of old.
> Ages ago I was set up,
> at the first, before the beginning of the earth.
> When there were no depths I was brought forth,
> when there were no springs abounding with water.
> Before the mountains had been shaped,
> before the hills, I was brought forth,
> before he had made the earth with its fields,
> or the first of the dust of the world.
> When he established the heavens, I was there;
> when he drew a circle on the face of the deep,
> when he made firm the skies above,
> when he established the fountains of the deep,
> when he assigned to the sea its limit,
> so that the waters might not transgress his command,
> when he marked out the foundations of the earth,
> then I was beside him, like a master workman,
> and I was daily his delight,
> rejoicing before him always,
> rejoicing in his inhabited world
> and delighting in the children of man."[3]

For this reason, it is unobjectionable—in fact, virtually self-evident—for John to say, "In the beginning was the Word, and the

[3] Prov. 8:22–31. Note, however, that John's assertion that the Word eternal both preexisted and coexisted with God and was at work with him at creation even goes beyond the personification of wisdom in the book of Proverbs. See Andreas J. Köstenberger, *John*, Baker Exegetical Commentary on the New Testament (Grand Rapids, MI: Baker, 2004), 25–29.

Word was with God, and the Word was God." For if the Word had not existed in the beginning, how could God have created everything *through his spoken Word*? For this reason, it is manifestly true that "the Word was with God" in the beginning. What is more, if the Word was already with God—the eternal, infinite, ever-living God—then the Word, too, shares God's eternal preexistence before all time. These are lofty thoughts to entertain, because all thinking about God—theology—takes us outside the realm of our own human creaturely existence and lifts us up into an entirely higher realm—the realm of the divine.

But wait! If "the Word was *with* God," does that mean that the Word enjoys an existence that is in some sense distinct *from* God? How else could it be said that "the Word was with God"? So are there then *two* gods? Impossible! Every Jewish child knows that "the LORD our God, the LORD is one."[4] But here John says, "and the Word *was God*." The Word was God! The Word through whom God spoke into being everything that exists, that Word was himself God. This is a remarkable declaration. What is only latent in the Genesis creation narrative[5] John makes glaringly explicit in the opening words of his Gospel, not that there are actually *two* gods—a notion irreconcilable with Jewish monotheism (the belief in only *one* God)—but that God exists *in community*: "the Word was *with* God." There are *two persons*, the *Word* and *God*, who are *both God* (Greek *theos*; i.e., they are both divine), yet these two persons are *one God* (i.e., they share one divine essence).[6]

All Things Were Made through Him

But who is this Word? Who is this Word who is not only *with* God but is *himself* God? John's introduction continues, "He was in the beginning with God. All things were made through him, and without him was not anything made that was made. In him was life,

[4] Deut. 6:4.

[5] See also the reference to "the Spirit of God . . . hovering over the face of the waters" in Gen. 1:2.

[6] As becomes clear later in John's Gospel, the Godhead, in fact, includes three persons, Father, Son, and Spirit; the Holy Spirit, like the Son, is invested with deity as well (cf. John 14:26; 16:7). See also Jesus's assertion in John 10:30, "I and the Father are one" (Greek *hen*, one entity).

and the life was the light of men. The light shines in the darkness, and the darkness has not overcome it."[7] It's as if John were saying, "Let that truth sink in for a moment. Let me repeat that one more time: 'He was in the beginning with God.'"[8] Do you understand how momentous a declaration this is? Not only was the Word "with" God in the beginning; the Word also had an integral part in God's creation of the universe: "*All* things were made *through him*."[9]

Conversely, "without him was not any thing made that was made."[10] Wow! Amazing! There is nothing in the universe that was made without the Word. The Word was the exclusive agent of creation, the only medium through which everything that exists came into being. So intimate is the relationship between the Creator and the Word that they work hand-in-glove throughout the process of creation. As the writer of the book of Hebrews affirms, grasping the truth of these assertions takes faith: "*By faith* we understand that the universe was created by the word of God, so that what is seen was not made out of things that are visible."[11] But more on that later.

Now let's get back to our original question. Who is that Word? Before revealing the identity of the preexistent, creative, *divine* Word, John takes a moment to elaborate on the life-giving characteristic of the Word. "In him was life."[12] He had life in himself. No one gave him life; he existed before all time, from eternity. What is more, if he had life in himself, he retained the prerogative to give life to whomever he, and God the Creator, chose to give it. This includes plants and animals, but first and foremost people, the man and the woman, who, according to the creation narrative, were made as God's very special creatures in his own likeness. So every human being owes his or her existence not only to God, but also to that Word who was in the beginning with God and served as his exclusive agent of creation.

---

[7] John 1:2–5.
[8] John 1:2.
[9] John 1:3a.
[10] John 1:3b.
[11] Heb. 11:3.
[12] John 1:4a.

As John continues, not only did the Word have life in himself, that life was "the light of men."[13] This motif mirrors the original creation narrative, which also began with light:

> And God said, "Let there be light," and there was light. And God saw that the light was good. And God separated the light from the darkness. God called the light Day, and the darkness he called Night. And there was evening and there was morning, the first day.[14]

Later, on the fourth day of creation, God made lights to rule the night and the day, so that life could exist and flourish.[15] But now John says that, ultimately, "the light of men" is none other than the Word himself. He illumines not only our physical surroundings but also our very hearts and souls. That light "shines in the darkness, and the darkness has not overcome it."[16]

The Light Shines in the Darkness, and the Darkness Has Not Overcome It

In the Genesis creation narrative, God "separated the light from the darkness" and "called the light Day, and the darkness he called Night."[17] It appears that both light and darkness, day and night, peacefully coexist in their respective God-assigned spheres. Night is not better than day, nor is day better than night; both have their place and exist in a noncompetitive relationship.

So why, then, does John say that "the light shines in the darkness, *and the darkness has not overcome it*?"[18] Why would the darkness want to *overcome* the light?[19] Here we see the first indication of a struggle between the light and the darkness in John's Gospel, a harbinger of the cosmos engaging in a titanic conflict

[13] John 1:4b.
[14] Gen. 1:3–5.
[15] Gen. 1:14–18.
[16] John 1:5.
[17] Gen. 1:4–5.
[18] John 1:5.
[19] Note that some translate the Greek word underlying "overcome" (*katalambanō*) as "has not *understood* it," but this translation is less likely. See Köstenberger, *John*, 31n37.

between darkness and light. But this is not a struggle between equal powers. Just as in the physical realm darkness is no match for light—try turning on a light switch in a dark room and see who wins!—so also in the spiritual realm light keeps on shining, and darkness cannot prevail against it. But now John affirms the light's victory over the darkness, not as a *timeless principle*, but as a *historical certainty*: "The darkness *has not overcome it* [i.e., the light]." In human history, the light has prevailed. The light has triumphed!

"Okay, then," you say, "tell me, who is this light?" Well, one of the things light does is *reveal*. As long as you're in the dark about something, you have no idea what is going on, but when you shine the light on it, you can see clearly. The fourth Evangelist is not quite ready to reveal the identity of "the light" (obviously, he is speaking of "light" in a personal sense that transcends the original reference to creation). But if you skip to the end of the introduction to John's Gospel, you can catch a glimpse of the revelatory function of the light: "No one has ever seen God; the only God, who is at the Father's side, *he has made him known*."[20] From this you learn that, while no one has ever seen God, who is invisible to the human eye, the only God—the Word—who is at the Father's side ("with" him),[21] *he* has made God known. This means that the Word, who has a privileged place and preeminent role in *creation*, also has an equally privileged place and preeminent role in *revelation*, specifically, in the end-time revelation of the invisible God in the form of human flesh.

JESUS IS THE WAY

You remember the interchange between Jesus and his followers in the upper room? Jesus had just told his disciples that they knew the way to where he was going. But Thomas retorted, "Lord, we do not know where you are going. How can we know the way?"[22]

[20]John 1:18.
[21]John 1:1.
[22]John 14:5.

Jesus went on to explain that he himself was the way to the Father. But Philip still didn't understand and asked Jesus to show him the Father. Then Jesus stated even more plainly, "Have I been with you so long, and you still do not know me, Philip? Whoever has seen me has seen the Father. How can you say, 'Show us the Father'? Do you not believe that I am in the Father and the Father is in me? The words that I say to you I do not speak on my own authority, but the Father who dwells in me does his works."[23]

How often are we like the disciples in that story? Like them, we fail to realize that, while no one has ever seen God, Jesus has come to reveal God to us and tell his story. Perhaps you have heard the anecdote of the child (I'm paraphrasing) who listened to her mother's bedtime story assuring her of God's presence and calling her to trust in him. When the mother was done, the child said, "Mom, I know God is always with me, but right now, I need someone with skin on." The great news is that Jesus is God "with skin on"! He's the incarnate Word, the Word made flesh, the Word that shows us the Father. When we want to know God and his ways, we look to the incarnate Word.

When I (Andreas) was a young Christian, I once spent several months engaging in a thorough study of Jesus's words and actions in all four Gospels. I wanted to see how Jesus responded to questions directed at him and how he handled unexpected or trying situations. I wish I had time to elaborate on my findings, but, in short, I found the study extremely rewarding and would challenge you to embark on a similar study. Still, one thing stands out: in Jesus I found a concrete picture of how God reacts to various human situations and models how we should live.

You see, the Gospels don't give us the gospel in the form of abstract propositions or a list of creedal formulas. Instead, God, through the four Evangelists, has given us an incredible treasure trove: reliable accounts of Jesus, God-in-the-flesh, pitching his tent among us and showing us how God would have us live. To be sure, we are not Jesus. But in the power of the Holy Spirit, we can aim

---

[23] John 14:9–10.

consciously to follow the example of the God-man who once lived in our midst and still empowers the mission of his people.

But we're getting ahead of ourselves in our story. In the flow of the narrative, the evangelist has still withheld the identity of the light. And to continue the suspense, he turns to introduce another character—a man who came to bear witness to that light, a man named John.

12

WITNESS: A MAN NAMED JOHN

JOHN 1:6–7, 15

There was a man sent from God, whose name was John. He came as a witness, to bear witness about the light, that all might believe through him. He was not the light, but came to bear witness about the light. . . .

(John bore witness about him, and cried out, "This was he of whom I said, 'He who comes after me ranks before me, because he was before me.'")

C. AD 29

A Man Sent from God

In the first verses of John's introduction, we read about the majestic, magnificent Word who is instrumental in God's monumental act of creation. It seems as if John is building up to reveal the precise identity of that Word at any moment. But then, the fourth Evangelist suddenly shifts course (or so it seems). Rather than tell us who the Word is, he introduces a new character, "a man . . . whose name was John."[1] In and of himself, this man might have been rather ordinary—unlike the Word, who was *God*, he was

[1] John 1:6.

a mere *man*. What made him important, as with Old Testament figures commissioned by God (such as prophets), was the fact that John was "sent from God."

In John's Gospel, the word *send* is exceedingly significant. The Gospel mentions four missions: (1) Jesus's mission; (2) the disciples' mission; (3) the Holy Spirit's mission; and (4) the mission of John the Baptist.[2] The fact that John's is one of only four missions featured in the Gospel highlights the importance of his mission. John was "sent from God." His mission was derived not from mere human appointment; God himself sent him. Later, we will hear that John was "the voice of one crying out in the wilderness," in keeping with Isaiah's prediction.[3] Here the fourth Evangelist (whose name was also John) introduces the Baptist simply as "a man . . . whose name was John."[4] This characterization is rather understated, since anytime God sends anyone to do anything, that person's mission takes on great significance because it was initiated by none other than God himself.

He Came as a Witness

So, then, what was John's mission? We have already seen that in the other Gospels, such as Luke, John's primary role was that of heralding the coming of the Messiah, specifically by baptizing people as a sign of repentance. He was "John *the Baptist*" (or, perhaps more accurately, "John *the Baptizer*"!). The fourth Evangelist, however, emphasizes a different aspect of John's purpose. John's baptism of Jesus is mentioned later in the narrative only in passing,[5] and John's Gospel nowhere calls John "the Baptist" or "the Baptizer." Instead, the primary function ascribed to him is that of *witness*. The following

---

[2] For more on the "mission motif" in John's Gospel, see Andreas Köstenberger's published dissertation, *The Missions of Jesus and the Disciples according to the Fourth Gospel* (Grand Rapids, MI: Eerdmans, 1998).

[3] John 1:23; cf. Isa. 40:3.

[4] The fourth Evangelist at times does not mention a prominent character in his Gospel by name so as to simplify the cast and prevent confusion between more than one character with the same name. In the present case, he calls John the Baptist simply John while identifying himself not as John but as "the disciple Jesus loved." He does the same with Jesus's mother, Mary, whom he calls simply "Jesus's mother." John's readers would have known that Jesus's mother was called Mary, in any case, just as they would have known that John wrote the Gospel.

[5] John 1:31. Even here his primary purpose is that of witness; see v. 34.

two verses attribute this function to John three times: "He came as a *witness*, to bear *witness* about the light, that all might believe through him. He was not the light, but came to bear *witness* about the light."[6]

What does this shift in characterization from baptizer to witness signify? In his Gospel, the fourth Evangelist is supremely concerned with the identity of Jesus. All that matters to him is who Jesus truly is, and the truth about Jesus is what must compel each person to render his or her own verdict. Who is Jesus? Is he the Messiah, the Son of God, as John's purpose statement claims?[7] Or is he a blasphemer, usurper, and deceiver, as the Jewish authorities alleged when clamoring for his crucifixion?[8]

To adjudicate this matter, John's Gospel presents Jesus's entire ministry as a gigantic court trial in which a series of witnesses testify against the unbelieving world (including the Jewish authorities) in support of Jesus's messianic claims.[9] John is one of these witnesses, who also include God the Father, Jesus's miracles, the Holy Spirit, Moses and the Scriptures, the disciples, and the fourth Evangelist himself.[10] This phalanx of witnesses constitutes

---

[6]John 1:7–8.

[7]John 20:30–31.

[8]John 19:7.

[9]See Andrew T. Lincoln, *Truth on Trial: The Lawsuit Motif in the Fourth Gospel* (Peabody, MA: Hendrickson, 2000); Andreas J. Köstenberger, *A Theology of John's Gospel and Letters*, Biblical Theology of the New Testament (Grand Rapids, MI: Zondervan, 2009), chap. 11.

[10]The preeminent passage indicating the series of witnesses to Jesus in John's Gospel is John 5:31–47:

> "If I alone bear witness about myself, my testimony is not true. There is another who bears witness about me, and I know that the testimony that he bears about me is true. You sent to *John*, and he has borne witness to the truth. Not that the testimony that I receive is from man, but I say these things so that you may be saved. He was a burning and shining lamp, and you were willing to rejoice for a while in his light. But the testimony that I have is greater than that of John. For the *works* that the Father has given me to accomplish, the very works that I am doing, bear witness about me that the Father has sent me. And the *Father* who sent me has himself borne witness about me. His voice you have never heard, his form you have never seen, and you do not have his word abiding in you, for you do not believe the one whom he has sent. You search the *Scriptures* because you think that in them you have eternal life; and it is they that bear witness about me, yet you refuse to come to me that you may have life. I do not receive glory from people. But I know that you do not have the love of God within you. I have come in my Father's name, and you do not receive me. If another comes in his own name, you will receive him. How can you believe, when you receive glory from one another and do not seek the glory that comes from the only God? Do not think that I will accuse you to the Father. There is one who accuses you: *Moses*, on whom you have set your hope. For if you believed Moses, you would believe me; for he wrote of me. But if you do not believe his writings, how will you believe my words?"

See also John 15:26–27: "But when the Helper comes, whom I will send to you from the Father, the *Spirit* of truth, who proceeds from the Father, he will bear witness about me. And *you also*

overwhelming proof that Jesus was in fact the Messiah and that the unbelieving world is eminently culpable for rejecting such a "great cloud of witnesses."[11] We will talk more about this matter in the next chapter.

To Bear Witness about the Light

For now, we will investigate John's witness a bit further. In what, exactly, did his witness consist? What did he bear witness *to*? In the context of the introduction to John's Gospel, the Evangelist simply says that John came to bear witness "about the light, that all might believe through him."[12] The question immediately arises: Docs the light really need a witness? Does "the light that shines in the darkness" and that the darkness cannot overcome[13] need any attestation, beyond the fact that it manifestly dispels darkness and prevails over all false rivals? In one sense, it does not. As Jesus himself later points out, his witness regarding his own identity is true in and of itself.[14]

Yet at the same time, it was firmly embedded in the Jewish consciousness that a man's testimony is invalid except for two or three witnesses.[15] For this reason, John's witness plays an exceedingly important role. For, you see, when Jesus appears on the scene just a few verses later, he does not come unheralded. He is unlike the missionary I (Andreas) encountered on the streets of Vienna, Austria, my hometown, shortly after becoming a Christian. When I asked him, "Who sent you?" he said, "No one. I just went." Jesus was not like that. He was sent. In fact, Jesus's favorite, ubiquitous appellation of God the Father in John's Gospel is "the one who sent me." John was also sent. And John bore witness to Jesus, "the light." Later, Jesus calls John "a lamp" that was shining "for a while."[16] The lamp illumined the light.

---

will bear witness, because you have been with me from the beginning"; and John 21:24: "This is the *disciple* who is bearing witness about these things [i.e., the fourth Evangelist], and who has written these things, and we know that his testimony is true."

[11] Heb. 12:1.
[12] John 1:7.
[13] John 1:5.
[14] John 8:14.
[15] Deut. 17:6; 19:15.
[16] John 5:35.

Now notice the difference: the witness's task is comparatively humble. He simply tells others what hc has seen and heard and what he knows. So John focused people's attention not on himself as the lamp but on what the lamp *illumines*, in this case, "the light." John bore witness to this light, which is somehow related to the Word who was with God in the beginning and who was himself God. Then, before moving on, the fourth Evangelist clarifies once again, "He [i.e., John the witness] was *not* the light, but came to bear witness *about* the light."[17]

That said, the Evangelist moves on, at last, to explore and unpack the identity of the light.[18] Later in the introduction, he returns to John's witness one more time by way of a brief aside: "John bore witness about him, and cried out, 'This was he of whom I said, "He who comes after me ranks before me, because he was before me."'"[19] In this way, the Evangelist makes clear that, even though John was slightly older in terms of physical age (perhaps by about six months), in light of the Word's eternal preexistence with God in the beginning, there was no contest: the Word was before John, and therefore ranked above him, even though the enfleshed Word commenced his ministry later than John.

In the remainder of John's Gospel, we hear of John the Baptist several more times. When the Evangelist commences his narrative of John's and Jesus's ministries, he recounts John's denial that he was the Messiah and records John's witness that Jesus is the "Lamb of God, who takes away the sin of the world."[20] He records how John pointed several of his followers to Jesus, and they stopped following the Baptist and began to follow Jesus instead.[21] Later, when questions arose as to the relative greatness of John and Jesus among John's followers, John called himself "the friend of the bridegroom" who must decrease so the groom (Jesus) may increase.[22] Then, as mentioned, Jesus called John a "burning and

[17]John 1:8.
[18]John 1:9–14.
[19]John 1:15; cf. vv. 26–27.
[20]John 1:29, 36.
[21]John 1:35–37.
[22]John 3:25–30.

shining lamp"[23] who had "borne witness to the truth."[24] The last time we encounter John in this Gospel is at the end of chapter 10, where many bear witness to John, testifying, "John did no sign, but everything that John said about this man was true."[25]

WITNESS THE WORD

John is the first—but certainly not the last—witness to Jesus in John's Gospel. He takes his place among a long procession of witnesses who appear on the witness stand to testify in support of Jesus's messianic claims in the grand trial that calls the world—including the Jewish people—to account for rejecting Jesus.

Plenty of evidence supports Jesus's messianic claims. First, God sent John, the "voice crying in the wilderness," to testify regarding Jesus. Then Jesus himself testified, as did his startling feats—turning water into wine, clearing the temple, healing the centurion's son, healing the lame man, feeding the multitudes, opening the eyes of the man born blind, and raising Lazarus from the dead. Moses and the Scriptures, God the Father, the Holy Spirit, and the disciples (including the fourth Evangelist) also testified. The evidence in support of Jesus's messianic claims is overwhelming.

This is the burden of John's "witness motif." God did not fail to back up Jesus's mission. He provided ample evidence for people to place their faith in him. If people still rejected Jesus, they had no one to blame but themselves and their own sinful rebellion. Theodicy—the justification of God—stands behind the fourth Evangelist's characterization of John the Baptist and the entire plot line of the Gospel. Will you and I believe? We have every reason to do so.

[23] John 5:35.
[24] John 5:33.
[25] John 10:41.

13

INCARNATION: THE WORD BECAME FLESH

JOHN 1:9–14

The true light, which gives light to everyone, was coming into the world. He was in the world, and the world was made through him, yet the world did not know him. He came to his own, and his own people did not receive him. But to all who did receive him, who believed in his name, he gave the right to become children of God, who were born, not of blood nor of the will of the flesh nor of the will of man, but of God.

And the Word became flesh and dwelt among us, and we have seen his glory, glory as of the only Son from the Father, full of grace and truth.

6 OR 5 BC

The Coming of the Light into the World

Now that John the Evangelist has cleared away the brush by identifying John the Baptist as a witness to the light, he is ready to move on to discuss the identity of the true light himself. Because the Word has light in himself,[1] he can give light to others. In fact, the true light "gives light to everyone."[2] This statement is open

[1]John 1:4.
[2]John 1:9a.

to misunderstanding, because it may suggest that everyone will actually receive the light and walk in it. As we will see shortly, however, this is not in fact what took place when that light "was coming into the world."[3] Some will receive the light, while others—many—will reject it.[4] But first, let's explore the significance of the "coming" of the light "into the world."

In a sense, this phraseology is still a rather inconspicuous, oblique way of referring to the creative Word's monumental, transformative visitation to the globe to which he gave birth in ages past. John takes his time to probe the magnitude of transcendence being transmuted into immanence, of the Creator entering his creation, of light invading the darkness—the moral darkness—into which the world has tragically fallen. The creative tension between light and darkness, present in the Genesis creation narrative, rears its head in a new, escalated fashion when applied to the stark contrast between the "true light"—the genuine, pristine, pure light—and the evil, fallen, sinful world that he entered.

The World's Rejection of the Light

"For God so loved the world . . . ," the fourth Evangelist writes later in his Gospel.[5] Wonderful news indeed! And yet, what we must not miss in this exhilarating declaration is that God loved the world not because it was so worthy and deserving of his love but because it was so needy and desperate for it, whether it realized it or not. As the fourth Evangelist writes, "He was in the world, and the world was made through him, yet the world did not know him. He came to his own, and his own people did not receive him."[6] How tragic! The very world the Word had made failed to recognize him when he paid his visit! The cosmos languished estranged from the Word. He came to his own but met mostly rejection.

Significantly, here the fourth Evangelist highlights that the

---

[3]John 1:9b.
[4]John 1:10–13. See Andreas J. Köstenberger, *John*, Baker Exegetical Commentary on the New Testament (Grand Rapids, MI: Baker, 2004), 35–36.
[5]John 3:16.
[6]John 1:10–11.

coming of the Messiah was an event of cosmic proportions, affecting not only Israel but all of humanity, and even all of creation. He also highlights the deep irony of both the Word's "own *things*"[7]—that is, the created universe and, in particular, sinful humanity at large—as well as his "own *people*,"[8] who reject the coming of the light. Later in his Gospel, John elaborates on the reason for this rejection:

> And this is the judgment: the light has come into the world, and people loved the darkness rather than the light *because their works were evil*. For everyone *who does wicked things* hates the light and does not come to the light, *lest his works should be exposed*. But whoever does what is true comes to the light, so that it may be clearly seen that his works have been carried out in God.[9]

Sinful humanity—including even God's own people Israel—rejected the visitation of the light because "their works were evil." Just as Adam and Eve hid in the garden after rebelling against God,[10] so even today humanity hides from the Creator. And when the Creator came into the world as light invades darkness, people scurried in every direction to avoid having their wickedness exposed in the light. This statement represents an incredibly profound analysis of the human predicament apart from God.

The Believing Remnant's Reception of the Light

And yet, in the midst of this tragic rejection of the light by a world in darkness, we see a bright spot, a silver lining. Not everyone had rejected the light. There were those—a believing remnant—who received the light: "But to all who did receive him, who believed in his name, he gave the right to become children of God, who were born, not of blood nor of the will of the flesh nor of the will of man, but of God."[11] In many ways, we have arrived at the

[7] Greek *idia*, neuter plural, John 1:11.
[8] Greek *idioi*, masculine plural, John 1:11.
[9] John 3:19–21.
[10] Gen. 2:8–10.
[11] John 1:12–13.

climactic affirmation of John's introduction to his Gospel. In fact, verse 12 has been called the "pivot" of John's prologue, the affirmation on which John's entire introduction—indeed, his entire story—turns.[12]

Some *received* the light and *believed* in his name, and in response, he gave them the right to become children of God. In the Old Testament, the phrase "children of God" referred in a special sense to God's people Israel.[13] They were God's chosen people. To be sure, Israel rejected God at many points in her history, but they were still God's chosen people by virtue of the series of covenants God had made with Abraham, Moses, and David, by virtue of the miraculous deliverance God effected at the exodus, and by virtue of his giving of the law at Sinai.

But now, it appears, the definition of "children of God" has shifted. "Children of God" now refers to everyone who has received *him*, who has believed in *his name*, whether that person is ethnically part of God's people Israel or not. Just like the reference to the light enlightening every person in verse 9, the reference to God's children as those who believe in the name of the Word strikes a decidedly universal (though not universalistic) note.[14] The light's coming into the world indeed has global implications and far-reaching consequences that far transcend the scope of the Jewish people. Their rejection of the Messiah has opened the door for everyone who receives the Messiah and believes in his name to become children of God and receive eternal life. Such people are "born, not of blood nor of the will of the flesh nor of the will of man, but of God."[15] They are, literally and spiritually, born of God as those who have received a second, spiritual birth through the Holy Spirit's work of regeneration.[16]

---

[12] R. Alan Culpepper, "The Pivot of John's Prologue," *New Testament Studies* 27 (1980–1981): 1–31.
[13] E.g., Deut. 14:1.
[14] By this we mean that the Bible, including the Gospel of John, does not teach *universalism*, that is, the notion that all people, regardless of their faith or lack thereof in Christ, will one day be saved. The exact opposite is the case. In John 14:6, Jesus states categorically, "I am the way, and the truth, and the life. No one comes to the Father except through me."
[15] John 1:13.
[16] John will develop this theme later in and through Jesus's conversation with Nicodemus in chap. 3 of his Gospel (see esp. vv. 3–8).

The Enfleshment of the Word

With this, we have arrived at the second major climax in the introduction to John's Gospel.[17] At last, the Word's identity is unpacked in further detail: "And the Word became flesh and dwelt among us, and we have seen his glory, glory as of the only Son from the Father, full of grace and truth."[18] So this is how the light came into the world! The Word became flesh. The Word—the exclusive agent of creation, God's powerful speech and self-expression, the way in which the Creator effected the coming into being of that which was nothing until God spoke—that Word clothed himself with flesh.

In the original Greek, the word translated "flesh" (*sarx*) is almost crude. The expression refers to creatureliness in its material nature opposite the realm of the spirit. As Jesus said to Nicodemus, "That which is born of flesh is flesh, and that which is born of spirit is spirit."[19] The fourth Evangelist chooses not the word *sōma* (translated "body") but the word translated "flesh," in order to distinguish it from the spiritual realm. The preexistent Word, John announces, entered the realm of the creatures he himself had made.

Now it is important here to understand what John is *not* saying. He is *not* saying that the Word, when he became flesh, *ceased to be the Word*. Instead, the Word *took on* flesh in the sense that he remained the Word while adding to himself a fleshly nature. Later on, the church would develop the doctrine of the dual natures of Jesus, the God-man, as combining within himself both a divine and a human nature. But that theological formulation came centuries later. For now, John presents the Messiah as the Word-become-flesh, as fully divine and fully human, *both at the same time*. While hard to grasp intellectually, it is nonetheless true historically and theologically. "The Word became flesh."

What does the Word's enfleshment signify? What does it all

---

[17] The first one, as just mentioned, occurs in v. 12 with the declaration that all those who received the light/Word and believed in his name were given the right to become God's children.
[18] John 1:14.
[19] John 3:6. Authors' translation.

mean? Why did the Word become flesh? Several aspects of an answer come to mind. First, the Word's enfleshment means a temporary leaving of the glory that the Word had from eternity with God the Father. This amounted to a sacrifice of astounding magnitude. At times, we marvel at missionaries leaving behind the comfort of their homes, extended families, and native cultures for the sake of proclaiming the gospel to an unreached people group. Any such sacrifice, while significant and noble, pales by comparison with the sacrifice of the Word leaving behind the glory he shared with the Father before the world began.[20]

Second, the Word's enfleshment means solidarity and identification. Rather than remaining in the realm of the spirit, with its glorious transcendence, loftiness, and bliss, untouched by human sin and exalted above all suffering, the Word entered experientially into the world of human beings, with all that this entails. The Word became a human being. He was tired from his journey.[21] He was thirsty.[22] He wept.[23] He died![24] In this way, Jesus could identify with our human predicament in a way he never could before.[25]

The writer of Hebrews explores a third, related entailment of Jesus's humanity, the ability to provide atonement for sin as a sinless divine-human high priest:

> Since therefore the children share in flesh and blood, he himself likewise partook of the same things, that through death he might destroy the one who has the power of death, that is, the devil, and deliver all those who through fear of death were subject to lifelong slavery. For surely it is not angels that he helps, but he helps the offspring of Abraham. *Therefore he had to be made like his brothers in every respect, so that he might become a merciful and faithful high priest in the service of God, to make propitiation for the sins of the*

[20]John 17:5, 24.
[21]John 4:6.
[22]John 4:7; 19:28.
[23]John 11:35.
[24]John 19:30.
[25]See Marianne Meye Thompson, *The Humanity of Jesus in the Fourth Gospel* (Philadelphia: Fortress, 1988).

> *people*. For because he himself has suffered when tempted, he is able to help those who are being tempted.[26]

The Word took on flesh because only in this way could he identify with humanity as a merciful and faithful high priest who makes atonement for the sins of the people. In other words, at the heart of the true meaning of the incarnation stands the cross. Why did Jesus enter the earth as a baby? Why did God come into the world as a crying infant in swaddling cloths, laid in a manger? *Because of the cross*. Because of our salvation. For this is what *Yeshua* ("Jesus") means: "the Lord is salvation."

The "Tenting" of the Word

We could reflect on the meaning of the incarnation much longer, but for now we must move on. Not only did the Word become flesh, the Word "dwelt among us, and we have seen his glory, glory as of the only Son from the Father, full of grace and truth."[27] By becoming flesh, the Word took up residence in the world, and in particular among God's people Israel. He "dwelt among us" (Greek *skēnoō*), or more literally, he "tented among us."

Apart from the universal sense of taking up residence in this dark and sinful world, the word *skēnoō* also has specialized meaning by harking back to manifestations of God's presence among his people Israel in Old Testament times. In the garden, of course, Adam and Eve enjoyed unmitigated fellowship with God.[28] Then, after their rebellion, God cast them out from his presence.[29] Later, God dwelt among his people in the tabernacle and still later in the temple. For the Jews in Jesus's day, the primary sanctuary where worship had to be rendered was the Jerusalem temple.

And yet, John's Gospel asserts that this Word who became flesh and "tented" among his people supplanted all previous manifestations of God's presence. In the second chapter of his Gospel, John

---

[26] Heb. 2:14–18.
[27] John 1:14.
[28] Cf. the description of "the Lord God walking in the garden in the cool of the day" (Gen. 3:8).
[29] Gen. 3:24.

records Jesus's clearing of the temple and his ensuing confrontation with the Jewish authorities who called him to account:

> So the Jews said to him, "What sign do you show us for doing these things?" Jesus answered them, "Destroy this temple, and in three days I will raise it up." The Jews then said, "It has taken forty-six years to build this temple, and will you raise it up in three days?" *But he was speaking about the temple of his body.*[30]

Similarly, in chapter 4, when the Samaritan woman seeks to divert Jesus from probing her sinful past (and present), Jesus tells her,

> Woman, believe me, the hour is coming when neither on this mountain nor in Jerusalem will you worship the Father. You worship what you do not know; we worship what we know, for salvation is from the Jews. But the hour is coming, and is now here, when the true worshipers will worship the Father in spirit and truth, for the Father is seeking such people to worship him. God is spirit, and those who worship him must worship in spirit and truth.[31]

All of this means that Jesus—the Word-become-flesh who "tented" among his people—has now become the new temple, the new and sole proper focus of all human worship. The Jerusalem temple, along with all other human sanctuaries, has become obsolete. Proper worship must now be rendered "in spirit and truth" and be directed toward the new "temple"—Jesus. For, as Paul writes in Colossians, in Jesus "all the fullness of Deity dwells in bodily form."[32]

The Glory of the Word

As we have seen, in Luke's Gospel the glory of the Lord shone around the shepherds when the angel appeared to them to announce the Messiah's birth.[33] In John's Gospel, glory is centered

[30] John 2:18–21.
[31] John 4:21–24.
[32] Col. 2:9 (NASB).
[33] Luke 2:9.

first and foremost on God the Father and then on Jesus the Son. Jesus reveals the Father's glory, as well as his own, in a variety of ways throughout his earthly ministry, most notably through a series of signs. Thus, after witnessing Jesus's first sign—the turning of water into wine at the wedding at Cana—we read that "[t]his, the first of his signs, Jesus did at Cana in Galilee, and manifested his glory. And his disciples believed in him."[34]

This later statement helps us understand the fourth Evangelist's pronouncement immediately following his declaration that the Word had now taken up residence among God's people: "we have seen his glory, glory as of the only Son from the Father, full of grace and truth."[35] The "we" in this statement most likely includes the fourth Evangelist (the apostle John) and the other apostles, who belonged to that Jewish remnant that received the Word-made-flesh and believed in his name. The word for "seen" (Greek *theaomai*, from which we derive our word *theater*) is perhaps better rendered "perceived" in that many *saw* Jesus physically but only few perceived the *true* significance of Jesus's words and actions, that these revealed his messianic identity.

The Only Son from the Father

Jesus's glory was "as of the only Son from the Father."[36] He was, as the traditional rendering puts it, "the only begotten Son of God." More accurately, Jesus was the "one-of-a-kind" Son, the *unique* Son of God the Father.[37] Just as an only child is of great value to his parents, so Jesus's relationship with the Father was one of a kind. There is no one like him. His divine sonship is unique. In one sense, all believers are God's children,[38] but only Jesus is the Son of God in a messianic sense that also entails his deity.[39]

What is more, while at the outset John had stated that the

---

[34]John 2:11.
[35]John 1:14b.
[36]John 1:14b.
[37]See Köstenberger, *John*, 44.
[38]John 1:12.
[39]See John 20:17, where Jesus tells Mary Magdalene to tell his "brothers": "I am ascending to my Father and your Father, to my God and your God."

Word was with God and the Word was God, he now unveils that the Word relates to God as a Son to his Father. This intimate personal communion, in turn, enables the Son to make the Father known in an unparalleled way: "No one has ever seen God; the only God, *who is at the Father's side*, he has made him known."[40] Later on, John will use this close proximity to the object of revelation in a similar fashion to set apart his own witness to Jesus.[41]

The climactic verse of the Johannine prologue concludes by asserting that the Word-become-flesh is himself full of grace and truth. Since John further develops this assertion in verses 16–17 (see below), we will reserve comment on this set of attributes for the following chapter.

THE INCARNATION AND THE BABY IN THE MANGER

Matthew presents Jesus as the virgin-born Messiah. Luke depicts him as a lowly babe born in a manger and as the light of the nations. John casts Jesus as the incarnate Word. Must we choose between these varying portrayals as if only one (or two) of them could be true? Or does each of these characterizations catch a glimpse of an important aspect of Jesus's coming?

Rather than pitting one portrait against another, we see how John deepens our understanding of the Matthean and Lucan birth narratives. Jesus can be the virgin-born Messiah and Immanuel ("God with us"), as well as the Savior, Christ the Lord, because he is himself God and was already active at creation.

While it boggles the mind how the Creator of the universe can be born as a crying baby in a small Jewish village to a young girl and his adoptive father, a construction worker, John invites us to embrace this mystery and to affirm it by faith. As Charles Wesley wrote in his famous hymn, "Hark! The Herald Angels Sing," the invitation still stands: "veiled in flesh the Godhead see, hail th' incarnate deity." Will you join your voice to throngs who praise God for the mystery of the Word made flesh?

---

[40]John 1:18.
[41]John 13:23.

14

CULMINATION: THE LAW, GRACE, AND TRUTH

JOHN 1:16-17

For from his fullness we have all received, grace upon grace. For the law was given through Moses; grace and truth came through Jesus Christ.

GRACE INSTEAD OF GRACE

Sometimes people focus on all the things they gave up in order to follow Jesus. Listen to what the apostle Peter told Jesus in that regard:

> Peter began to say to him, "See, we have left everything and followed you." Jesus said, "Truly, I say to you, there is no one who has left house or brothers or sisters or mother or father or children or lands, for my sake and for the gospel, who will not receive a hundredfold now in this time, houses and brothers and sisters and mothers and children and lands, with persecutions, and in the age to come eternal life.[1]

Those who receive Jesus and believe in his name may have to leave behind their earthly possessions and even family relationships,

[1] Mark 10:28–30.

but they have received from his fullness "grace upon grace."[2] Jesus himself is full of grace and truth, and so believing in the One who is grace and truth conveys abundant grace and truth also to us.

In fact, the phrase "grace upon grace" has an important salvation-historical dimension. You see, we might think of the law as just a compilation of rules and regulations, in contrast to the grace Jesus introduced at his coming. But this is not John's point here. Rather, he is saying that, in the past, God conveyed his grace to Israel through the giving of the law. The law set Israel apart from other nations, for God had uniquely communicated to them his expectations, most notably in the "Ten Words" (the literal sense of "Ten Commandments"). Now, John continues, in the Messiah God has extended his grace to his people once again, this time in a climactic, eschatological (end-time) sense. It is, as the Greek reads more literally, an exchange of "grace *instead of* grace."[3]

This is indeed a great exchange. As the book of Hebrews elaborates in some detail, the old covenant sacrificial system and stipulations were rather cumbersome. Now, in Jesus, we have once-and-for-all forgiveness of sins and the indwelling Holy Spirit, who enables us to live our lives in keeping with God's expectations of us from within (albeit imperfectly). God has given us a new heart and a new Spirit! While we still sin due to our sin nature, God has set us free from the *bondage* of sin and introduced us already to the new, abundant life of the age to come.[4] This truly is amazing grace.

TRUTH

Jesus is also the truth. When Jesus stood before Pilate, the Roman governor asked dismissively, "What is truth?" and, without waiting for an answer, walked away.[5] This callousness or at least skepticism toward the possibility of absolute truth characterizes contemporary culture as well. We live in an age where pluralism, relativism, and postmodernism reign supreme. The "new tolerance" and

[2] John 1:16.
[3] The Greek word for "instead of" is *anti*.
[4] John 10:10.
[5] John 18:38.

the fascination with diversity claim that the only "heresy" that remains is belief in absolute truth.[6] Truth, our culture asserts, is merely perspectival in nature. Truth exists for *me*, and truth exists for *you*, but no truth compels all of us. We choose the truth we like and discard the truth we deem inconvenient or unpalatable. We are the masters of our fates and the captains of our souls, and no deity has the right to interfere. The only truth that stands is the truth we choose for ourselves. This libertarian notion enthrones the individual and endows that person with the right to choose what is right or wrong *for him or her*.

This view, of course, is a far cry from *Jesus's* truth, who is *the* truth. The notion of Jesus as truth centers on his revelation of God in and through his teaching, which emerges from his eternal communion with the Father. As John affirms, "No one has ever seen God; the only God, who is at the Father's side, he has made him known."[7] The truth conveyed by Jesus revolves around his sacrifice on the cross and entails his demand that his adherents deny themselves, take up their cross, and follow him. Truth is correspondence to reality. If the Gospels' witness to Jesus is true, Jesus is that reality. He is God, and we are not. He is our Maker and our Lord, and we owe our very existence and full allegiance to him.

GRACE AND TRUTH

Then, at last, in the penultimate verse of John's introduction, he finally reveals the secret. Who is the Word who was in the beginning with God, the light that came into the world, the Word who became flesh and dwelt among us, the Only Son from the Father? It is none other than Jesus Christ: "For the law was given through Moses; grace and truth came through Jesus Christ."[8] It is hard to think of a better way to sum up the two Testaments, the two covenants, and the two eras of salvation history. The law was the stan-

[6] On this issue, see Andreas J. Köstenberger and Michael J. Kruger, *The Orthodoxy of Heresy: How Contemporary Culture's Fascination with Diversity Has Reshaped Our Understanding of Early Christianity* (Wheaton, IL: Crossway, 2010).
[7] John 1:18.
[8] John 1:17.

dard of God's expectations for his people in Old Testament times. Now, grace and truth have come in and through Jesus Christ.

As mentioned, we best conceive of the relationship between these two periods—the era of the law and the age of Jesus Christ—not as stark contrast (though they possess undeniable differences) but as escalation and fulfillment. We can be glad we live in the age of Jesus Christ, in the era of full-orbed grace and truth. The person who lives in the sphere of grace and truth has nothing to fear. What is more, the gospel of Jesus Christ has the power to set us free. As Jesus told his would-be followers, "If you abide in my word, you are truly my disciples, and you will know the truth, and the truth will set you free."[9]

JOHN'S PROLOGUE AND MATTHEW'S AND LUKE'S BIRTH NARRATIVES

We're almost at the end of our study of the first days of Jesus. It's time to take stock of what we have learned. In the conclusion, we will reflect a bit more on the implications of Jesus's coming for us today. But first, now that we have finished looking at each of the stories of Jesus's first days in their own right (reading the birth narratives vertically), it will be helpful, perhaps even intriguing, to consider the Gospels with reference to each other (reading them horizontally).[10]

What is the relationship between John's opening words and Matthew's and Luke's birth narratives? Some of you may have been surprised even to find a treatment of John's Gospel in a book on the first days of Jesus, since conventionally we think of only Matthew and Luke as contributing to the subject. In fact, John doesn't even mention any of the things Matthew and Luke talk about: the virgin birth, the angels, the shepherds, the visit of the *magoi*, the escape to Egypt, and so on. John is completely silent about all these things. How can we account for this silence, and why did we choose to include a treatment of John's Gospel?

[9] John 8:31–32.

[10] On reading the Gospels vertically and horizontally, see Andreas J. Köstenberger and Justin Taylor, with Alexander Stewart, *The Final Days of Jesus: The Most Important Week of the Most Important Person Who Ever Lived* (Wheaton, IL: Crossway, 2014), 13–21.

We believe John makes an absolutely vital, even indispensable, contribution to the biblical witness regarding the origins of Jesus. While the fourth Evangelist omits an account of the virgin birth,[11] John probes the origins of Jesus far beyond his humble birth as a baby in a small Jewish village. John wants us to know that there is so much more than meets the eye when we behold the little baby in the manger. That baby who, of his own volition, lies helplessly in Mary's arms and nurses at her breast is in fact the Lord of the entire universe, the Maker of all things, and the Lord of all creation.[12]

As John makes clear, the story of Jesus begins not with the virgin birth, nor even with the miraculous virgin conception. The story of Jesus begins "in the beginning," when the Word already existed in eternity past with God in unspeakable glory. John lifts up our eyes far above the manger, the shepherds, the baby, and even the angels. He wants us to see the deity in the baby and the cross in the cradle, and he wants to help us understand that the birth of Jesus marks the arrival of grace and truth incarnate.

We have reason to believe that John was aware of Matthew's and Luke's Gospels, including their birth narratives, when he wrote. If so, John deliberately chose not to duplicate their material but instead opted to supplement their presentation by providing a deeper theological discussion of the meaning and significance of Jesus's coming into this world. You may think of John's method as "theological transposition," like transposing a melody from one

[11] We might note, though, that, if he wrote a decade or two after the other Gospels—as is commonly believed—and knew that two Gospels already included birth narratives of Jesus, he may have felt little reason to add a third, similar account. People may ask, then, why John—like the other Evangelists—still included an account of Jesus' death, but clearly, no telling of Jesus's life would be complete without recounting his death and resurrection, since those events are central to the gospel narrative.

[12] Cf. the last stanza of "Mary Did You Know?" (by Mark Lowry and Buddy Greene; copyright © 1991 Word Music, LLC, Rufus Music; all rights reserved; used by permission):

> Mary, did you know
> that your Baby Boy is Lord of all creation?
> Mary, did you know
> that your Baby Boy would one day rule the nations?
> Did you know
> that your Baby Boy is heaven's perfect Lamb?
> The sleeping Child you're holding is the Great I Am.

key to another.[13] What this means is that John presupposes the kind of material contained in the other Gospels—including the birth narratives—but takes their presentation one step—or several steps—further. As Clement of Alexandria famously put it, John wrote a "spiritual Gospel," by which he meant, essentially, a Gospel containing a deeper interpretation of the theological significance of Jesus's coming.[14]

Let's flesh this out a bit more and explore the ways in which John supplements and theologically transposes some of the material found in the Matthean and Lucan birth narratives.

No Place in the Inn

As we saw, Luke mentions, almost in passing, that there was no place for Mary and Joseph in the inn when the time had come for Jesus to be born.[15] In the flow of his narrative, Luke does not make it clear whether he is striking an ominous note or is merely recording a historical fact without drawing any theological significance from this detail.

John probes the matter further. Following his reference to the light coming into the world, John adds, "He was in the world, and the world was made through him, yet the world did not know him. He came to his own, and his own people did not receive him."[16] These verses make clear that Jesus's coming into the world was met with rejection, both by the world at large and by the Jewish people in particular. John later highlights that the world is a dark and inhospitable place and that people hide from the light because their deeds are wicked.[17] Together these comments provide a penetrating

[13] See Andreas J. Köstenberger, "John's Transposition Theology: Retelling the Story of Jesus in a Different Key," in *Earliest Christian History: History, Literature, and Theology. Essays from the Tyndale Fellowship in Honor of Martin Hengel*, ed. Michael F. Bird and Jason Maston, Wissenschaftliche Untersuchungen Zum Neuen Testament 2, book 320 (Tübingen: Mohr Siebeck, 2012), 191–226.

[14] Clement of Alexandria's full quote is as follows: "John, last of all, conscious that the outward facts had been set forth in the Gospels, was urged on by his disciples, and, divinely moved by the Spirit, composed a spiritual Gospel." Quoted in Eusebius, *Hist. eccl.*, trans. J. E. L. Oulton, vol. 2, Loeb Classical Library (1932; repr., Cambridge, MA: Harvard University Press, 1980), 6.14.7.

[15] Luke 2:7.

[16] John 1:10–11

[17] John 3:19–21.

analysis of the human condition, on which Luke's reference "no place for them in the inn" touches only obliquely.

God with Us

Matthew mentions that Jesus was Immanuel, "God with us,"[18] and Luke records the angelic testimony that "unto you is born this day in the city of David a Savior, who is Christ the Lord."[19] In these references to "God with us" and "Lord,"[20] Matthew and Luke hint at the deity of Jesus.

Again, John elaborates on Jesus's deity and on the way in which he manifests God's presence with his people. He speaks of the Word who was in the beginning with God[21] and affirms that this Word became flesh in Jesus and took up residence ("tented") among his people.[22] In this way, as discussed in the previous chapter, John establishes a biblical theology of the manifestation of God's presence with his people across salvation history, culminating in the incarnate Jesus's revelation of God the Father as the one-of-a-kind Son.[23]

The Glory of the Lord

As mentioned, in his birth narrative Luke speaks of the glory accompanying the appearance of the angels to the shepherds in the field. This "glory of the Lord" is mediated through the angels, who announce the good news of the Savior's birth to the shepherds.[24]

John, for his part, makes clear that the ultimate glory belongs to God and Jesus. In the introduction to his Gospel, the fourth Evangelist writes that "we have seen his glory, glory as of the only Son from the Father, full of grace and truth."[25] Jesus's glory consists in his revelation of God the Father in all his grace and truth. By making this statement at the very outset, John signals to

---

[18] Matt. 1:23.
[19] Luke 2:11.
[20] Greek *kyrios*.
[21] John 1:1.
[22] John 1:14.
[23] John 1:18; cf. Heb. 1:2.
[24] Luke 2:9.
[25] John 1:14.

his readers that, as they read his Gospel, they should view everything Jesus says and does throughout the Gospel as manifestations of God's glory, a glory characterized by grace and truth. As we noted briefly earlier, Philip, one of Jesus's first followers, failed to understand this reality. When Jesus declared that he is the way, the truth, and the life, Philip immediately questioned him:

> "Lord, show us the Father, and it is enough for us." Jesus said to him, "Have I been with you so long, and you still do not know me, Philip? Whoever has seen me has seen the Father. How can you say, 'Show us the Father'? Do you not believe that I am in the Father and the Father is in me? The words that I say to you I do not speak on my own authority, but the Father who dwells in me does his works. Believe me that I am in the Father and the Father is in me, or else believe on account of the works themselves."[26]

God's glory pervades Jesus's entire ministry and is revealed in and through the Word made flesh.

Light to the Nations

Luke makes reference to Jesus not only as the restorer of Israel and the fulfillment of God's promises to Abraham and David but also as a "light for revelation to the Gentiles."[27]

John further highlights the global and universal dimension of Jesus's coming. Jesus is "the true light, which gives light to everyone."[28] On the one hand, whoever receives him and believes in his name has the right to be counted among God's children.[29] On the other hand, the Jewish rejection of the Messiah represents the world's rejection of the light. In his "universal Gospel,"[30] John presents Jesus's coming on a cosmic scale, transcending the humble birth of a baby boy in a small Jewish village.[31]

---

[26] John 14:8–11; cf. v. 6.
[27] Luke 2:32; cf. Isa. 49:6.
[28] John 1:9.
[29] John 1:12.
[30] This title comes from Chester Warren Quimby, *John: The Universal Gospel* (New York: Macmillan, 1947).
[31] See, e.g., John 3:16: "God so loved *the world* . . . ," on which see Andreas J. Köstenberger, "Lifting Up the Son of Man and God's Love for the World: John 3:16 in Its Historical, Literary, and

My Father's House

Luke's narration of the story of the twelve-year-old Jesus in the temple reads as follows:

> After three days they found him in the temple, sitting among the teachers, listening to them and asking them questions. And all who heard him were amazed at his understanding and his answers. And when his parents saw him, they were astonished. And his mother said to him, "Son, why have you treated us so? Behold, your father and I have been searching for you in great distress." And he said to them, "Why were you looking for me? Did you not know that I must be in my Father's house?" And they did not understand the saying that he spoke to them.[32]

When Jesus's parents confront him in their anguish, Jesus responds, "Did you not know that I must be in my Father's house?" This reply provides a fascinating glimpse into the early consciousness of Jesus, who identified God explicitly as his "Father."

John develops Jesus's relationship as the Son of the Father in much greater detail. In his introduction, he speaks of Jesus's glory as being "of the only Son from the Father"[33] and later mentions that Jesus, who is "at the Father's side," has made him known.[34] John develops this characterization of Jesus as "the Son" throughout the remainder of his Gospel. In this way, John deepens Luke's presentation of Jesus as needing to be in his "Father's house."

BEARING WITNESS

Aren't you glad we have the story of the incarnation on good authority? Matthew could draw on a tradition going back to Joseph, Luke may well have heard it directly from Mary, and John was the closest disciple to Jesus during his earthly ministry. Each of these eyewitnesses bore testimony to Jesus's true identity, sharing their

---

Theological Contexts," in *Understanding the Times: New Testament Studies in the 21st Century: Essays in Honor of D. A. Carson on the Occasion of His 65th Birthday*, ed. Andreas J. Köstenberger and Robert W. Yarbrough (Wheaton, IL: Crossway, 2011), 141–59.

[32] Luke 2:46–50.

[33] John 1:14.

[34] John 1:18.

experiences, perceptions, and perspectives on the significance of Jesus's birth and even his preexistence.[35] But while the apostolic witness is primary, we must bear witness as well. As Jesus told his first followers, "But when the Helper comes, whom I will send to you from the Father, the Spirit of truth, who proceeds from the Father, he will bear witness about me. And you also will bear witness, because you have been with me from the beginning."[36] True, this statement pertains first to those who followed Jesus from his early days of ministry; but on a secondary level, the invitation—even obligation—also extends to us.

We, too, must bear witness because we have received the apostolic testimony regarding the incarnation. We recognize that, just as there was no place in the inn for God Incarnate when he was born into this world, so we, like Jesus, must endure rejection as we identify with him. We believe that, even though he is now exalted with God in heaven, Jesus is God with us, and his promise is true that he will be with us until the end of the age as we bear witness to him. We behold the glory of God in his Son, whom he gave to die for us on the cross, and we long for our loved ones and others to catch a glimpse of his glory in and through us. We understand that Jesus, while born as a Jew in a tiny Judean village, came as the light to the nations to enlighten every person, regardless of culture, race, or ethnic identity. And just as Jesus must be in his Father's house, we believe that he has gone to prepare a place for us so that we will spend eternity with him in heaven. This is our glorious hope and expectation.

CONCLUSION

Together, Matthew, Luke, and John provide a wonderful threefold witness to the first days of Jesus, presenting him as the virgin-born Messiah, the light to the nations, and the incarnate Word. Each

---

[35] While John clearly refers to Jesus's preexistence with God in the beginning, references to his preexistence in Matthew, Mark, and Luke are more indirect. But see Simon J. Gathercole, *The Pre-existent Son: Recovering the Christologies of Matthew, Mark, and Luke* (Grand Rapids, MI: Eerdmans, 2006).

[36] John 15:26–27.

in his own way bears witness to the unique event represented by Jesus's coming into this world to save us from our sins. Rather than looking for divergences between the Gospel witnesses to Jesus's birth, we should stand amazed at the richness resulting from the diverse and complementary ways in which the Gospel writers testify to the events surrounding Jesus's birth, and we should probe their significance for us today. We turn now to reflect briefly on the King's rejection and return.

15

THE KING'S REJECTION AND RETURN

THE SCANDAL OF JESUS'S COMING

Jesus embodies God's greatest gift to his creation. In Genesis 1 we see how God created a beautiful and good world and crowned his creative activity by breathing life into his image-bearing representatives, commissioning them to extend his reign throughout his creation.[1] Yet Genesis 3 describes how God's plan seemed to be derailed as his image bearers rejected his rule and embraced the slavery of sin and death. God, however, did not walk away from his creation but set a plan in motion to rescue and restore it through a human being,[2] a descendent of Abraham,[3] a descendent of David.[4] The infancy narratives powerfully proclaim Jesus as the realization of these hopes and expectations, the fulfillment of God's ancient promises.

God, however, didn't do things the way everyone expected. He didn't fit into everyone's preconceived boxes. He didn't act in accordance with human wisdom. Paul makes this exact point:

[1] Gen. 1:26–28.
[2] Gen. 3:15.
[3] Gen. 12:3.
[4] 2 Sam. 7:14.

> For the word of the cross is folly to those who are perishing, but to us who are being saved it is the power of God. For it is written,
>
> > "I will destroy the wisdom of the wise,
> > and the discernment of the discerning I will thwart."
>
> Where is the one who is wise? Where is the scribe? Where is the debater of this age? Has not God made foolish the wisdom of the world? For since, in the wisdom of God, the world did not know God through wisdom, it pleased God through the folly of what we preach to save those who believe. For Jews demand signs and Greeks seek wisdom, but we preach Christ crucified, a stumbling block to Jews and folly to Gentiles, but to those who are called, both Jews and Greeks, Christ the power of God and the wisdom of God. For the foolishness of God is wiser than men, and the weakness of God is stronger than men. . . .
>
> But God chose what is foolish in the world to shame the wise; God chose what is weak in the world to shame the strong; God chose what is low and despised in the world, even things that are not, to bring to nothing things that are, so that no human being might boast in the presence of God.[5]

The foolishness of God that is wiser than the wisdom of men begins in the infancy narratives and carries through to the end of each Gospel. Jesus fulfilled God's promises in a way that exploded and exceeded all contemporary expectations. Our familiarity with the Christmas story could unwittingly cause us to miss the unexpected wonder, shock, and newness that accompanied these events. In this chapter we will seek to revive that sense of surprise.

THE SCANDAL OF THE VIRGIN CONCEPTION

Matthew provides Joseph's perspective on Mary's unexpected pregnancy. When he was planning to divorce her, Joseph apparently assumed some form of infidelity, an assumption that others would have shared. Joseph would have carried through on the divorce if

[5] 1 Cor. 1:18–25, 27–29.

an angel had not revealed to him the true nature of Mary's pregnancy in a dream.

By the end of the second century, over a century after Matthew and Luke wrote their Gospels, Origen reports that Celsus, a Jew opposing Christianity, lodged the following charges:

> He accuses Him of having "invented his birth from a virgin," and upbraids Him with being "born in a certain Jewish village, of a poor woman of the country, who gained her subsistence by spinning, and who was turned out of doors by her husband, a carpenter by trade, because she was convicted of adultery; that after being driven away by her husband, and wandering about for a time, she disgracefully gave birth to Jesus, an illegitimate child, who having hired himself out as a servant in Egypt on account of his poverty, and having there acquired some miraculous powers, on which the Egyptians greatly pride themselves, returned to his own country, highly elated on account of them, and by means of these proclaimed himself a God."[6]

From the end of the second century, this account of Jesus's birth became established as the Jewish counterstory to the accounts we find in Matthew and Luke. The story finds no evidential support from contemporary first-century sources, and it appears that it was fabricated in response to the Gospel accounts to discourage Jews from believing in Jesus. Mary's fate may indeed have reflected these false charges if God had not revealed the reality of the virgin conception to Joseph.

This controversy raises the question: Why a virgin conception? Why didn't God send Jesus in some way that was less open to misunderstanding and scandal? Celsus was just the first (as far as we know) of many skeptics to ridicule the virgin conception of Jesus. Many modern critics reject it on the basis of its miraculous character. The reality remains, however, that this was how God chose to go about saving the world through his Son, Jesus. The Savior would be fully God and fully man.

[6] Origen, *Against Celsus*, in *The Ante-Nicene Fathers*, ed. Alexander Roberts and James Donaldson, 10 vols. (Grand Rapids, MI: Eerdmans, 1951), 4:408 (*Cels.* 1.28).

THE SCANDAL OF THE INCARNATION

We are so used to speaking about Jesus as God that we forget how earth-shattering this idea was. Gabriel announced to Zechariah that John would prepare the way for the Lord, for Yahweh, the God of Israel, to come to his people.[7] When Yahweh came, he came as Jesus. God became man in order to be Immanuel, God with us.[8]

Trypho the Jew, as recorded by Justin Martyr, accused Christians of being influenced by Greco-Roman religion: "And you ought to feel ashamed when you make assertions similar to theirs, and rather [should] say that this Jesus was born man of men."[9] Historians generally believe that Justin created this dialogue and the character of Trypho as a literary setting for his apologetic presentation, but some of the objections voiced by Trypho likely represented legitimate early Jewish attacks against Christianity. Trypho further argued, "You endeavor to prove an incredible and well-nigh impossible thing; [namely], that God endured to be born and become man."[10]

It is incredible and amazing but not impossible; "[f]or nothing will be impossible with God."[11] God was born as a baby, grew as a human being, and walked this earth as a man. This historical reality represents perhaps one of the strongest responses to the problem of evil. Rather than remain aloof and distant, God entered our world of pain, frailty, vulnerability, suffering, and death. He walked alongside us in every way and endured the full fury of evil, oppression, and injustice. When we suffer and when we have to watch those whom we love suffer, we do so knowing that God suffered alongside us and on our behalf in order to rescue us from suffering and provide an eternal home with no tears, death, mourning, crying, or pain.[12]

---

[7] Luke 1:16–17.
[8] Matt. 1:23.
[9] Justin, *Dialogue with Trypho*, in *The Ante-Nicene Fathers*, ed. Alexander Roberts and James Donaldson, 10 vols. (Grand Rapids, MI: Eerdmans, 1950), 1:231 (*Dial.* 67).
[10] Ibid., 1:232 (*Dial.* 68).
[11] Luke 1:37.
[12] Rev. 21:4.

THE SCANDAL OF A LOWLY BIRTH

How would God come to his people? He would come with power, strength, might, glory, majesty. The opening vision of Revelation describes the Jesus we would expect.

> I saw . . . a son of man, clothed with a long robe and with a golden sash around his chest. The hairs of his head were white, like white wool, like snow. His eyes were like a flame of fire, his feet were like burnished bronze, refined in a furnace, and his voice was like the roar of many waters. In his right hand he held seven stars, from his mouth came a sharp two-edged sword, and his face was like the sun shining in full strength.[13]

This vision captures Jesus following his resurrection; when he came to earth for the first time, however, his eyes were not like flames of fire nor his face like the sun shining in full strength. Despite popular Christmas cards, he wasn't glowing in Mary's arms or in the manger with a bright yellow halo around his head. He came in weakness and vulnerability. A baby depends totally and completely upon its mother for survival.

Not only did Jesus come as a vulnerable baby to rescue his people, the setting of his birth hardly reflects his power. The Creator of the universe breathed his first breath excluded from normal human habitation (no room) and was promptly laid in a feeding trough for animals. His first visitors were lowly, dirty, ceremonially unclean shepherds. Why would God visit his people in this manner? Why didn't he have the angels reveal the birth to the Jewish religious leadership at the temple? Why didn't God plan ahead to reserve a decent room? All of these questions reflect the difference between our expectations and God's plan.

In his birth, Jesus "emptied himself, by taking the form of a servant, being born in the likeness of men. And being found in human form, he humbled himself by becoming obedient to the point of death, even death on a cross."[14] The lowly and humble

---

[13] Rev. 1:12–16.
[14] Phil. 2:7–8.

birth anticipated the complete humiliation and shame of the cross.

THE SCANDAL OF THE CROSS

The *Magnificat* and *Benedictus* beautifully express how everything would turn out. We noted in the discussion of these texts that Mary and Zechariah even used past-tense instead of future-tense verbs to communicate their certainty that the events would surely come to pass. In Jesus God had raised up a horn of salvation to rescue his people from the hands of their enemies.[15] Everyone at the beginning of the first century knew how this would end. Jesus would establish a physical kingdom, proclaim Jewish independence, and subjugate the rest of the Gentile nations. He would be a light to the nations by ruling over them with a rod of iron.[16] This plan left no room for the most shameful and humiliating death possible, crucifixion on a Roman cross. It simply could not turn out that way: God would never, ever, under any circumstances allow his Messiah to die on a Roman cross. That was not how the Messiah's story would end.

All four Gospels agree with this assessment; that was not how the Messiah's story would end. Resurrection triumphed over death! Crucifixion did not have the final word, and the shame and humiliation of the cross accomplished God's scandalous plan to rescue the human race by taking our punishment upon himself. But the plan did include unexpected suffering and disgrace. The Old Testament anticipated this complexity in God's plan in a passage that the Jews either overlooked or explained away because it conflicted with their expectations for God's Messiah:

> He was despised and rejected by men;
> a man of sorrows, and acquainted with grief;
> and as one from whom men hide their faces
> he was despised, and we esteemed him not.

[15] Luke 1:69.
[16] Ps. 2:8–12.

Surely he has borne our griefs
 and carried our sorrows;
yet we esteemed him stricken,
 smitten by God, and afflicted.
But he was pierced for our transgressions;
 he was crushed for our iniquities;
upon him was the chastisement that brought us peace,
 and with his wounds we are healed.
All we like sheep have gone astray;
 we have turned—every one—to his own way;
and the LORD has laid on him
 the iniquity of us all.

He was oppressed, and he was afflicted,
 yet he opened not his mouth;
like a lamb that is led to the slaughter,
 and like a sheep that before its shearers is silent,
 so he opened not his mouth.
By oppression and judgment he was taken away;
 and as for his generation, who considered
that he was cut off out of the land of the living,
 stricken for the transgression of my people?
And they made his grave with the wicked
 and with a rich man in his death,
although he had done no violence,
 and there was no deceit in his mouth.

Yet it was the will of the LORD to crush him;
 he has put him to grief;
when his soul makes an offering for guilt,
 he shall see his offspring; he shall prolong his days;
the will of the LORD shall prosper in his hand.
Out of the anguish of his soul he shall see and be satisfied;
by his knowledge shall the righteous one, my servant,
 make many to be accounted righteous,
 and he shall bear their iniquities.
Therefore I will divide him a portion with the many,
 and he shall divide the spoil with the strong,
because he poured out his soul to death

> and was numbered with the transgressors;
> yet he bore the sin of many,
> and makes intercession for the transgressors.[17]

This passage was essential and foundational for the earliest Christians as they reflected on the death and resurrection of the man who they knew without a doubt was God's Messiah. Why would God let his Messiah be tortured and experience such humiliation and shame? Why would God let his Messiah die? This passage in the book of Isaiah answers that question: God's Messiah had to die to rescue his people from sin, iniquity, and guilt and bring about healing, peace, and righteousness. The Davidic Messiah could not rule forever over a kingdom of sinful people. God's plan was to purify his people through a perfect sacrifice before bringing them into his eternal kingdom.

THE SCANDAL OF UNMET EXPECTATIONS

God's plan would have been scandalous to early first-century Jewish ears in two more ways. Both are implicit in the disciples' question recorded in the book of Acts: "Lord, will you at this time restore the kingdom to Israel?"[18] First, what's up with the Gentiles? Jesus was a Jewish Messiah who was rejected by many of his own people but accepted by outsiders who didn't follow the law. Why would God allow this to happen? Second, why the delay? Once Jesus conquered death through resurrection and made righteousness possible through the forgiveness of sins, what more was there to do? Why not bring in the kingdom now?

Many New Testament texts wrestle with the Jewish rejection and Gentile acceptance of the gospel message. In a very real sense, this was *the* issue that faced the earliest Christians. Some Jews, including Paul, did accept Jesus as the Messiah, so it is a question not of all or nothing but of majority and minority (remnant). God had originally created the entire human race to represent him as his

[17] Isa. 53:3–12.
[18] Acts 1:6.

image bearers and extend his rule and reign throughout his creation. Sin and rebellion thwarted this goal and rendered humanity unable to fulfill this mission. Now Jesus's work on the cross and the outpouring of the Holy Spirit have enabled us, as human beings, to extend God's rule and his reign throughout his creation as those who are being conformed into the image of God's Son.[19] God's plan was always universal and always included the Gentiles, even though this rescue was accomplished through a particular family (i.e., Abraham's seed).

The universal element in God's rescue mission leads directly to the reason for the delay. Jesus made it quite clear that the purpose of the delay was to spread his rule and reign throughout God's creation.[20] This is the mission of God that Jesus has called and enabled us to join. Peter rightly expresses the reason for the delay as follows: "The Lord is not slow to fulfill his promise as some count slowness, but is patient toward you, not wishing that any should perish, but that all should reach repentance."[21]

THE RETURN OF THE KING TO BRING FINAL AND COMPLETE SALVATION

The delay, however, won't last forever. Jesus will return to establish his kingdom. In this future kingdom God's promises will find final fulfillment. In this kingdom God will accomplish the economic and political salvation celebrated in the *Magnificat* and *Benedictus*. This expectation leads to what is perhaps the final scandal associated with Jesus's birth. Not everyone will take part in this future kingdom; some will be eternally excluded in judgment. The birth narratives anticipate this judgment in Herod's rejection of Jesus and in Simeon's prophecy of opposition to Jesus.

Jesus divides humanity between those who submit to his rule through allegiance and belief and those who reject his rule over their lives. Every human being falls into one of these two catego-

[19] Rom. 8:39.
[20] Matt. 28:18–20; Luke 24:47; John 20:21; Acts 1:8; cf. chap. 1 above.
[21] 2 Pet. 3:9.

ries. There is no third or neutral option. The baby who was born in humility and vulnerability will one day return to rule with power and strength. For now, people still have time to embrace his rule, to change sides, but that period won't last forever. God will not postpone his final salvation and judgment indefinitely. If this study of Jesus's birth has done anything, we hope it has helped you assess your choice and align with Jesus—the virgin-born Messiah, the light to the nations, the incarnate Word.

EPILOGUE

THE END OF GOD'S STORY?

In chapter 1 we looked at the unfolding of God's story in the Old Testament leading up to the birth of Jesus. We claimed that "our involvement in *God's* story has the ability to rewrite *our* stories—to change their endings. Put another way, become a part of God's story, and he will write yours." Here in the epilogue we want to briefly pick up God's story as it unfolded in Jesus's life and look at how God's story can and must impact the stories of our individual lives.

Jesus's resurrection raised a legitimate question: Is this the end of God's story? Jesus wins—happily ever after? Jesus's disciples thought so. God's Messiah had come and conquered death; surely it was time for the complete fulfillment of all the Old Testament prophecies. But then, why are we still here?

In accordance with the prophecy of enmity in the book of Genesis,[1] each of the four Gospels recounts how the Messiah engaged in a life-or-death battle with God's adversary, the prince of this world, the Serpent who originally deceived Eve. Jesus cast out demons, supernaturally healed sicknesses, raised the dead, and exercised control over nature. Meanwhile, God's adversary did not remain idle. The book of Revelation pictures Satan symbolically as a seven-headed dragon who was waiting to devour Jesus as soon as he was born.[2]

We have yet to see a church incorporate this depiction into the

[1] See Gen. 3:15.
[2] See Revelation 12.

manger scene at their children's Christmas pageant. Somehow a huge, seven-headed dragon waiting next to the donkey and sheep to devour cute, sweet, little baby Jesus as soon as he appears on the scene doesn't connect very well with audiences! Yet John's vision in Revelation found concrete realization in history as Herod sought to kill the infant rival king.

Each Gospel recounts how God's adversary appeared to gain the upper hand—he manipulated people and events to kill God's promised hero, his Messiah. In the words of the ancient promise, he "bruise[d] his heel."[3] But not even death could keep our God in its grip! The resurrection powerfully displays God's victory over death and confirms our hope for resurrection life following death. Through resurrection, Jesus crushed the Serpent's head and began God's new creation right in the midst of this fallen, broken world.

OUR STORIES JOIN GOD'S CONTINUING STORY

Suffering, sickness, and death often plague our personal life stories, as does the widespread reality of evil and pain throughout the world. Our hearts resonate with the disciples' longing for Jesus to establish God's kingdom on earth concretely and fully. We cannot wait for God's story with his creation to reach the final chapter. Why the delay? How long, O Lord? Different answers have been offered, but we can do no better than examine Jesus's post-resurrection words.[4]

According to the book of Acts, Jesus made various appearances to his disciples during the forty days between his resurrection and ascension.[5] What did Jesus talk about the most over the course of those forty days? What do you think he *should* have talked about? As we might expect, Jesus spoke of how he was the fulfillment of Old Testament prophecies with greater clarity than he could before his death and resurrection.[6] The conversation with the two disciples on the road to Emmaus likely provided the foundation for

[3] Gen. 3:15.
[4] See also Peter's discussion of the delay in 2 Peter 3:1–13.
[5] Acts 1:3.
[6] See Luke 24:25–27.

the early Christian interpretation of the Old Testament. Another theme, however, featured far more prominently.

John records how Jesus appeared to his disciples the first night following his resurrection and commissioned them to join him in God's mission to the world: "Jesus said to them again, 'Peace be with you. As the Father has sent me, even so I am sending you.'"[7] John 3:16 famously recounts how God sent his Son, Jesus, on a mission motivated by his love for a lost and dying world. After his resurrection, Jesus entrusted this mission to his followers. The continuation of Jesus's mission through his followers hints that God's mission to rescue and restore the world he created would be delayed to some degree.

A few weeks later, Jesus appeared to his disciples in Galilee and again commissioned them to their mission: "All authority in heaven and on earth has been given to me. Go therefore and make disciples of all nations, baptizing them in the name of the Father and of the Son and of the Holy Spirit, teaching them to observe all that I have commanded you. And behold, I am with you always, to the end of the age."[8] As a result of his resurrection, Jesus asserted his reign as the world's true King who possesses all authority. He commissioned his followers to go to the entire world as his representatives to announce his rule and to call the nations to obedience. Significantly, he promised his indispensable presence.

Finally, right before his ascension, Jesus affirmed this mission in response to the disciples' question of when he would usher in his kingdom: "It is not for you to know times or seasons that the Father has fixed by his own authority. But you will receive power when the Holy Spirit has come upon you, and you will be my witnesses in Jerusalem and in all Judea and Samaria, and to the end of the earth."[9] The delay of the kingdom serves the purpose of enabling the global witness of God's people in the power of his Spirit!

---

[7] John 20:21.
[8] Matt. 28:18–20.
[9] Acts 1:7–8.

BECOMING PART OF GOD'S STORY

God's story is thus still being written. It didn't end with the writing of the New Testament but continues to unfold as Jesus, from his exalted position with the Father, empowers and directs his people to engage in his mission to reclaim and restore a lost world. This mission progresses in anticipation of Jesus's return when he will finally and fully set everything right in the world and usher in God's kingdom.

How do we, as Jesus's followers two thousand years later, participate in God's ongoing story? We join God's story and allow him to write our stories by engaging in his mission to the world as his image bearers and commissioned representatives. Those who confess their sin to God and ask for his forgiveness become members of God's people. God forgives their sins. They experience both the peace that comes from being in a right relationship with God in the present and the hope of a future in resurrection life after death. Once we are in God's family, we let God write our stories by becoming part of his story, engaging in his mission. That is, we don't simply live our lives for ourselves—to be comfortable, to own a nice home and a nice car, and to have a "perfect" family—but we live our lives for God, for Jesus, for him who died for us. Every Christian is God's representative, his ambassador, communicating God's presence and kingdom in the workplace, the home, and anywhere else we find ourselves.

How are you allowing God to write your story? How are you actively participating in his story? It doesn't happen by accident but requires intentional activity and effort. It is not for the lazy or cowardly but for those who know God is real, have had a life-saving encounter with him, and have given their lives for his service. There is really no other way to live—or at least to live well. Anyone can survive with food and water, but you were not created for sheer survival—you were created for more, so much more! As a Christian, you are supernaturally united to Christ, filled with the divine Spirit, and empowered by him to live a life of freedom, victory, and peace participating with God in his mission. Why settle for less?

CONCLUSION

God's story stretches from eternity past to eternity future, but the story of his involvement with this world pivots at one place and at one time in history: *the coming of Jesus Christ.*

Looking backward, Jesus's coming is the *fulfillment of the entire Old Testament narrative.* Every narrative in the Old Testament serves to move history forward while narrowing down the identity of God's coming Messiah, the offspring of the woman, the descendant of Abraham, the seed of David. This backward connection is summarized in the opening of Matthew's Gospel, "Jesus Christ, the son of David, the son of Abraham," and elaborated in his genealogy.[10]

Jesus alone completely fulfilled the prophecy and promise of Immanuel, God with us. The theological term for this communion is "incarnation," a term that captures how God in Jesus became a human being and walked among us. He personally entered into our world, identified with our pain and suffering, and bore our sins on a cross in order to rescue us.

Beyond the limited time period of his physical life, Jesus promised his followers, "behold, I am with you always, to the end of the age."[11] Through the Holy Spirit, Jesus *continues* to be Immanuel, God with us. And the New Testament closes with a powerful vision of the future time after Christ will return finally to restore his creation:

> Behold, the dwelling place of God is with man. He will dwell with them, and they will be his people, and God himself will be with them as their God. He will wipe away every tear from their eyes, and death shall be no more, neither shall there be mourning, nor crying, nor pain anymore, for the former things have passed away.[12]

Even as we reflect upon the past when God walked among us in the person of Jesus and rejoice in the present time in God's

[10] Matt. 1:1–17.
[11] Matt. 28:20b.
[12] Rev. 21:3–4.

presence with us through the Holy Spirit, we long for the future day when God will physically and concretely walk among us again, wiping every tear from every eye and killing death forever.

> O come, Thou Day-spring, come and cheer
> Our spirits by Thine advent here;
> Disperse the gloomy clouds of night,
> And death's dark shadows put to flight.
> Rejoice! Rejoice! Emmanuel
> Shall come to thee, O Israel![13]

Looking forward beyond Christ's first coming, we find that we, as Jesus's followers, have a role to play in God's story as well. Those of us who have trusted Christ and have embarked with him and our fellow believers on his mission are characters in the unfolding story. As we fulfill his purposes for us in his plan, we eagerly look for Christ's return to set everything right once and for all.

[13] Verse 2 of "O Come, O Come, Emmanuel," translated from Latin into English by John Mason Neale (1851). A modern rendition is available in *Worship His Majesty* (Alexandria, IN: Gaither Music Company, 1987), 120.

APPENDIX
MESSIAH IS COMING!

SECOND TEMPLE JEWISH MESSIANIC EXPECTATIONS

NOT SO SILENT

The four hundred or so years separating the Old Testament from the New were far from silent, and a large number of historical events unfolded during the course of these years, many of which fundamentally molded the world Jesus entered.[1] God's Son wasn't born into a historical vacuum—far from it.

Foreign Rule

The Old Testament ends with Israel under Persian rule (539–331 BC).[2] The most important events of this period in relation to Palestine were bound up with Cyrus's foreign policy allowing the Jews to return to Palestine and rebuild the city of Jerusalem and the temple originally built by Solomon. Apart from the biblical material, we know little else about life in Palestine during this period.

Matters changed quite rapidly with the conquests of Alexander the Great (333–323 BC). Alexander himself had little interest in

---

[1] For further details about events in the historical period between the Old and New Testaments, see Andreas J. Köstenberger, L. Scott Kellum, and Charles L. Quarles, *The Cradle, the Cross, and the Crown: An Introduction to the New Testament* (Nashville, TN: B&H Academic, 2009), chap. 2.

[2] Several Old Testament books describe events in the first part of this period, including 2 Chronicles, Ezra, Nehemiah, Esther, Daniel, Haggai, Zechariah, and Malachi.

Palestine, and shortly after his death, his vast kingdom was divided. Ptolemy, one of the several generals who then vied for territory, established control of Egypt, and his ruling dynasty governed Palestine from 323 to 198 BC. Historical details in Judea during this period are fairly obscure, but the people likely enjoyed relative peace with a measure of heavy taxation and self-governance under the high priest.

Fortunes deteriorated for Jews living in Palestine when the Seleucid Empire seized control of the land from the Ptolemies in 198 BC. Although Syrian rule lasted only thirty-one years, it was quite brutal; the Seleucid ruler Antiochus IV aggressively sought to spread Greek culture and eventually waged war directly against Judaism. He banned the Torah, circumcision, Jewish festivals, and sacrifices to Yahweh. To top it off, he dedicated the Jerusalem temple to Zeus, erected a statue of Zeus in the temple, and sacrificed a pig on the altar. Pious Jews who resisted these changes were persecuted, beaten, or killed.[3]

Jewish Self-Rule

Things seemed to take a turn for the better when the Maccabean revolt established Jewish self-rule, which lasted from 167 to 63 BC. The success of the rebellion filled many Jews with hope that God was fulfilling his ancient promises to his people, but such hopes proved illusory. During this period, one of the early rulers, Simon, exercised both executive and religious power after being invested with the high priesthood.[4] Although this period is known for Jewish independence, it was also characterized by constant infighting, corruption, and even brutality.

Jewish independence ended when Rome stepped in to determine the outcome of a power struggle between two brothers, Hyrcanus II and Aristobulus II. Rome decided in favor of Hyrcanus,

---

[3] Our best ancient historical sources for this period include Josephus's *Jewish Antiquities* and the book of 1 Maccabees.

[4] The sectarian community associated with the Dead Sea Scrolls likely formed during this period (the middle of the second century BC) in direct response to the corruption of the Jerusalem priesthood.

but from that point forward, Palestine was a client kingdom of Rome. This period meets up with the birth of Jesus under the rule of Herod the Great, whom Rome appointed "king of Judea" in 40 BC.

These centuries of foreign rule with the interval of independence gave the Jewish people ample time to reflect upon the promises that Yahweh had made through his prophets. The years of nonfulfillment and oppression did not cause the Jews to abandon the hope that their God would one day intervene decisively in history in their favor; instead, the years of waiting only intensified this hope.

The Old Testament provided the Jewish people with many expectations as to how God was going to act in the future to deliver, guide, and restore the nation. Most of these prophecies and promises centered on a coming figure—a prophet, messiah ("anointed one"), king, shepherd, or divine "son of man" (a term used for a mysterious divine-human figure descending from heaven in the book of Daniel)—who would bring restoration and establish God's rule among his people in order to bring blessing and light to the entire world.

The recollection of these divine prophecies and promises fueled intense speculation and hope during the days leading up to and following the birth of Jesus. The Jewish people in Palestine knew that they were not currently living in the time of fulfillment and longed for God to send his Messiah and make good on his ancient promises to his people. Their longing is communicated well by the Christmas hymn, "O Come, O Come, Emmanuel":

> O come, O come, Emmanuel,
> And ransom captive Israel
> That mourns in lonely exile here
> Until the Son of God appear.
> Rejoice! Rejoice! Emmanuel
> Shall come to thee, O Israel.[5]

[5] "O Come, O Come, Emmanuel," translated from Latin into English by John Mason Neale (1851).

OLD TESTAMENT MESSIANIC EXPECTATIONS

Looking at some Old Testament passages will help us get a taste of the hope that could not be extinguished by the long passage of time or the then-present reality of oppression and lack of fulfillment. These Old Testament prophecies can be grouped into four main categories: (1) a *prophet like Moses*; (2) an *ideal priest*; (3) a *Davidic ruler*; and (4) a *son of man*. Diverse Jewish communities and writings emphasized one aspect or another.[6]

The Prophet Like Moses

Before he died, Moses prophesied that one day God would raise up another prophet like himself from among the people:

> The Lord your God will raise up for you a prophet like me from among you, from your brothers—it is to him you shall listen. . . . And the Lord said to me, "They are right in what they have spoken. I will raise up for them a prophet like you from among their brothers. And I will put my words in his mouth, and he shall speak to them all that I command him. And whoever will not listen to my words that he shall speak in my name, I myself will require it of him."[7]

This prophecy, inscribed in Scripture, was never forgotten, and people during the time of Jesus were still waiting for the prophet like Moses to come, someone from among them who would speak the very words of God to his people once again. Before Jesus began his public ministry, the Jewish leaders wondered whether John the Baptist was "the prophet."[8] After Jesus miraculously fed the five thousand, the people were naturally amazed and said, "This is indeed the Prophet who is to come into the world."[9] The Jewish

[6] The community responsible for the Dead Sea Scrolls, for example, seems to have expected two messiahs, one royal and one priestly. See in particular 1QS 9:10–11 (*Rule of the Community*); CD 12:22–23 (*Damascus Document* [Cairo Genizah copy]); 1QSa (*Rule of the Congregation*).
[7] Deut. 18:15, 17–19.
[8] John 1:21, 25.
[9] John 6:14; cf. 7:40, 52.

people were looking for the "prophet like Moses" to arrive and declare God's powerful word afresh, anew.

The Ideal Priest

From the time of Aaron onward, the high priest played a very important role within Judaism. The book of Leviticus describes the priest as anointed using the same language from which we get our term *messiah* ("anointed one").[10] When the Jews returned from Babylonian exile, Zechariah described Zerubbabel the descendent of David and Joshua the high priest as two "anointed ones" or "sons of new oil."[11] During most of the period between the Testaments, the high priest in Jerusalem led the nation in the absence of a Davidic monarch.

Although the Old Testament offers little evidence of a future messianic priest, this expectation developed within some Jewish communities leading up to Jesus's birth.[12] The book of Hebrews also develops, at length, Jesus's role as the eschatological high priest on the basis of Psalm 110: "The Lord has sworn and will not change his mind, You are a priest forever after the order of Melchizedek."[13] The author of Hebrews doesn't replace Jesus's Davidic kingly role with a priestly one but rather combines both roles into one.[14]

The Davidic Ruler

Much more than looking for God's end-time prophet or ideal priest, the common Jewish people were longing for the Davidic Messiah, an anointed ruler who would rescue them from foreign rule and govern them with justice and wisdom. This expectation came from God's promise to David to establish his kingdom forever.[15] Focused on the permanence of David's lineage, this promise

---

[10] Lev. 4:3, 5, and 16.
[11] Zech. 4:14.
[12] The community associated with the Dead Sea Scrolls likely expected the priestly messiah to hold a higher rank than the anticipated kingly messiah.
[13] Ps. 110:4; cf. Heb. 5:6.
[14] Heb. 1:3; 5:5.
[15] 2 Sam. 7:12–17.

was reaffirmed by later prophets throughout the Old Testament, particularly Isaiah:

> For to us a child is born,
> to us a son is given;
> and the government shall be upon his shoulder,
> and his name shall be called
> Wonderful Counselor, Mighty God,
> Everlasting Father, Prince of Peace.
> Of the increase of his government and of peace
> there will be no end,
> *on the throne of David and over his kingdom,*
> *to establish it and to uphold it*
> *with justice and with righteousness*
> *from this time forth and forevermore.*
> The zeal of the LORD of hosts will do this.[16]
>
> There shall come forth a shoot from the stump of Jesse,
> and a branch from his roots shall bear fruit.
> And the Spirit of the LORD shall rest upon him,
> the Spirit of wisdom and understanding,
> the Spirit of counsel and might,
> the Spirit of knowledge and the fear of the LORD.
> And his delight shall be in the fear of the LORD.
> He shall not judge by what his eyes see,
> or decide disputes by what his ears hear,
> but with righteousness he shall judge the poor,
> and decide with equity for the meek of the earth;
> and he shall strike the earth with the rod of his mouth,
> and with the breath of his lips he shall kill the wicked.
> Righteousness shall be the belt of his waist,
> and faithfulness the belt of his loins.[17]

Similarly, Psalm 2 promises universal rule to this "King" and directly labels the King as both God's "Son" and his Messiah or "Anointed."[18] The reality that none of David's sons ever achieved

---

[16] Isa. 9:6–7.
[17] Isa. 11:1–5.
[18] Ps. 2:2, 6, 7, 12.

universal rule and the lack of a functioning Davidic king in the first century enabled readers to interpret this psalm as referring to a future coming son of God, messiah, and king.

The prophet Micah also foretold of a future ruler:

> But you, O Bethlehem Ephrathah,
> who are too little to be among the clans of Judah,
> from you shall come forth for me
> *one who is to be ruler in Israel,*
> whose coming forth is from of old,
> from ancient days.
> Therefore he shall give them up until the time
> when she who is in labor has given birth;
> then the rest of his brothers shall return
> to the people of Israel.
> And *he shall stand and shepherd his flock* in the strength of the LORD,
> in the majesty of the name of the LORD his God.
> And they shall dwell secure, for now he shall be great
> to the ends of the earth.[19]

The words of this prophecy fostered a sense of expectation for a future king among some, if not many, Jews in the first century.

These prophecies, and others like them, filled the Jewish people with an undefeatable hope that God would send a deliverer from the line of David to throw off foreign oppression and restore the fortunes of his people.[20] Even centuries of foreign occupation, oppression, and rule could not easily snuff out or diminish this hope, no matter how unlikely it appeared.

Three symbols also became closely associated with messianic hope in the centuries surrounding Jesus's birth: (1) the *scepter*; (2) the *star*; and (3) the *branch*. These symbols find their source in the Old Testament. On his deathbed, Jacob prophesied that the "*scepter* shall not depart from Judah,"[21] and later in Jewish history,

[19] Mic. 5:2–4.

[20] Other important texts that fueled expectation for a coming Messianic ruler include Hag. 2:20–23; Zech. 9:9–10; 12:7–13:1.

[21] Gen. 49:10.

the pagan prophet Balaam declared, "I see him, but not now; I behold him, but not near: a *star* shall come out of Jacob, and a *scepter* shall rise out of Israel."[22] These two symbols became a shorthand for the Messiah. During the final Jewish revolt against Rome in AD 132–136, the Jewish leader Simon took on the name Bar Kokhba ("son of a star") in order to legitimize his claim to leadership. His followers believed that he fulfilled Balaam's prophecy. It is no accident that a star features significantly in the narrative of the Messiah's birth in Matthew's Gospel.[23]

The symbol of a *branch* also carried messianic overtones. Jeremiah prophesied that "the days are coming, declares the LORD, when I will raise up for David a righteous *Branch*, and he shall reign as king and deal wisely, and shall execute justice and righteousness in the land. In his days Judah will be saved, and Israel will dwell securely. And this is the name by which he will be called: 'The LORD is our righteousness.'"[24] This passage describes the future Davidic King as a "branch" (see also Zech. 3:8; 6:12). Although using slightly different language, Isaiah 11:1–9 begins with the promise that "there shall come forth a *shoot* from the stump of Jesse, and a *branch* from his roots shall bear fruit." Ezekiel 17 portrays the Davidic King as the top of a cedar carried off by an eagle (Babylon) from which God would plant a shoot that would again grow into a "noble cedar."[25] These various images combine to produce the idea that God would one day restore the kingdom to an heir (shoot, branch) of David.

In addition, the promise of a coming good *shepherd* contributed to first-century Jewish hopes that God would restore the Davidic kingship. Old Testament literature often associated kings with shepherds because they were expected to care for, protect, and provide for their people, God's flock. Thus we saw above in

---

[22] Num. 24:17a.

[23] The use of these texts in ancient Israelite enthronement ceremonies (Psalm 2; 110; Isaiah 9) or to establish the legitimacy of the Davidic line (Num. 24:15–19; Gen. 49:10) does not detract from the way first-century Jews commonly interpreted them as pointing forward to a coming messianic Davidic king.

[24] Jer. 23:5–7; cf. 33:14–16.

[25] Ezek. 17:23.

Micah's prophecy that the future ruler of Israel would "*shepherd his flock* in the strength of the LORD."[26]

Ezekiel 34 powerfully confirms this connection. The chapter begins with a scathing critique of the current Jewish shepherds (leadership) who served themselves and devoured the flock.[27] God responded by promising that he would shepherd his people directly: "Behold, I, I myself will search for my sheep and will seek them out. As a shepherd seeks out his flock when he is among his sheep that have been scattered, so will I seek out my sheep, and I will rescue them from all places where they have been scattered on a day of clouds and thick darkness."[28] This promise of direct involvement quickly expanded to include a Davidic shepherd. "And I will set up over them *one shepherd, my servant David*, and he shall feed them: he shall feed them and *be their shepherd*. And I, the LORD, will be their God, and my servant David shall be prince among them. I am the LORD; I have spoken."[29]

Significantly, Ezekiel concluded his powerful vision of the valley of dry bones with the image of a shepherd. This vision pointed symbolically to a complete restoration of the people in their land, and in it God promised that "my servant David shall be king over them, and they shall all have *one shepherd*. They shall walk in my rules and be careful to obey my statutes."[30] Jesus built upon this motif and expectation by explicitly declaring himself to be the "good shepherd."[31] Hearers alert to the prophetic promises of the Old Testament would have likely perceived the messianic overtones of Jesus's metaphor.

The Son of Man

Although many of the above expectations could be fulfilled in some way by a human prophet, priest, or king, this final category points, to a certain degree, toward a heavenly or divine figure.

---

[26] Mic. 5:4.
[27] Ezek. 34:1–10.
[28] Ezek. 34:11–12.
[29] Ezek. 34:23–24.
[30] Ezek. 37:24.
[31] John 10:14.

Daniel recounts the following vision: "I saw in the night visions, and behold, with the clouds of heaven there came one like a son of man, and he came to the Ancient of Days and was presented before him. And to him was given dominion, and glory and a kingdom, that all peoples, nations, and languages should serve him; his dominion is an everlasting dominion, which shall not pass away, and his kingdom one that shall not be destroyed."[32]

Extensive scholarly debate has taken place concerning the meaning of this vision both within its original context in Daniel and in Jesus's use of the phrase "son of man" to refer to himself. While the "one like a son of man" could represent God's people, the phrase more probably refers to the ruler of God's people, since Daniel 7 contrasts it with four beasts (or representatives of kingdoms).

In either case, by the first century this text took its place among the other texts discussed above and was read as a prediction of a coming messianic individual who was in some way more than human.[33] The earliest Christians directly connected Jesus's self-reference as the "Son of Man" with this prophecy from the book of Daniel. Jesus's explicit claim to be this promised individual during the Jewish phase of his trial sealed his execution on the charge of blasphemy.[34]

THE EXTENT OF MESSIANIC EXPECTATION

Was every first-century Jew sitting on the edge of his or her seat, waiting and longing for the coming of God's Messiah? It's hard to determine the exact extent of messianic expectation among average Jews at this time. Certainly many Jews were quite content with the status quo and had no desire to see everything turned upside down, particularly those with some degree of political or religious power in the Sanhedrin (the ruling Jewish council), such as members of the Sadducees (Jerusalem's leading aristocracy). We can reasonably assume that, in contrast to the economic, political,

[32] Dan. 7:13–14.

[33] *1 Enoch* 46:1; 70:1; *4 Ezra* 13. Both of these Jewish texts interpret Daniel's "son of man" as the preexistent Messiah and view him as an individual and not as a collective symbol for God's people.

[34] Matt. 26:63–68.

and religious elite, many ordinary people cherished some form of messianic expectation.

This assessment is supported by evidence in Jewish literature, records of failed messianic movements, and the revolt that led to the destruction of Jerusalem by the Romans in AD 70.[35] Grounded in the above-mentioned Old Testament prophetic texts, this hope intensified over centuries of nonfulfillment and oppression by other nations and godless rulers. Widespread expectation centered on a political Davidic messiah who would overthrow Roman rule, destroy the enemies of Israel, and establish peace and prosperity in an independent Jewish state. Messianic expectation filled the Palestinian air throughout the first century; all that was needed was a spark, or, as we see with the hindsight of history, the birth of a royal child.

JEWISH MESSIANIC EXPECTATIONS PRECEDING JESUS'S BIRTH[36]

First-century Palestinian Judaism was characterized by intense longing for God to deliver his people based on Old Testament promises. The Gospels bear witness to this expectation, but they are not alone. The desperate yearning of an oppressed people finds expression in many other texts from the same period. Messianic expectations in Second Temple Judaism were both diverse and pervasive.[37] We cite several primary sources below to serve as a resource that gives you access to some of the most important Jewish texts from this period.

This small sampling of Jewish texts attests to messianic expectations in the literature of this period. These significant texts

[35] Allusions to some kind of messianic figure (whether prophet, priest, king, or son of man) is widespread in Second Temple Jewish literature. See, for example, Sirach 51:12–13; *Psalms of Solomon* 17–18; *Sibylline Oracles* 3:652–56; *1 Enoch* 45–57; *Testament of Judah* 24:1–5; *4 Ezra* 12:31–32; 13; 2 *Baruch* 40, 72. Evidence from the Dead Sea Scrolls includes CD 12:22–23 (*Damascus Document* [Cairo Genizah copy]); 1QS 9:10–11 (*Rule of the Community*); 1Q28a 2:11–22 (*Rule of the Congregation*); 4Q174 10–13 (*Florilegium*); 4Q252 5:1–7 (*Commentary on Genesis A*); 4Q175 1–13 (*Testimonia*); 4Q246 2:1–9 (*4QAramaic Apocalypse [Apocryphon of Daniel]*).

[36] All of the following texts were in circulation before the birth of Jesus except for 4 *Ezra* and 2 *Baruch*. We start with *Psalms of Solomon* (70–45 BC); the following texts are cited in presumed chronological order. The Dead Sea Scrolls are grouped together, while later Jewish texts (4 *Ezra*, 2 *Baruch*) come last.

[37] Scholars use the term *Second Temple Judaism* to refer to the period between the reconstruction of the temple in 516 BC and the Roman destruction of Jerusalem and the temple in AD 70.

bear witness to active expectations that God would act through his agents to fulfill his promises around the time of Jesus's birth. The Gospel infancy narratives echo this same expectation and proclaim boldly that Jesus fulfilled all these hopes and dreams. The first Christians did not invent these expectations or foist messianic interpretations on Old Testament texts; such expectations were widespread during the centuries preceding Jesus's birth and the century following it.

Psalms of Solomon 17:21–18:9

The text from the *Psalms of Solomon* is representative of the kind of messianic expectation presupposed in the Gospel narratives and can be dated confidently to between 70 and 45 BC (it was not written by the biblical Solomon).

> See, Lord, and raise up for them their king,
> the son of David, to rule over your servant Israel
> in the time known to you, O God.
> Undergird him with the strength to destroy the unrighteous rulers,
> to purge Jerusalem from gentiles
> who trample her to destruction;
> in wisdom and in righteousness to drive out
> the sinners from the inheritance;
> to smash the arrogance of sinners
> like a potter's jar;
> To shatter all their substance with an iron rod;
> to destroy the unlawful nations with the word of his mouth;
> At his warning the nations will flee from his presence;
> and he will condemn sinners by the thoughts of their hearts.
>
> He will gather a holy people
> whom he will lead in righteousness;
> and he will judge the tribes of the people
> that have been made holy by the Lord their God.
> He will not tolerate unrighteousness (even) to pause among them,

and any person who knows wickedness shall not live
with them.
For he shall know them
that they are all children of their God.
He will distribute them upon the land
according to their tribes;
the alien and the foreigner will no longer live near them.
He will judge peoples and nations in the wisdom of his
righteousness.
Pause.
And he will have gentile nations serving him under his yoke,
and he will glorify the Lord in (a place) prominent (above)
the whole earth.
And he will purge Jerusalem
(and make it) holy as it was even from the beginning,
(for) nations to come from the ends of the earth to see his glory,
to bring as gifts her children who had been driven out,
and to see the glory of the Lord
with which God has glorified her.
And he will be a righteous king over them, taught by God.
There will be no unrighteousness among them in his days,
for all shall be holy,
and their king shall be the Lord Messiah.
(For) he will not rely on horse and rider and bow,
nor will he collect gold and silver for war.
Nor will he build up hope in a multitude for a day of war.
The Lord himself is his king,
the hope of the one who has a strong hope in God.

He shall be compassionate to all the nations
(who) reverently (stand) before him.
He will strike the earth with the word of his mouth forever;
he will bless the Lord's people with wisdom and happiness.
And he himself (will be) free from sin, (in order) to rule a
great people.
He will expose officials and drive out sinners
by the strength of his word.
And he will not weaken in his days, (relying) upon his God,
for God made him

powerful in the holy spirit
and wise in the counsel of understanding,
with strength and righteousness.
And the blessing of the Lord will be with him in strength,
and he will not weaken;
His hope (will be) in the Lord.
Then who will succeed against him,
mighty in his actions
and strong in the fear of God?
Faithfully and righteously shepherding the Lord's flock,
he will not let any of them stumble in their pasture.
He will lead them all in holiness
and there will be no arrogance among them,
that any should be oppressed.
This is the beauty of the king of Israel
which God knew,
to raise him over the house of Israel
to discipline it.

His words will be purer than the finest gold, the best.
He will judge the peoples in the assemblies,
the tribes of the sanctified.
His words will be as the words of the holy ones,
among sanctified peoples.
Blessed are those born in those days
to see the good fortune of Israel
which God will bring to pass in the assembly of the tribes.

May God dispatch his mercy to Israel;
may he deliver us from the pollution of profane enemies;
The Lord Himself is our king forevermore.

O Lord, your mercy is upon the works of your hands forever.
(You show) your goodness to Israel
with a rich gift.
Your eyes (are) watching over them and none of them will be
in need.
Your ears listen to the hopeful prayer of the poor,
Your compassionate judgments (are) over the whole world,

and your love is for the descendants of Abraham, an Israelite.
Your discipline for us (is) as (for) a firstborn son, an only child,
to divert the perceptive person from unintentional sins.
May God cleanse Israel for the day of mercy in blessing,
for the appointed day when his Messiah will reign.
Blessed are those born in those days,
to see the good things of the Lord
which he will do for the coming generation;
(which will be) under the rod of discipline of the Lord Messiah,
in the fear of his God,
in wisdom of spirit,
and of righteousness and of strength,
to direct people in righteous acts, in the fear of God,
to set them all in the fear of the Lord[;]
A good generation (living) in the fear of God,
in the days of mercy.[38]

Sirach 51

Ben Sira penned the book known as Sirach sometime before 180 BC. In between verses 12 and 13 of chapter 51, someone inserted a Hebrew psalm of thanksgiving of uncertain date and authorship, which bears witness to hopes for a Davidic messiah. Line H of the Psalm reads: "Give thanks to him who makes a horn to sprout for the house of David, for his mercy endures forever."[39]

Sibylline Oracles 3:652-56

The third book of the Sibylline Oracles dates from 163 to 45 BC and voices Alexandrian Jews' expectations for an apparently Ptolemaic messiah.

And then God will send a King from the sun
who will stop the entire earth from evil war,
killing some, imposing oaths of loyalty on others;

---

[38] R. B. Wright, trans., "Psalms of Solomon: A New Translation and Introduction," in *The Old Testament Pseudepigrapha*, ed. James H. Charlesworth, 2 vols. (New York: Doubleday, 1983, 1985), 2:667–70.

[39] Bruce Metzger and Roland Murphy, eds., *The New Oxford Annotated Apocrypha* (New York: Oxford University Press, 1991), 159.

and he will not do all these things by his private plans
but in obedience to the noble teachings of the great God.[40]

1 Enoch 45–57

The book of *1 Enoch* was written by various authors from different time periods, but the sections we will look at from the so-called Similitudes were written between 105 to 64 BC. It is not possible to reproduce everything reflecting messianic expectations in *1 Enoch*; the following selections are representative.

> On that day, my Elect One shall sit on the seat of glory
> and make a selection of their deeds,
> their resting places will be without number,
> their souls shall be firm within them when they see my
> Elect One,
> those who have appealed to my glorious name.
> On that day, I shall cause my Elect One to dwell among
> them,
> I shall transform heaven and make it a blessing of light
> forever.
> I shall (also) transform the earth and make it a blessing,
> and cause my Elect One to dwell in her.
> Then those who have committed sin and crime shall not
> set foot in her.
> For in peace I have looked (with favor) upon my righteous
> ones and given them mercy,
> and have caused them to dwell before me.
> But sinners have come before me so that by judgment
> I shall destroy them from before the face of the earth.

At that place, I saw the One to whom belongs the time before time. And his head was white like wool, and there was with him another individual, whose face was like that of a human being. His countenance was full of grace like that of one among the holy angels. And I asked the one—from among the angels—who was going with me, and who had revealed to me all the secrets regard-

[40] J. J. Collins, trans., "Sibylline Oracles: A New Translation and Introduction," in *Old Testament Pseudepigrapha*, 1:376.

ing the One who was born of human beings, "Who is this, and from whence is he who is going as the prototype of the Before-Time?" And he answered me and said to me, "This is the Son of Man, to whom belongs righteousness, and with whom righteousness dwells. And he will open all the hidden storerooms; for the Lord of the Spirits has chosen him, and he is destined to be victorious before the Lord of the Spirits in eternal uprightness. This Son of Man whom you have seen is the One who would remove the kings and the mighty ones from their comfortable seats and the strong ones from their thrones. He shall loosen the reins of the strong and crush the teeth of the sinners. He shall depose the kings from their thrones and kingdoms. For they do not extol and glorify him, and neither do they obey him, the source of their kingship.[41]

At that hour, that Son of Man was given a name, in the presence of the Lord of the Spirits, the Before-Time; even before the creation of the sun and the moon, before the creation of the stars, he was given a name in the presence of the Lord of the Spirits. He will become a staff for the righteous ones in order that they may lean on him and not fall. He is the light of the gentiles and he will become the hope of those who are sick in their hearts. All those who dwell upon the earth shall fall and worship before him; they shall glorify, bless, and sing the name of the Lord of the Spirits. For this purpose he became the Chosen One; he was concealed in the presence of (the Lord of the Spirits) prior to the creation of the world, and for eternity. And he has revealed the wisdom of the Lord of the Spirits to the righteous and the holy ones, for he has preserved the portion of the righteous because they have hated and despised this world of oppression (together with) all its ways of life and its habits in the name of the Lord of the Spirits; and because they will be saved in his name and it is his good pleasure that they have life.[42]

On the day of their weariness, there shall be an obstacle on the earth and they shall fall on their faces; and they shall not rise up (again), nor anyone (be found) who will take them with his hands

[41] E. Isaac, trans., "1 (Ethiopic Apocalypse of) Enoch: A New Translation and Introduction," in *Old Testament Pseudepigrapha*, 1:34 (*1 Enoch* 45:3–46:5).
[42] Ibid., 1:35 (*1 Enoch* 48:2–7).

> and raise them up. For they have denied the Lord of the Spirits and his Messiah. Blessed be the name of the Lord of the Spirits![43]

> And he said to me, "All these things which you have seen happen by the authority of his Messiah so that he may give orders and be praised upon the earth."[44]

> After this, the Righteous and Elect One will reveal the house of his congregation. From that time, they shall not be hindered in the name of the Lord of the Spirits. And these mountains shall become (flat) like earth in the presence of his righteousness, and the hills shall become like a fountain of water. And the righteous ones shall have rest from the oppression of sinners.[45]

Testament of Judah 24:1-6

We can date both this passage from the *Testament of Judah* and the following passage from the *Testament of Levi* to the second century BC. Scholars widely believe that this text includes some later Christian additions or interpolations—particularly in reference to the sinlessness of the Messiah and the descent of the Spirit—but nonetheless reflects a solid pre-Christian Jewish core.

> And after this there shall arise for you a Star from Jacob in peace: And a man shall arise from my posterity like the Sun of righteousness, walking with the sons of men in gentleness and righteousness, and in him will be found no sin. And the heavens will be opened upon him to pour out the spirit as a blessing of the Holy Father. And he will pour the spirit of grace on you. And you shall be sons in truth, and you will walk in his first and final decrees. This is the Shoot of God Most High; this is the fountain for the life of all humanity. Then he will illumine the scepter of my kingdom, and from your root will arise the Shoot, and through it will arise the rod of righteousness for the nations, to judge and to save all that call on the Lord.[46]

---

[43] Ibid., 1:36 (*1 Enoch* 48:10).
[44] Ibid., 1:37 (*1 Enoch* 52:4).
[45] Ibid., 1:37–38 (*1 Enoch* 53:6–7).
[46] H. C. Kee, trans., "Testaments of the Twelve Patriarchs: A New Translation and Introduction," in *Old Testament Pseudepigrapha*, 1:801.

Testament of Levi 18:1-14

When vengeance will have come upon them from the Lord, the priesthood will lapse.
And then the Lord will raise up a new priest
to whom all the words of the Lord will be revealed.
He shall effect the judgment of truth over the earth for many days.
And his start shall rise in heaven like a king;
kindling the light of knowledge as day is illumined by the sun.
And he shall be extolled by the whole inhabited world.
This one will shine forth like the sun in the earth;
he shall take away all darkness from under heaven,
and there shall be peace in all the earth.
The heavens shall greatly rejoice in his days
and the earth shall be glad;
the clouds will be filled with joy
and the knowledge of the Lord will be poured out on the earth like the water of the seas.
And the angels of glory of the Lord's presence will be made glad by him.
The heavens will be opened,
and from the temple of glory sanctification will come upon him,
with a fatherly voice, as from Abraham to Isaac.
And the glory of the Most High shall burst forth upon him.
And the spirit of understanding and sanctification
shall rest upon him [in the water].
For he shall give the majesty of the Lord to those who are his sons in truth forever.
And there shall be no successor for him from generation to generation forever.
And in his priesthood the nations shall be multiplied in knowledge on the earth,
and they shall be illuminated by the grace of the Lord,
but Israel shall be diminished by her ignorance
and darkened by her grief.
In his priesthood sin shall cease
and lawless men shall rest from their evil deeds,
and righteous men shall find rest in him.

> And he shall open the gates of paradise;
> he shall remove the sword that has threatened since Adam,
> and he will grant to the saints to eat of the tree of life.
> The spirit of holiness shall be upon them.
> And Beliar shall be bound by him.
> And he shall grant to his children the authority to trample on wicked spirits.
> And the Lord will rejoice in his children;
> he will be well pleased by his beloved ones forever.
> Then Abraham, Isaac, and Jacob will rejoice,
> and I shall be glad, and all the saints shall be clothed in righteousness.[47]

The Dead Sea Scrolls

The Dead Sea Scrolls were discovered in various caves near Qumran between 1946 and 1956 and were translated during the latter half of the twentieth century. We can confidently date most of the scrolls from 200 BC to AD 70, though the vast majority were written prior to the Christian era. Although scholars continue to debate the nature of the community that produced the scrolls, this Jewish group appears to have become convinced that the Jerusalem priesthood and sacrifices had been corrupted following the successful Maccabean rebellion. They subsequently withdrew from normal society in order to worship and obey God faithfully until he acted by sending his messiahs to fulfill the Old Testament prophecies and promises.

In many ways, the Qumran community paralleled the early Christian movement. Both viewed the current religious establishment in Jerusalem as corrupt and interpreted Old Testament prophecies as being fulfilled in their own community and history. Christians, however, claimed that Jesus was God's Messiah who had triumphed over death through his resurrection and who had ushered in the time of fulfillment. The Qumran community did not survive the tumultuous first century AD, particularly the Roman conquest of Palestine and destruction of Jerusalem in response to the

[47] Ibid., 1:794–95.

Jewish revolt of AD 66–73. While this war devastated Palestine—and likely the Qumran community—the early Christian movement had already spread far beyond Palestine by that point and had established churches throughout the Roman Empire.

DAMASCUS DOCUMENT (CAIRO GENIZAH COPY; CD 20:1)

The beginning of this column is lost, but the text we have reads, "of the unique teacher until there arises the messiah out of Aaron and Israel."[48]

RULE OF THE COMMUNITY (1QS 9:9B–11)

> They should not depart from any counsel of the law in order to walk in complete stubbornness of their heart, but instead shall be ruled by the first directives which the men of the Community began to be taught until the prophet comes, and the Messiahs of Aaron and Israel.[49]

RULE OF THE CONGREGATION (1Q28A 2:11–22)

> At [a ses]sion of the men of renown, [those summoned to] the gathering of the community council, when [God] begets the Messiah with them: [the] chief [priest] of all the congregation of Israel shall enter, and all [his] br[others, the sons] of Aaron, the priests [summoned] to the assembly, the men of renown, and they shall sit be[fore him, each one] according to his dignity. After, [the Mess]iah of Israel shall [enter] and before him shall sit the heads of the th[ousands of Israel, each] one according to his dignity, according to [his] po[sition] in their camps and according to their marches. And all the heads of the cl[ans of the congre]gation with the wise [men . . .] shall sit before them, each one according to his dignity. And [when] they gather [at the tab]le of community [or to drink the n]ew wine, and the table of the community is prepared [and the] new wine [is mixed] for drinking, [no-one should stretch out] his hand to the first-fruit of the bread and of [the new wine] before the priest, for [he is the one who bl]esses the first-fruit of bread and of the new win[e and stretches out] his hand

[48] Florentino García Martínez and Eibert J. C. Tigchelaar, eds., *The Dead Sea Scrolls: Study Edition*, 2 vols. (Brill: Leiden, 1997, 1998), 1:579.
[49] Ibid., 1:91–93.

towards the bread before them. Afterwar[ds,] the Messiah of Israel [shall str]etch out his hands towards the bread. [And afterwards they shall ble]ss all the congregation of the community, each [one according to] his dignity. And in accordance with this precept one shall act at each me[al, when] at least ten me[n are gat]hered.[50]

FLORILEGIUM (4Q174 10–13)

[And] YHWH [de]clares to you that "he will build you a house. I will raise up your seed after you and establish the throne of his kingdom [for ev]er. I will be a father to him and he will be a son to me." This [refers to the] "branch of David," who will arise with the Interpreter of the law who [will rise up] in Zi[on in] the [l]ast days, as it is written: "I will raise up the hut of David which has fallen," This (refers to) "the hut of David which has fall[en" w]hich he will raise up to save Israel.[51]

TESTIMONIA (4Q175 1–13)

And **** spoke to Moses saying: "You have heard the sound of the words of this people, what they said to you: all they have said is right. If (only) it were given (that) they had /this/ heart to fear me and keep all my precepts all the days, so that it might go well with them and their sons for ever!" "I would raise up for them a prophet from among their brothers, like you, and place my words in his mouth, and he would tell them all that I command him. And it will happen that /the/ man who does not listen to my words which the prophet will speak in my name, I shall require a reckoning from him." And he uttered his poem and said: "Oracle of Balaam, son of Beor, and oracle of the man of penetrating eye, oracle of him who listens to the words of God and knows the knowledge of the Most High, who sees the vision of Shaddai, lying down and with an open eye. I see him, but not now, I espy him, but not close up. A star has departed from Jacob, and a scepter /has arisen/ from Israel. He shall crush the temples of Moab, and cut to pieces all the sons of Sheth."[52]

---

[50] Ibid., 1:103.
[51] Ibid., 1:353.
[52] Ibid., 1:357.

4QARAMAIC APOCALYPSE (APOCRYPHON OF DANIEL) **(4Q246 2:1-9)**

> He will be called son of God, and they will call him son of the Most High. Like the sparks that you saw, so will their kingdom be; they will rule several year[s] over the earth and crush everything; a people will crush another people, and a province another provi[n]ce. Until the people of God arises and makes everyone rest from the sword. His kingdom will be an eternal kingdom, and all his paths in truth. He will jud[ge] the earth in truth and all will make peace. The sword will cease from the earth, and all the provinces will pay him homage. The great God is his strength, he will wage war for him; he will place the peoples in his hand and cast them all away before him. His rule will be an eternal rule, and all the abysses. . . .[53]

COMMENTARY ON GENESIS A **(4Q252 5:1-7)**

> [. . .] The scepter shall [no]t depart from the tribe of Judah. While Israel has the dominion, there [will not] be cut off someone who sits on the throne of David. For "the staff" is the covenant of royalty, [and the thou]sands of Israel are "the standards." Until the messiah of righteousness comes, the branch of David. For to him and to his descendants has been given the covenant of the kingship of his people for everlasting generations, which he observed [. . .] the Law with the men of the Community, for [. . .] it is the assembly of the men of [. . .] [. . .] He gives.[54]

Later Jewish Texts

Both *4 Ezra* and *2 Baruch* can be dated to the end of the first century or the beginning of the second century AD. They were written after the destruction of the temple in AD 70 and reflect later first-century Jewish messianic expectations that seem to have escaped Christian influence.

4 EZRA 7:12-13 **(C. AD 90-100)**

> For behold, the time will come, when the signs which I have foretold to you will come to pass; the city which now is not seen

53 Ibid., 1:495.

54 Ibid., 1:505.

shall appear, and the land which now is hidden shall be disclosed. And everyone who has been delivered from the evils that I have foretold shall see my wonders. For my son the Messiah shall be revealed with those who are with him, and those who remain shall rejoice four hundred years. And after these years my son the Messiah shall die, and all who draw human breath. And the world shall be turned back to primeval silence for seven days, as it was at the first beginnings; so that no one shall be left. And after seven days the world, which is not yet awake, shall be roused, and that which is corruptible shall perish. And the earth shall give up those who are asleep in it; and the chambers shall give up the souls which have been committed to them. And the Most High shall be revealed upon the seat of judgment, and compassion shall pass away, and patience shall be withdrawn; but judgment alone shall remain, truth shall stand, and faithfulness shall grow strong.[55]

And as for the lion that you saw rousing up out of the forest and roaring and speaking to the eagle and reproving him for his unrighteousness, and as for all his words that you have heard, this is the Messiah whom the Most High has kept until the end of days, who will arise from the posterity of David, and will come and speak to them; he will denounce them for their ungodliness and for their wickedness, and will cast up before them their contemptuous dealings. For first he will set them living before his judgment seat, and when he has reproved them, then he will destroy them. But he will deliver in mercy the remnant of my people, those who have been saved throughout my borders, and he will make them joyful until the end comes, the day of judgment, of which I spoke to you at the beginning. This is the dream that you saw, and this is its interpretation.[56]

"This is the interpretation of the vision: As for your seeing a man come up from the heart of the sea, this is he whom the Most High has been keeping for many ages, who will himself deliver his creation; and he will direct those who are left. And as for

[55] B. M. Metzger, trans., "The Fourth Book of Ezra: A New Translation and Introduction," in *Old Testament Pseudepigrapha*, 1:537–38 (*4 Ezra* 7:26–34).
[56] Ibid., 1:550 (*4 Ezra* 12:31–35).

your seeing wind and fire and a storm coming out of his mouth, and as for his not holding spear or weapon of war, yet destroying the onrushing multitude which came to conquer him, this is the interpretation: Behold, the days are coming when the Most High will deliver those who are on the earth. And bewilderment of mind shall come over those who dwell on the earth. And they shall plan to make war against one another, city against city, place against place, people against people, and kingdom against kingdom. And when these things come to pass and the signs occur which I showed you before, then my son will be revealed, whom you saw as a man coming up from the sea. And when all the nations hear his voice, every man shall leave his own land and the warfare that they have against one another; and an innumerable multitude shall be gathered together, as you saw, desiring to come and conquer him. But he will stand on the top of Mount Zion. And Zion will come and be made manifest to all people, prepared and built, as you saw the mountain carved out without hands. And he, my Son, will reprove the assembled nations for their ungodliness (this was symbolized by the storm), and will reproach them to their face with their evil thoughts and with the torments with which they are to be tortured (which were symbolized by the flames); and he will destroy them without effort by the law (which was symbolized by the fire). And as for your seeing him gather to himself another multitude that was peaceable, these are the ten tribes which were led away from their own land into captivity in the days of King Hoshea, whom Shalmaneser the king of the Assyrians led captive; he took them across the river, and they were taken into another land. . . ."

He said to me, "Just as no one can explore or know what is in the depths of the seas, so no one on earth can see my Son or those who are with him, except in the time of his day."[57]

2 BARUCH 39-40, 72 (C. AD 100)

And it will happen when the time of its fulfillment is approaching in which it will fall, that at that time the dominion of my Anointed One which is like the fountain and the vine, will be revealed. And when it has revealed itself, it will uproot the

[57] Ibid., 1:552–53 (4 *Ezra* 13:25–40, 52).

multitude of its host. And that which you have seen, namely the tall cedar, which remained of that forest, and with regard to the words which the vine said to it which you heard, this is the meaning.

The last ruler who is left alive at that time will be bound, whereas the entire host will be destroyed. And they will carry him on Mount Zion, and my Anointed One will convict him of all his wicked deeds and will assemble and set before him all the works of his hosts. And after these things he will kill him and protect the rest of my people who will be found in the place that I have chosen. And his dominion will last forever until the world of corruption has ended and until the times which have been mentioned before have been fulfilled. This is your vision, and this is its explanation.[58]

Now, hear also about the bright waters which come at the end after these black ones. This is the word. After the signs have come of which I have spoken to you before, when the nations are moved and the time of my Anointed One comes, he will call all nations, and some of them he will spare, and others he will kill. These things will befall the nations which will be spared by him. Every nation which has not known Israel and which has not trodden down the seed of Jacob will live. And this is because some from all the nations have been subjected to your people. All those, now, who have ruled over you or have known you, will be delivered up to the sword.[59]

CONCLUSION

This brief overview of some of the chief primary sources related to Jewish messianic hopes illustrates the diverse expectations present within Judaism during the time of Jesus. Despite the diversity, several elements unify the texts. The most significant unifying theme was the belief that God would indeed act through his Messiah to establish his kingdom in the last days. The earliest Christians declared Jesus to be this Messiah based upon their reading of the

[58] A. F. J. Klijn, trans., "2 (Syriac Apocalypse of) Baruch: A New Translation and Introduction," in *Old Testament Pseudepigrapha*, 1:633 (2 *Baruch* 39:7–40:4).
[59] Ibid., 1:645 (2 *Baruch* 72:1–6).

Old Testament in light of Jesus's life, miracles, teaching, and, most importantly, resurrection.

Jewish messianic expectations were not finally crushed in Palestine until the Jewish revolt under Simon Bar Kokhba in the years AD 132–135. Simon chose the name Bar Kokhba ("son of a star") to connect himself with the messianic prophecy in Numbers 24:17 that a star would arise out of Jacob. Akiva ben Joseph, a famous rabbi during the time of the Bar Kokhba revolt, apparently endorsed him as the long-awaited Messiah, and some at the time described Simon Bar Kokhba's brief rule of two and a half years as the era of the redemption of Israel. The massive devastation that followed Rome's decisive response effectively ended Jewish messianic expectation and gave rise to rabbinic Judaism.

ADVENT READING PLAN

The following Advent Reading Plan includes four readings from the Old Testament, six from Matthew, ten from Luke, four from John's Gospel, and one from the book of Revelation. The readings move from some of the major Old Testaments texts expressing messianic expectations to the infancy narratives in Matthew and Luke to John's prologue. Ideally, these Scripture passages should be read in conjunction with the respective chapters in this volume.

DATE	SCRIPTURE PASSAGE	TOPIC	*FIRST DAYS OF JESUS*
December 1	Luke 1:1–4	An account from eyewitnesses	Introduction
December 2	Genesis 49:8–12	The scepter of Judah	Chapter 1
December 3	Isaiah 9:6–7; 11:1–5	A child is born; a branch of Jesse	Chapter 1
December 4	Micah 5:2–4	A ruler is born in Bethlehem	Chapter 1
December 5	Matthew 1:1–17	Jesus's ancestry	Chapter 1
December 6	Matthew 1:18–25	The virgin birth	Chapter 2
December 7	Matthew 2:1–12	The visit of the *magoi*	Chapter 3
December 8	Matthew 2:13–15	Escape to Egypt	Chapter 4

DATE	SCRIPTURE PASSAGE	TOPIC	*FIRST DAYS OF JESUS*
December 9	Matthew 2:16-18	Herod's order	Chapter 4
December 10	Matthew 2:19-23	Return to Nazareth	Chapter 4
December 11	Luke 1:5–25	John the Baptist's birth foretold	Chapter 5
December 12	Luke 1:26-38	Jesus's birth foretold	Chapter 5
December 13	Luke 1:39–45	Mary's visit to Elizabeth	Chapter 6
December 14	Luke 1:46–56	Mary's song (*Magnificat*)	Chapter 6
December 15	Luke 1:57–66	Birth of John the Baptist	Chapter 7
December 16	Luke 1:67–80	Zechariah's song (*Benedictus*)	Chapter 7
December 17	Luke 2:1–7	Birth of Jesus Christ	Chapter 8
December 18	Luke 2:8–21	The angelic announcement	Chapter 9
December 19	Luke 2:22–40	Simeon's and Anna's prophecies	Chapter 10
December 20	John 1:1–5, 18	The preexistent Word	Chapter 11
December 21	John 1:6–8, 15	John the Baptist's witness	Chapter 12
December 22	John 1:9–14	The Word-become-flesh	Chapter 13
December 23	John 1:16–17	The law, grace, and truth	Chapter 14
December 24	Isaiah 52:13-53:12	The suffering servant	Chapter 15
December 25	Revelation 21:1–8	A new heaven and a new earth	Epilogue

GENERAL INDEX

SCRIPTURE INDEX

ANCIENT SOURCES INDEX

Apocryphal/Deuterocanonical Books

Old Testament Pseudepigrapha

Dead Sea Scrolls